Supporting Students' Motivation

This is a book about teachers' classroom motivating styles. Motivating style is the interpersonal tone and face-to-face behavior the teacher relies on when trying to motivate students to engage in classroom activities and procedures. The over-arching goal of the book is to help teachers work through the professional development process to learn how to provide instruction in ways that students will find to be motivationally enriching, satisfying, and engagement-generating.

To realize this goal, the book features six parts: Part 1: Introduction, introduces what teachers are to support—namely, student motivation; Part 2: Motivating Style, explains what a supportive motivating style is; Part 3: "How to," overviews the recommended motivationally-supportive instructional strategies one-by-one and step-by-step; Part 4: Workshop, walks the reader through the skill-building workshop experience; Part 5: Benefits, details all the student, teacher, and classroom benefits that come from an improved motivating style; and Part 6: Getting Started, discusses ways to begin using these skills in the classroom.

Based on a successful workshop program run by the authors, teachers successfully improve their classroom motivating style. In doing so, they experience gains in their teaching skill and efficacy, job satisfaction, a renewed passion for teaching, and a more satisfying relationship with their students. This multiauthored book provides teachers with the practical, concrete, step-by-step, skill-based "how to" they need to develop a highly supportive motivating style.

Johnmarshall Reeve is a Professor in the Institute for Positive Psychology and Education, Australian Catholic University, Australia.

Richard M. Ryan is a Professor in the Institute for Positive Psychology and Education, Australian Catholic University, Australia. He is also a Professor Emeritus in the Department of Psychology, University of Rochester, USA. He is the President of the Center for Self-Determination Theory.

Sung Hyeon Cheon is an Associate Professor in the Department of Physical Education, Korea University, South Korea.

Lennia Matos is a Professor in the Department of Psychology, Pontifical Catholic University of Peru, Peru.

Haya Kaplan is a Senior Lecturer and Head of the Center for Motivation and Self-Determination at the Kaye Academic College of Education, Israel.

Supporting Students' Motivation

Strategies for Success

Johnmarshall Reeve,
Richard M. Ryan,
Sung Hyeon Cheon,
Lennia Matos and Haya Kaplan

LONDON AND NEW YORK

Cover image: Getty images

First published 2022
by Routledge
2 Park Square, Milton Park, Abingdon, Oxon OX14 4RN

and by Routledge
605 Third Avenue, New York, NY 10158

Routledge is an imprint of the Taylor & Francis Group, an informa business

British Library Cataloguing-in-Publication Data
A catalogue record for this book is available from the British Library

Library of Congress Cataloging-in-Publication Data
Names: Reeve, Johnmarshall, author. | Ryan, Richard M., author. | Cheon, Sung Hyeon, author. | Matos, Lennia, author. | Kaplan, Haya, author.
Title: Supporting students' motivation: strategies for success / Johnmarshall Reeve, Richard M. Ryan, Sung Hyeon Cheon, Lennia Matos, and Haya Kaplan.
Description: Abingdon, Oxon; New York, NY: Routledge, 2022.
Identifiers: LCCN 2021036712 (print) | LCCN 2021036713 (ebook) | ISBN 9780367550486 (hardback) | ISBN 9780367550493 (paperback) | ISBN 9781003091738 (ebook) | ISBN 9781032187877 (ebook other)
Subjects: LCSH: Motivation in education. | Classroom environment. | Teacher-student relationships.
Classification: LCC LB1065 .R396 2022 (print) | LCC LB1065 (ebook) | DDC 370.15/4—dc23
LC record available at https://lccn.loc.gov/2021036712
LC ebook record available at https://lccn.loc.gov/2021036713

ISBN: 9780367550486 (hbk)
ISBN: 9780367550493 (pbk)
ISBN: 9781003091738 (ebk)
ISBN: 9781032187877 (eebk)

DOI: 10.4324/9781003091738

Typeset in Sabon
by KnowledgeWorks Global Ltd.

Dedication

To the approximately
1,300 teachers,
38,000 students,
400 schools,
24 classroom observers,
35 research team members,
13 family members, and
7 universities
that made this program of research possible.

Contents

Detailed contents

Figures

Tables

Preface

ORIGINS OF THE BOOK

The book's authors are long-time research collaborators who share the same theoretical framework about the nature of student motivation and how teachers can support it. Together, we have learned that the best way to motivate students is to work with their teachers. This insight led us to develop a teacher-focused professional development workshop to help teachers learn how to develop a more supportive classroom motivating style. This book tells the story about this approach to supporting students' motivation—what it is, how to do it, why it works, what teachers learn, and its benefits to teachers and students alike. Because this workshop worked so well and teachers received it so positively, we decided to put all our research and classroom experiences together into this book.

VIEW OF MOTIVATION

Our view on motivation is that all students naturally possess a full repertoire of engagement-fostering inner motivational resources, especially intrinsic motivation and the psychological needs for autonomy, competence, and relatedness. Students further acquire experience-based motivations, such as personal goals and self-endorsed values. Because of this, the teacher's instructional challenge is not to "motivate students" but, rather, to support the motivation students already have.

GOAL OF THE BOOK

The goal of this book is to help teachers develop an effective motivating style. This is a skill that needs to be learned, refined, personalized, and put into practice. This book therefore describes what an effective motivating style is, and it explains how to develop it step-by-step.

AUDIENCE

The intended audience is the classroom teacher—primarily in-service (practicing) teachers but also pre-service teachers. Preservice teachers are "teachers-in-training" and include mostly undergraduate students enrolled in Colleges of Education in universities around the world. The supplemental audience includes college and university instructors, educational administrators and policy makers, school psychologists, school counselors, tutors, parents, athletic coaches, workplace managers, and health care professionals. We also hope motivational researchers around the globe—especially educational psychologists—will find the book and our research both interesting and of value.

The teacher is an audience we know well. When we visit schools and ask teachers what they need from us, they make four requests: (1) keep the recommendations uncomplicated, clear, explicit, concrete, realistic, and effective; (2) emphasize the practical "how to"—not just the theoretical principles; (3) provide evidence-based recommendations that actually work—not just our opinions and idealism; and (4) speak to the really difficult-to-solve teaching situations, such as serious misbehavior (e.g., aggression, bullying).

We wrote the book for a global audience of teachers, and this is because we have worked with teachers, observed their classrooms, and conducted our research all around the globe. Each of the book's five authors, for instance, lives and works in a different nation, including Australia, Korea, Peru, Israel, and the United States.

Part 1

Introduction

Origins

At 7:00 am on a chilly Monday morning in February 2002, one of the authors and a team of four graduate students met together in the College of Education's parking lot at the University of Iowa (United States). Together, we drove 30 miles north to a high school in nearby Cedar Rapids. Upon arrival, we pulled out our schedule of classes and, working in pairs, observed maths, English, science, and economics classes throughout the day. That was the first day of what became this book.

By the end of the week, the research team had closely observed 20 teachers in action. Most of what was observed was the unfolding of a typical classroom script in which the teacher took 5 minutes to introduce a task and a learning objective and then another 15 minutes to explain how students could complete that activity and attain the learning objective, as the teacher offered a demonstration, a videoclip, a lecture, or something similar. For the next 30 minutes, students worked to complete their assigned task, such as a biology laboratory project, a series of math problems, a writing activity, or a class discussion on how an economic principle explained a current news event. Most classes ended with a wrap-up group discussion or Q&A (question and answer). While all this was going on, two members of the research team sat in the background with a stack of rating sheets to score how engaged students were throughout the lesson and also everything the teacher said and did to motivate and support that engagement.

Our research question was this: If the teacher made a special effort to support students' needs, interests, and initiatives throughout the 55-minute class period, would students' engagement be unusually high?

During that first week, the classroom observers simply recorded what was typical of teachers and students in this Cedar Rapids high school. The filled-in rating sheets told the story of how engaged and how motivationally supportive these students and teachers typically were. After that first week, we then did something special. We conducted an experiment. In late February, we randomly assigned 10 of the 20 high school teachers to participate in a workshop designed to help them develop a more supportive motivating style. Using motivation theory and research, we recommended specific acts of instruction the teachers might put into practice. For the other ten teachers, they were placed into a waitlist control group. Throughout March, these ten teachers provided instruction in their usual way (i.e., "practice as usual"). A month later (after the experiment ended), these teachers were provided the same workshop experience.

In the last week in March, we revisited all 20 classes for a second time. As before, the pair of raters scored how engaged students were and everything the

DOI: 10.4324/9781003091738-2

teacher said and did to motivate that engagement. The raters did not know which teachers were in the experimental group (participated in the workshop) and which teachers were in the control group (did not participate in the workshop). The critical question was this: Would the students of teachers who participated in the workshop show significantly greater classroom engagement than the students of teachers who did not participate in the workshop? If so, how closely related would the teacher's use of motivationally supportive teaching practices be to students' level of classroom engagement? If this relation existed, would this effect be a mild, moderate, or strong one?

In the classrooms of the ten teachers in the control group, students' classroom engagement in March declined a bit from its earlier February level. This is not an unusual occurrence in a high school classroom. What was unusual, however, was that students' engagement in the classrooms of the ten teachers in the experimental group spiked higher. When we analyzed the data, two findings were clear. First, teachers who participated in the workshop were able to provide instruction in a more motivationally supportive way. In doing so, they took their students' perspective, supported their interests and initiatives, and helped students discover personal value in the classroom activities. Second, a strong linear relation emerged to show that the more teachers taught in this motivationally supportive way, the more engaged their students were. Some teachers (those in the control group) did not make a special effort to support their students' motivation, and their students' engagement was correspondingly low to moderately low. The teachers in the experimental group made a special effort to support their students' motivation, and their students responded by showing an unusually high level of engagement. The full study and its findings can be found in a published journal article (Reeve, Jang, Carrell, Jeon, & Barch, 2004).

Twenty years have now passed, and these positive findings have been replicated many times in many different schools across different grade levels and even in different nations. As we shared our findings with researchers in education and psychology, we learned that the questions we were asking and our approach to helping teachers improve their motivating style were just as interesting to those in other nations as they were to us. So, we expanded our small research team to include international collaborations. We conducted our first international studies in Seoul, South Korea. At the same time we were doing this, researchers in Israel were conducting similar classroom-based research that produced similar positive results. Next, we joined forces with researchers to conduct investigations in Peru and then in Australia. To give the reader a sense of the international nature of our current research, Figure 1.1 shows the nationalities of the five authors who came together to produce this book. In addition to our team, similar investigations to help teachers improve their classroom motivating style have now been conducted by other research teams in 18 different nations, including Australia, Belgium, Brazil, China, Columbia, Estonia, Finland, France, Germany, Greece, Israel, Korea, Norway, Peru, Singapore, Spain, the United Kingdom, and the United States (reviewed in Reeve & Cheon, 2021).

This book is the story of what we learned and what we now recommend. We have worked closely with about 2,000 teachers, and just about all of them have

FIGURE 1.1 Nationalities of the Book's Five Authors

been able to develop a highly supportive motivating style. After each investigation, we talked with the participating teachers to ask what we might do differently to provide a more helpful, effective, and satisfying workshop experience. With each successive study, our goal has been to provide a new-and-improved workshop that becomes increasingly able to help teachers work through the professional development experience of upgrading the quality of their classroom motivating style. Fortunately, we have learned a lot, and the workshop we provide today is a much stronger version than what we were able to provide to those Cedar Rapids teachers all those years ago.

In watching teachers in action and in listening to their stories and experiences, we have noticed that each teacher seems to go through a similar three stage professional development process. First, teachers understand what a supportive motivating style is. This is an accomplishment of knowledge and theory. Teachers come to understand what student motivation is, where it comes from, why it changes, and under which conditions it changes. Teachers also understand what a supportive motivating style is, what motivationally-supportive teachers say, and what motivationally-supportive teachers do. Teachers further come to understand the close connection between the motivational support they provide and their students' motivational thriving.

After a teacher learns all this theoretical knowledge, he or she still needs practical skills. This takes a good deal of deliberate practice in an authentic classroom setting. It takes access to expert role models—What do highly motivationally supportive teachers say and do? It takes a good deal of mentoring and guidance to advance one's skill level from clumsy to proficient to mastery. And it takes feedback, still more guidance, and personal reflection to figure out how to do today what one was not able to do yesterday. At this point, the teacher has gained both knowledge and skill (theory and practice), but there is yet a third process that lies ahead.

When teachers successfully support their students' motivation, it soon becomes obvious to the teacher how beneficial such an approach to teaching really is. Students respond with greater motivation, engagement, learning, and personal growth. With some reflection, it becomes equally obvious how much more satisfying and fulfilling it is to be a teacher when one's students are so enthusiastically engaged. At some point, the teacher realizes that a supportive motivating style is not just a luxury possessed by a few special teachers but is, instead, a necessity for all teachers. With this insight, the teacher's professional journey to develop a more supportive motivating style is complete.

As we have helped teachers work through this professional development experience, we have learned that most teachers initially see the instructional effort to support students' motivation to be a somewhat mysterious process. When we first collaborate with a teacher, we frequently hear this: "Okay, fine. Supporting students' motivation sounds well and good; but what *specifically* could I do?" Teachers want clear, explicit, concrete, realistic, effective, and tried-and-true recommendations. With each successive study, we have worked hard to provide the next group of teachers with recommended teaching practices that are clearer, more explicit (step-by-step), more concrete, more realistic, more effective, and more evidence-based. If this "What *specifically* could I do?" question resonates with you, then we provide the next 22 chapters to guide you through your own professional journey to become a more motivationally supportive teacher. Let's start!

CHAPTER 2
Student motivation

One of the authors was once an 8th grade student sitting in English class taking the weekly vocabulary quiz. The quiz was always on Friday and offered the same challenge: Define 33 words and use each in a sentence. The words varied from week to week, of course, except for #33. Word 33 was always the same: Motivation. The English teacher's preferred definition was: "The stuff that permeates your entire being when you have a clear, vivid picture in your mind of what you want to do and an intense burning, all-consuming desire in your heart to fight for it." No student ever missed question #33.

Contemporary motivation researchers do not use the English teacher's colorful definition. Still, "intense burning, all-consuming desire" does conjure up some rich imagery, and it does convey a sense of purpose that goes beyond the standard definition of *an internal process that gives behavior its energy, direction, and persistence* (Schunk, Meece, & Pintrich, 2014). The English teacher's definition also makes it clear that motivation is foundational for all forms of skilled performance and adaptive functioning. Most teachers can help students generate "a clear, vivid picture in your mind of what you want to do." They will say, "Memorize 33 vocabulary words" or "Make an A on Friday's quiz." The difficulty begins when teachers try to help students generate the elusive "intense burning, all-consuming desire" that gives behavior its energy, direction, and persistence.

To understand what most teachers do, one group of researchers visited the classrooms of 30 late-elementary school teachers to observe which motivational strategies they most used (Newby, 1991). The observers also recorded how effective each strategy was, as judged by the rise or fall in students' engagement following each particular strategy. The four most frequently used motivational strategies were, in order, offer extrinsic rewards and punishments (used 58% of the time), capture students' attention—as by a dramatic statement or a quiet pause (27%), build students' confidence (7%), and explain the relevance of the learning activity to students' lives (7%). In terms of effectiveness, *emphasize relevance* was the only motivational strategy that actually worked (generated engagement), while *offer rewards and punishers* actually backfired (decreased engagement). *Gain attention* and *build confidence* were somewhere in between (i.e., both were mildly engagement-fostering). The unfortunate take-home message was this: Teachers least frequently used motivational strategies were the most effective, while their most frequently used strategies were the least effective.

These are discouraging results, and they cast skepticism on doing "what everyone else does." A better starting point would be to conduct the classroom-based research

DOI: 10.4324/9781003091738-3

necessary to identify what actually works. Once a teacher knows this, the road to best practices then becomes a matter of developing the skill needed to put those evidence-based teaching practices into action. So that is what this book will do. This chapter explains the nature of student motivation—what it is, where it comes from, how it works, why it changes, under what conditions it changes, and why it is so important. Coming chapters will identify what those evidence-based engagement-generating motivational strategies are and how to do them.

TEACHER-STUDENT DYNAMICS

Talk to a typical teacher about student motivation and you are likely to hear yearnings such as, "I wish my students were more motivated." Most teachers—perhaps all teachers—walk into their classrooms with some level of worry about how students will respond to the day's lesson in terms of their motivation, engagement, and learning. The fear is that students will respond with apathy, minimal engagement, and token learning. Similarly, most students walk into the classroom with some level of anticipation that the teacher has prepared some interesting things to do and that the teacher will be there to encourage and support them (rather than offer long boring lectures and endless worksheets). Mostly, teachers wish for motivated students, while students wish for motivating teachers.

When things go well, teachers and students support each other. As shown in the left and upper parts of Figure 2.1, students' classroom engagement flows out of their motivational resources, including their needs, interests, goals, and values (the arrow on the top). Teachers, on the other hand, offer a particular motivating style, and the right and lower parts of the figure illustrate that teachers' motivational teaching practices flow out of their motivating style (the arrow on the bottom).

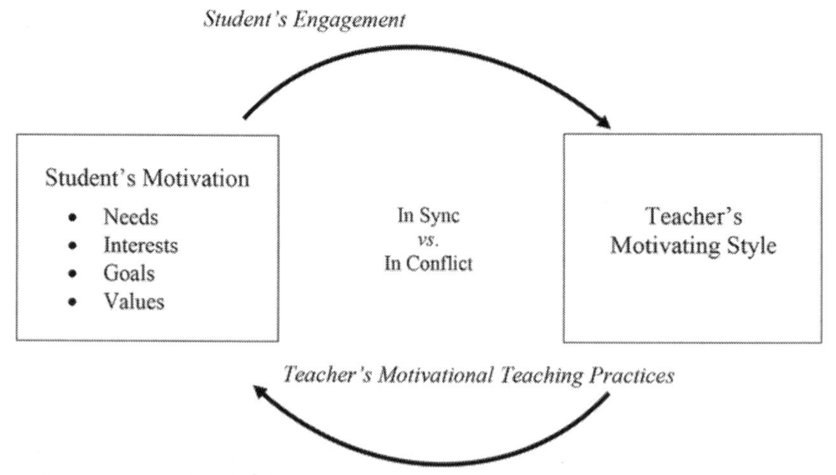

FIGURE 2.1 Student-Teacher Motivational Dynamics

What students say and do (display engagement) affects what teachers say and do (introduce motivational teaching practices) and vice versa. When teachers appreciate and support students' motivational resources, things go well. Similarly, when students value and respond favorably to the teacher's learning activities and behavioral requests, things also go well. In these classrooms, students give voice to their needs, interests, goals, and values and the teacher responds by offering learning activities that are relevant to those needs, interests, goals, and values. The teacher and students are in sync and mutually support each another (see center of diagram). In other classrooms, however, the teacher fails to support students' interests and goals and students resist the teacher's motivational strategies. This is when things do not go well, as the teacher and students are in conflict and mutually oppose one another.

To understand student motivation, it is helpful to look inside Figure 2.1's "Student's Motivation" box. What is in there are motivational resources. Some of these are inherent motivations that all students possess in roughly equal measure (e.g., need for relatedness). Others are acquired resources—motivations that students learn through experience and thus vary from student to student (e.g., one student has a goal to learn how to speak Spanish fluently, while another does not).

INHERENT MOTIVATIONS

All students, indeed all humans, have a rich repertoire of inherent (i.e., inborn) inner motivational resources that, when supported, are fully capable of energizing and directing their productive behavior. These endowed sources of motivation include psychological needs and intrinsic motivation.

Psychological needs

A psychological need is an inherent condition whose fulfillment is necessary and essential for psychological growth and well-being (Ryan & Deci, 2017; Vansteenkiste, Ryan, & Soenens, 2020). Everyone is familiar with biological needs such as hunger and thirst and that bodily health and wellness depend on attaining nutriments such as food and water. Similarly, everyone has psychological needs, including three that are quite basic and important, namely those for autonomy, competence, and relatedness. With a psychological need, what the person needs to be well is to pursue and fulfill a particular psychological experience.

Autonomy is the need to experience personal ownership during one's behavior

Autonomy is the psychological need to experience self-direction and personal endorsement in the initiation and regulation of one's behavior. When deciding what to do, we want the behavior to originate from within us. We want ownership over our behavioral initiatives, rather than have someone tell or make us do something.

We want to be the one who decides what to do, when to do it, how to do it, when to stop doing it, and when and whether to do something else. We want the choice to put ourselves in one situation rather than in another. The tell-tale signs of autonomy satisfaction are the feelings of volition and self-endorsement. Volition is an unpressured willingness to engage in an activity, one that centers on how free (vs. how coerced) we feel while acting (e.g., playing, studying, attending school) and while putting ourselves in one situation rather than in another (e.g., "I want to participate in choir but not band"). Personal endorsement is a heartfelt sense of ownership over an action. It is an affirmative answer to questions such as, Is this my choice? Is this what I want to do?

Competence is the need to experience effectance during environmental interactions

Competence is the psychological need to seek out optimal challenges, take them on, and exert persistent effort and strategic thinking to make progress in mastering them. Everyone wants and strives to be competent—to interact effectively with his or her surroundings. This desire extends into all aspects of our lives—at school, at work, in relationships, and during recreation and sports. We all want to develop and grow our skills, abilities, and talents. When we make progress toward that growth experience, we feel satisfied, even happy. The tell-tale signs of competence satisfaction are the feelings of effectance and mastery. Effectance is a feeling of producing an intentional effect on the environment. For instance, an art student may want to draw a face (an optimal challenge). She exerts effort to draw on paper the ideal image she has in her mind, and as the product on the paper moves closer to her ideal mental image, she feels effectance from a job well done. Mastery is a feeling that our skills and capacities are improving and expanding to the extent that we can handle (i.e., gain mastery over) (a) the challenge we presently face and (b) whatever future challenges are likely to come our way.

Relatedness is the need to experience acceptance and closeness in our relationships

Relatedness is the psychological need to establish close emotional bonds and attachments with the important people in our life. It reflects the desire to be socially and emotionally involved in warm, caring, and loving relationships—to be appreciated, accepted, and prized by others. Everyone needs to feel that they belong—to feel that they are included rather than excluded. When interacting with someone who truly understands and accepts us, we feel an emotional connection that is deeply satisfying. And we not only want others to care about our well-being, be sensitive to our concerns, and be responsive to our needs, we also want our relationships to be reciprocal, as we want to care about the other's well-being, be sensitive to their concerns, and be responsive to their needs. The tell-tale signs of relatedness satisfaction are the feelings of warmth and a sense of closeness that comes from interacting with someone who truly understands and accepts us for who we really are—flaws and all.

The "satisfaction" in need satisfaction

Motivation is an internal, private experience. Because it is private, teachers cannot see students' motivation. What they can see, however, are the outward signs of motivational satisfaction. With competence and relatedness satisfaction, students smile and laugh as they show their greater energy and enthusiasm. The satisfaction is obvious. Autonomy is a little different, as the satisfaction is more subtle. With autonomy, students also show greater energy and enthusiasm, but the satisfaction express itself through doing what is interesting, meaningful, fulfilling, and self-defining (Ryan, Huta, & Deci, 2008).

Intrinsic motivation

Recently, one of the authors was at a playground populated by a dozen elementary-aged school children. The motivation on that playground was any classroom teacher's dream, as all the children all the time were showing initiative, effort, challenge-seeking, problem-solving, and eager enthusiasm. They were all exploring, trying out and learning new skills, and showing social competence. For 45 uninterrupted minutes, these children were intrinsically motivated with no motivational problems in sight. But intrinsic motivation is not just the motivation of children. The same is often true for adolescents engaged in recreation, sports, games, smartphone apps, and whenever they find themselves in environments that offer interesting, challenging, and relationship-enriching things to do.

Intrinsic motivation is the motivation to engage in an activity out of interest and enjoyment. It is the inherent desire to seek out novelty and challenges, to explore new environments, to take interest in activities, and to stretch and extend one's abilities (Ryan & Deci, 2017). Psychological needs are the source of intrinsic motivation. That is, students find art, music, and a good game of basketball to be intrinsically motivating because these are the activities that allow them to feel autonomous, competent, and related to others. When intrinsically motivated, students do not necessarily say, "I feel autonomy, competence, and relatedness" but, rather, they express the emotional aftermath from such need satisfaction: "That was fun"; "This was so interesting!," and "I enjoyed doing that."

ACQUIRED MOTIVATIONS

Motivation starts with what people need to survive and thrive (i.e., physical and psychological needs). This is why the central concept in "supporting students' motivation" involves creating opportunities for students to fulfill their (psychological) needs—through autonomy support, competence support, and relatedness support. But students also take action to fulfill their own needs, and they do this by creating desired future states in their minds and then working to advance their current state of affairs to become that ideal state of affairs. This means that goals and values add

to and expand the motivational capacity of needs and intrinsic motivation. Thus, in addition to having a rich repertoire of inherent motivations, students further develop a rich repertoire of acquired (learned) motivations in the form of personal goals and self-endorsed values.

Personal goals

A goal is a future-focused mental representation of a desired end state that guides behavior (Hulleman, Schrager, Bodmann, & Harackiewicz, 2010). Goals are aspirations. Goals are guides and hopes for who we want to become and what we want to accomplish. A goal informs us what we need to do today to attain a desired future ("desired end state").

The tricky part of personal goals, motivationally speaking, is that they come in two forms—intrinsic and extrinsic. According to self-determination theory (Ryan & Deci, 2017), not all goals are equal, as some goals energize and benefit people (intrinsic goals) more than do other goals (extrinsic goals). A goal is intrinsic if it puts the goal-striver on an inwardly oriented pathway of activity that opens up frequent and recurring opportunities to experience psychological need satisfaction. That means that intrinsic goals are ideal states that are in close harmony with the students' psychological needs. Prototypical intrinsic goals are those that encourage the pursuit of autonomy satisfaction (e.g., "I want to join a school club that lets me pursue my personal interests"), competence satisfaction (e.g., "I want to learn how to play the guitar really well"), and relatedness satisfaction (e.g., "I want to develop a deeper friendship with my classmate."). The reason why intrinsic goal pursuits are especially beneficial is because they generate need satisfactions along the way and, because of this motivational support, the intrinsic goal-striver displays greater effort, makes more goal progress, and experiences greater well-being (Koestner, 2008).

A goal is extrinsic if it puts the goal-striver on an outwardly oriented pathway of activity to seek social approval, social status, or extrinsic reward. This means that extrinsic goals are ideal states that are divorced from students' inherent psychological needs. Prototypical extrinsic goals are the pursuit to become rich (financial success), popular (high social status), or famous (highly desirable social image). There is nothing wrong with goals to become rich, popular, and famous—unless and until they put students in a position of having to sacrifice or suppress their psychological needs (Niemiec, Ryan, & Deci, 2009). For instance, a high-achieving student who seeks to become the school valedictorian might suppress personal interests (i.e., suppress autonomy) and treat classmates as rivals (i.e., suppress relatedness). In one telling study, motivational researchers interviewed highly accomplished fashion models (who pursued *and attained* extrinsic goals for fame, fortune, and popularity). These men and women (*M* age = 24 years old) experienced unusually low daily need satisfaction and well-being and surprisingly high maladjustment—anxiety, depression, and a lack of confidence (Meyer, Enström, Harstveit, Bowles, & Beevers, 2007). The old saying is, "Be careful what you wish for."

Students do not typically pursue "financial materialism." Instead, they sometimes pursue "educational materialism," such as striving for high test scores, entrance to prestigious schools, winning a competitive scholarship, and achieving a high class ranking. Again, there is nothing inherently problematic about these educational pursuits—unless and until they put the student in a position of having to sacrifice or suppress their personal interests and psychological needs.

Self-endorsed values

A value is a belief as to what is desirable and attractive (Rokeach, 1973). Once acquired, values serve as guiding principles for how to live a desirable and attractive life. Values do this by guiding and informing the person's choices, goals, attitudes, lifestyle, identity, and sense of self (Feather, 1995; Hitlin, 2003).

No one is born with a particular value. Instead, people come to understand what is desirable, attractive, and important in life from their personal experiences and from the guidance of others, such as their parents, teachers, friends, and larger society. These social agents suggest that some beliefs, standards, events, and behaviors are good, attractive, and important, while other ways of thinking and behaving are bad, unattractive, or unimportant. Because students have different experiences and different socializing agents, values differ from one student to the next.

As the teacher interacts with a group of 20-30 diverse students, she might introduce the classroom values that "sharing is good" while "cheating is bad." Some students will fully accept the teacher's recommended values and take them on as their own (i.e., internalization). Other students, however, might not agree with or even reject the teacher's recommended values. The student's rejection reflects anti-internalization (i.e., defiance; Aelterman, Vansteenkiste, & Haerens, 2019). The importance of self-endorsed (internalized) vs. rejected (anti-internalized) values can be seen when students see homework, class participation, and the learning activity of the day to be important and personally useful things to do—or not. If valued and internalized, students willingly engage in and benefit from the teacher-recommended activity (Jang, 2008). If devalued and anti-internalized, students experience the teacher-recommended activity as something imposed on them against their will (i.e., against their values). If so, then students may do exactly the opposite of what the teacher requests.

THE RELATION BETWEEN STUDENT MOTIVATION AND THE TEACHER'S MOTIVATING STYLE

As illustrated in the upper part of Figure 2.2, when students walk into any classroom, they bring with them their motivational resources. Sometimes teachers think that students walk into class without any motivational resources—or teachers are unaware of these resources. Still, what students bring to the classroom is an impressive repertoire, as it includes all the motivational resources listed in the middle of

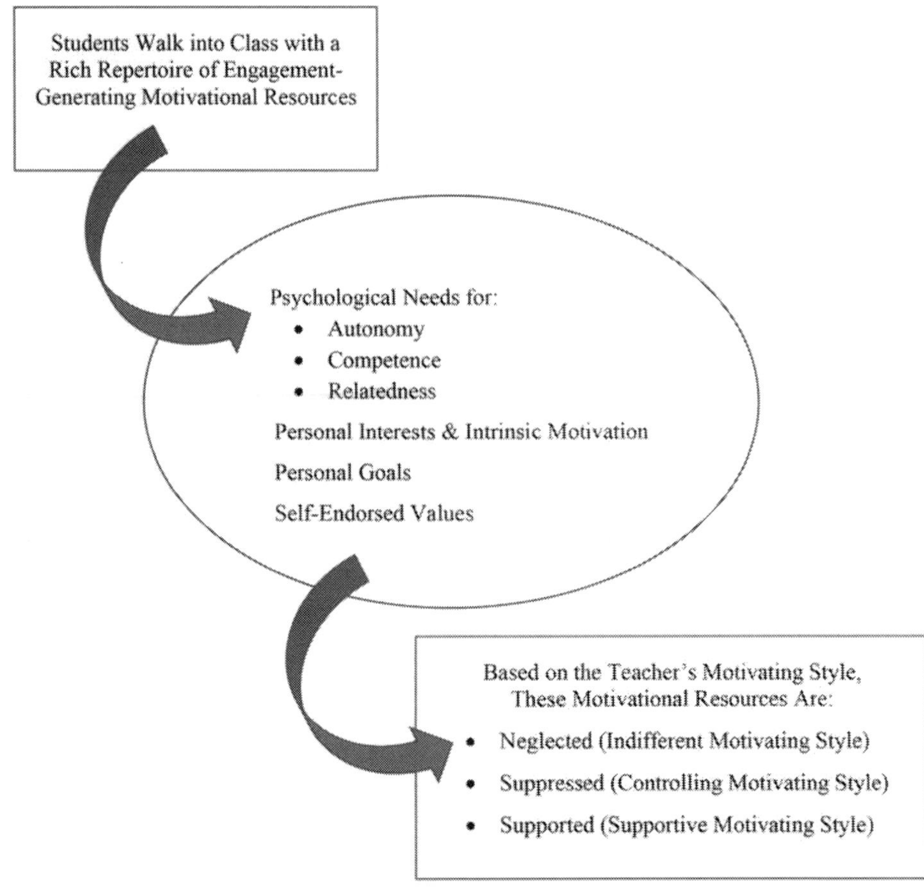

FIGURE 2.2 Three Different Ways that Teachers React to Students' Motivational Resources

Figure 2.2 (and Figure 2.1). Once in the classroom, students encounter a teacher who appreciates and supports their motivational resources—more or less.

Teachers sometimes neglect students' inner motivational resources. Sometimes teachers provide instruction in a way that simply by-passes or ignores (does not take into consideration) students' motivational resources. They are indifferent to students' psychological needs, personal interests, personal goals, and self-endorsed values. Rather than being in sync or in conflict, teachers and students are like strangers.

Teachers sometimes suppress students' inner motivational resources. They teach in ways that frustrate students' psychological needs, personal interests, personal goals, and self-endorsed values (e.g., "No, you are interested in the wrong thing; stop what you are doing and do what I tell you to do."). This is a controlling motivating style, as the teacher tries to control students' motivation and classroom activity. In these cases, teachers and students tend toward conflict (e.g., a "me vs. you" relationship).

Teachers sometimes support students' inner motivational resources. They are aware of what students want, need, and are interested in, they appreciate the engagement-generating potential of these resources, and they build their daily instruction around introducing learning activities in ways that involve and satisfy students' psychological needs, intrinsic motivation, personal goals, and self-endorsed values. This is a supportive motivating style. In these cases, teachers and students tend to be in sync with each other.

IS MOTIVATIONAL SUPPORT IMPORTANT?

Motivation is important in its own right. It is an end in and of itself. But motivation also produces benefits. It fuels gains in effective functioning, skilled performance, and well-being. As shown in the upper part of Figure 2.3, when teachers support students' motivation, such as greater need satisfaction and the internalization of goals and values, these motivations catalyze gains in a wide range of educationally-important outcomes (e.g., greater engagement, more positive self-concept). Similarly, as shown in the lower part of Figure 2.3, when teachers lessen students' motivational frustrations, such as lesser need frustration and anti-internalizations, educationally problematic outcomes diminish (e.g., lesser negative feelings, lesser bullying).

Chapter 15 ("Student benefits") explains all the motivationally enhanced and motivationally diminished outcomes featured on the right side of Figure 2.3. The key point here is to highlight that the teacher's essential task is not so complicated and multitasked as to increase all the positive outcomes and to decrease all the negative outcomes on the right side of Figure 2.3. Instead, the teacher's essential challenge is this: Provide instruction and relate to students in (a) more need-satisfying and internalization-promoting (the plus sign in Figure 2.3) and (b) less need-frustrating

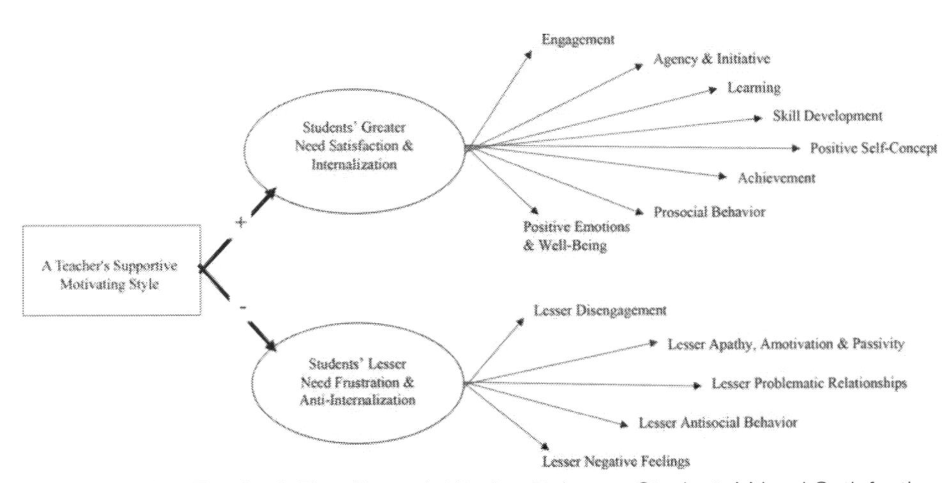

FIGURE 2.3 The Teacher's Two Essential Tasks: Enhance Students' Need Satisfaction and Lessen Students' Need Frustration

and anti-internalization promoting (the negative sign in Figure 2.3) ways. *Once teachers are able to do this, students' motivations will take care of the rest* (i.e., all the outcomes on the right side of Figure 2.3). Therefore, all the pages to come are designed to help teachers learn how to support students' motivational satisfactions and lessen students' motivational frustrations (the two boldfaced lines on the left side of the figure).

CONCLUSION

All students enter the classroom with a rich repertoire of engagement-generating motivational resources, including psychological needs, intrinsic motivation, personal goals, and self-endorsed values. When teachers appreciate these motivations and incorporate them into the delivery of their instruction, things usually go well.

Part 2

Motivating style

CHAPTER 3

Motivating and demotivating teachers

You are invited to a workshop. If you are willing, let's begin. Please look around and find someone who you do not know or who you do not usually get an opportunity to interact with. Pair up with that person, and briefly introduce yourself.

Now, I would like for one person in each pair to take three minutes each to describe *the most motivating* teacher you ever had. That teacher can be from any grade level, or any educational setting. No names are needed. Instead, try to describe what the teacher did that was so motivating in the most vivid way possible. When that person finishes, have the other person tell their story of their most motivating teacher.

Next, I would like for each person to tell a different story. This time take three more minutes each to describe *the least motivating* teacher you ever had. Again, no names are needed, and this teacher can be from any educational setting. The key thing is to describe what made this teacher so unmotivating.

After everyone tells their stories, each individual group is asked to pick one exemplary story of each type of teacher to report to the group as a whole. As teachers retell their stories, and as they emphasize defining adjectives (e.g., "He was *so critical*!"), a member of the workshop team writes these adjectives on a whiteboard. One teacher might tell a story such as, "She was really warm—she cared about each of us. She tried to make things interesting." Another teacher might tell a story such as, "He was really cold. He wouldn't listen to students. He just rambled on and on and the class was disorganized."

What is so interesting about this activity is that, after teachers have told their stories and emphasized 20–30 defining adjectives, a predictable pattern will emerge. A first group of adjectives will likely cluster around the theme of supporting relatedness (e.g., friendly, really cared, genuinely concerned for my welfare, made me feel special) vs. frustrating it (e.g., cold and distant, ignored us—didn't have time for us or our concerns, discriminated against me). A second group of adjectives will likely cluster around a theme of supporting autonomy (e.g., good listener, understood me, made class so interesting, patient) vs. frustrating it (e.g., intimidating, oppositional, really boring, put a lot of pressure on me). A third group of adjectives will likely cluster around the theme of supporting competence (e.g., helped me improve, believed in my potential, challenged me to be my best) vs. frustrating it (e.g., used sarcasm and ridicule as weapons to put students in their place, said I'll never be good enough).

DOI: 10.4324/9781003091738-5

The utility of this activity is that it begins to demystify what it means to be a motivating or unmotivating teacher, because it highlights three essential ingredients to a motivating teacher. A motivating teacher is one who supports my relatedness, autonomy, and competence. It also highlights three defining characteristics of an unmotivating teacher—one who undermines my relatedness, autonomy, and competence.

WHAT STUDENTS SAY ABOUT MOTIVATING AND DEMOTIVATING TEACHERS

Students have a front-row seat to observe teachers in action. After thousands of hours in the classroom, students form ideas about which teacher characteristics and which teaching practices empower vs. deflate their motivation. Over time, students come to understand what makes a "motivating teacher" and what makes a "demotivating teacher."

Students from all around the globe have been asked to reflect back years, even decades, to remember the (1) best and (2) worst teacher they ever had (see Box 3.1 and Christopher Niemiec's presentation at https://www.youtube.com/watch?v=4KlOgPTozuQ&t=771s). Just about every student can do this. Inspired by this exercise, we too asked students from different nations and grade levels (grades: 3 – 16) to write brief essays in response to the same questions in Box 3.1. Here is what these students told us.

BOX 3.1

Remembering your best and worst teachers

My best teacher

Think back to all the teachers that you have had in your educational history. Among all those teachers, which one stands out as your best teacher? With that one teacher in mind, ask yourself two questions:

1. How did he or she relate to you?
2. What type of opportunities did he or she provide to you?

My worst teacher

Once again, think back to all the teachers that you have had in your educational history. Among all those teachers, which one stands out as your worst teacher? With that one teacher in mind, ask yourself two questions:

1. How did he or she relate to you?
2. What type of opportunities did he or she provide to you?

My best teacher

A ninth-grade student in Australia:

BOX 3.2

An australian middle schooler's best teacher

My best teacher

1. How did this best teacher relate to you?
   He treated the students on a personal level instead of holding a place of superiority above us. The teacher was engaged with all the students and wanted to be involved with each and every person no matter if there were issues or not.
2. What types of opportunities did this best teacher provide to you?
   Learning was always entertaining with him, and he made me look forward to class. The opportunity of looking forward to learning was what this teacher provided me with.
   He helped me learn and helped me engage in the classroom. He dramatically changed my perspective on learning in the classroom.

When asked which personal characteristics and which teaching practices elevated one particular teacher to the status of "best teacher," students generally identified the following:

- She cared for us—not just as students but as people.
- He listened to me.
- I could trust her—I felt free to tell her what I really felt and thought.
- We were on the same level. It wasn't hierarchical.
- The teacher was always respectful of us.
- She understands us.
- He made class very interesting—fun too.
- He always explained things—everything had a reason behind it.
- The teacher constantly asked if we understood the material.
- Very passionate, enthusiastic.
- Made me laugh.
- Varied classroom activities. He had great strategies to teach me subjects.
- Good relationship.
- Supportive, willing to help.
- Interested in students' opinions.
- Personal connection with each student.

- She allowed me to believe in myself and get better.
- She believed in my potential and helped me improve.
- Provided me with extra opportunities.
- Gave me good feedback.
- Told me what I did was good.

One unifying theme shared by all best teachers is that they offer students a high-quality relationship. According to students, best teachers listen, care, trust, and respect. Best teachers understand what students want, take an interest in students' opinions, and develop a personal connection with each student. A second unifying theme is that best teachers have an excellent relationship with their subject matter, as they exude joy, curiosity, and a love of learning. They show interest, enthusiasm, and passion, as they seem to draw energy from the subject matter. A third unifying theme is that best teachers use interest- and engagement-generating teaching strategies, as they know how to make class interesting and fun, explain things clearly, vary classroom activities, and provide extra opportunities for students to learn and pursue their personal interests.

My worst teacher

An eight-grade student in Australia:

BOX 3.3

An australian middle schooler's worst teacher

My worst teacher

1. How did this best teacher relate to you?
   She didn't. That's why she was bad.
2. What types of opportunities did this best teacher provide to you?
   None. That's why I did not like them.

When asked which personal characteristics and which teaching practices relegated one particular teacher to the status of "worst teacher," students generally identified the following:

- He yells.
- He was boring, monotonous, used worksheets nearly exclusively.
- He only talked—he never turns around to see if we understand or not.
- He just talked and talked and talked but didn't care if you were listening or not.

- She wasn't interested in what we thought.
- It was always hard to deal with him.
- Didn't relate to me. Couldn't bother to.
- Only related to/spent time with students he liked.
- She would say, "You have to do it."
- Put a lot of pressure on me to behave properly.
- She was so confusing.
- Never gave any time to ask questions.
- Always too busy and in a hurry.
- If you asked a question, he would say "That's a silly question."
- Made fun of some students.
- Made me feel inadequate and doesn't give the help I need.
- She made us lose interest.
- She would threaten us by taking away our points.
- I was scared to ask a question because I didn't want to see that unpleasant expression.

One unifying theme shared by all worst teachers is that they offer students a low-quality and deteriorating relationship. Not-so-good teachers do not seem to care about students—what they want, what they think, and whether they understand. But to warrant the status of "worst teacher," the teacher needs to go beyond just indifference to actually inject some poison into the teacher-student relationship—such as yelling, showing favoritism, rejecting the student in some way (because of poor behavior, poor performance, or being different), being hard to deal with (bossy), and instilling fear in students. Worst teachers also identify themselves through their ineffective teaching strategies, such as by being boring, monotonous, confusing, and using worksheets exclusively.

We can learn a lot from asking students about their best and worst teachers. The more we listen, the more we understand the grand themes that elevate some teachers to "best" status and those that plunge others to "worst" status. One takeaway from such an exercise tends to be an awareness that near-universals exist as to what personal characteristics and what teaching practices coalesce into the forming of best teachers and worst teachers.

Most of the qualities that define best and worst teachers speak to the issue of student motivation. Essentially, best teachers support students and their motivations, while worst teachers ignore or dominate over students and ignore or squash their motivations. This raises the issue of the teacher's motivating style. Motivating teachers (best teachers) tend to have a motivationally supportive style. As the students said earlier, "He listened to me"; "She understands us"; and "He made class very interesting—fun too." Demotivating teachers tend to have a motivationally suppressive style. As the students said earlier, "She would say, 'You have to do it.'"; "Put a lot of pressure on me to behave properly"; and "She would threaten us by taking away our points."

MOTIVATING VS. DEMOTIVATING TEACHING PRACTICES: HOW TO TELL THE DIFFERENCE

Sometimes it is easy to spot demotivating teachers. They yell, ignore, discriminate, confuse, criticize, and are just really boring. Other times, however, it takes a trained eye. Like "Tiger Moms" (Chua, 2011), difficult-to-spot demotivating teachers actually might appear to be very motivating at first, as they push and pressure students to win, succeed, and be the best. Such a laser focus on achievement and results (e.g., high grades, get into a prestigious school) paired with admonishments to a "toughen up" and "be a winner" can be motivating (energizing). Because it can sometimes be difficult to tell the difference between a motivating vs. demotivating teacher (Boggiano, Barrett, Weiher, McClelland, & Lusk, 1987), we need a way to tell the difference.

All motivational strategies are designed to energize students and give their behavior a sense of purpose. So, it is understandable to ask, "What is so wrong with pushing students hard to make good grades, get into Harvard, be the valedictorian, become an M.D., and make the family proud?" The problems start when the teacher begins to force students to sacrifice their psychological needs, intrinsic motivation, personal goals, self-endorsed values, and even their well-being in order to achieve these teacher-desired outcomes (e.g., "I don't care whether you like it or not. Just do what I told you to do!"). Sacrificing one's needs, interests, goals, values, and well-being are serious side-effects. As they say, "It's not the earthquake that hurts you, but the fire that follows."

Motivational psychologists take these side effects very seriously because (1) the sacrificed needs, personal goals, and well-being are the very sources of motivation the teacher is trying to generate in the first place (e.g., killing the goose that lays the golden eggs) and (2) these sacrifices are totally unnecessary. A teacher (or parent) does not have to pressure, threaten, or coerce students to motivate them. There are other approaches that support both students' needs and well-being *and* their productivity and achievement.

An apt analogy occurs in the pharmaceutical industry's development of new drugs. New drugs are developed to produce a particular benefit, but human biology (like student motivation) is incredibly complex such that drugs never produce a single effect. Benadryl, for instance, eases allergy symptoms, but it also creates drowsiness. Antidepressant Paxil is a wonder drug, but it has a black box warning on its label that warns of increased suicidal ideation. Given side effects like drowsiness and suicide ideation, it becomes a fair question to ask whether the benefits of the drug are worth it. When the answer is no, pharmaceutical researchers roll up their sleeves and go to work to find a "new and improved" next-generation drug that can produce the intended beneficial effect without the harmful side effects.

When translated into motivation research, what educators want are motivational strategies that enhance both achievement and well-being. An effective motivational strategy is one that gives students the energy and direction they need to be "productive and happy." In motivation research, "productive and happy" is the equivalent of "effective and safe" in pharmaceutical research. A motivational strategy that yields "productive" but sacrifices "happy" is problematic. Yelling, threatening, or shaming may grab students' attention and energize them into immediate action, but they also produce side effects that can be so detrimental that they overwhelm any potential benefit from the motivational strategy—side effects such as crushing the student's interest and poisoning the teacher-student relationship. So, one yardstick to differentiate a motivating from a demotivating teaching practice is this: Does it leave students productive *and happy*? You can spot this yardstick by hearing its mixed message, as in "Sure, my teacher pushes and pressures me but, hey, 'no pain, no gain', right?"

Similarly, a motivational strategy that yields "happy" but sacrifices "productive" is also problematic, but in a different way. Here the issue is not one of side effects, but effectiveness. A motivational strategy that does not spark students' enthusiasm and engagement is about as effective as an aspirin that does not alleviate a headache (e.g., self-esteem affirmations). Being happy is good, but school provides opportunities to learn, develop skills, experience growth, and realize potential. So, a second yardstick to differentiate a motivating from a demotivating teaching practice is this: Does it leave students happy *and productive*? You can spot this yardstick by hearing its mixed message, as in "My teacher just wants me to be happy, so it is okay if I do not get my work done."

PROFESSIONAL DEVELOPMENT

Worst teachers can get better, just as best teachers can (Borko, 2004). Motivating style is not a static condition. Imagine, for instance, this exercise. A teacher videotapes his or her classroom instruction at one point in time—say, at the beginning of the school year. On the videotape, the teacher can see his or her often-used motivational strategies and also how students react to them. At some later time, the teacher is then given an opportunity to participate in a professional development experience to develop greater skill in using evidence-based motivational strategies (e.g., for one of our favorites, see deCharms, 1976). Afterward, the teacher videotapes his or her classroom for a second time—say, in the middle or end of the school year. As the teacher views this second video recording, the critical questions are "What has changed?" and "Are these changes beneficial?"

If the professional learning opportunity bears fruit, the teacher will see three changes. First, the teacher will now rely on a more supportive (and less pressuring) motivating style. During instruction and during teacher-student interactions, the teacher will show more understanding, perspective taking, and student support. Second, the students will show an obvious rise in how actively and productively they engage themselves in the learning activities. In viewing the second video, the students will be noticeably more productive and happier. Third, the teacher and students will be more in sync and less in conflict with each other. On the second video, the teacher and students will enjoy each other's company and both teacher and students will find their relationship satisfying and mutually enriching.

CONCLUSION

The most basic question in any relationship is this: Is the other person a blessing or a curse? Best teachers are a blessing. They are supportive and purposeful, and their way of teaching and relating allows students to be increasingly motivated, productive, and happy. Worst teachers are a curse. They are authoritarian or disengaged, and their way of teaching and relating eventually diminishes, and sometimes crushes, students' motivation, productivity, and well-being.

CHAPTER 4

Your motivating style

Watch as a teacher interacts with her students, such as the teacher in Figure 4.1. During her instruction, she will likely introduce a learning activity, request that students engage in that activity, and help students understand it and make some progress. For instance, the teacher may say, "Today, we will write a persuasive paragraph," introduce some models of excellent writing to get students started, and provide feedback on students' progress. As you watch this teacher in action, it may take a moment or two, but you will soon notice that she relies on a particular style to motivate and engage her students. This is a very important observation to make because, as we shall see, some motivating styles are better than others.

Motivating style is the interpersonal tone and face-to-face behavior teachers rely on when they try to motivate their students to engage in the learning activities they provide. One style is to identify, appreciate, and provide opportunities for students to act on their inner motivational resources (e.g., psychological needs, intrinsic motivation, and personal goals; recall Figure 2.2). Such a motivating style—autonomy support—is the focus of this chapter.

AUTONOMY SUPPORT

Autonomy-supportive teaching is the adoption of a student-focused attitude and an understanding interpersonal tone that enables the skillful enactment of seven autonomy-satisfying instructional behaviors that serve two purposes—support intrinsic motivation and support internalization (Reeve & Cheon, 2021, p. 56). Its essence appears in Figure 4.2.

Autonomy-supportive teaching begins with taking the students' perspective, which itself originates out of a student focus and an understanding interpersonal tone. A student focus and an understanding tone are prerequisites that set the table for the first autonomy-supportive instructional behavior (*ASIB #1*; Chapter 6), which is to take the students' perspective. Taking the students' perspective is the "foundational activity" to autonomy-supportive teaching (Ryan & Deci, 2017, p. 443). It may sound simple, but in the context of busy classrooms and teaching pressures, the room for being student focused and understanding the students' view on classroom activity is easily crowed out. Once they understand students' perspectives, teachers are better positioned to support both intrinsic motivation and internalized motivation.

As detailed in Figure 4.2, teachers can support students' intrinsic motivation in two ways—invite students to pursue their personal interests (*ASIB #2*; Chapter 7)

DOI: 10.4324/9781003091738-6

FIGURE 4.1 Indigenous Teacher in Australia

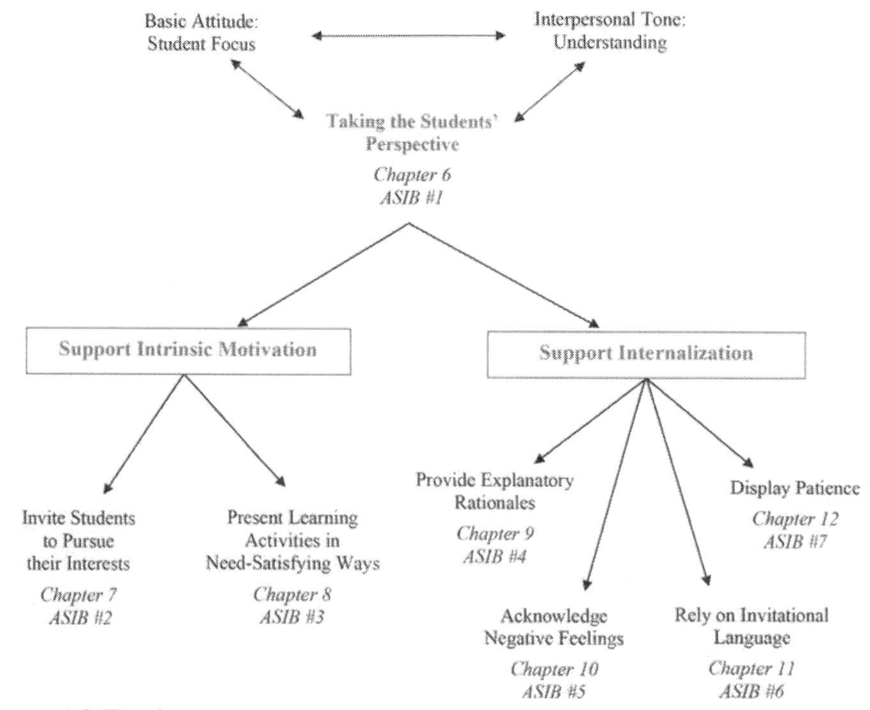

FIGURE 4.2 The Seven Autonomy-Supportive Instructional Behaviors and Their Origins (Student Focus, Understanding Tone) and Purposes (Support Intrinsic Motivation, Support Internalization)

Note: ASIB = Autonomy-Supportive Instructional Behavior

and present learning activities in need-satisfying ways (*ASIB #3*; Chapter 8). Not all educational activities can be intrinsically motivating, so teachers need to be able to support students' internalizations as well, and they do this in four interrelated ways—provide explanatory rationales (*ASIB #4*; Chapter 9), acknowledge negative feelings (*ASIB #5*; Chapter 10), rely on invitational language (*ASIB #6*; Chapter 11), and display patience (*ASIB #7*; Chapter 12). With all that said, we then turn to the issues of discipline, limit setting, and classroom management to discuss how teachers can introduce elements of classroom structure (e.g., setting rules, communicating expectations) in an autonomy-supportive way (Chapter 13).

Student focus, understanding tone

Teachers display a basic attitude vis-à-vis their students (Vansteenkiste, Aelterman, Haerens, & Soenens, 2019). This basic attitude tends toward either a mostly student-focus or a mostly self-focus (i.e., teacher-focus) during instruction and during teacher-student interactions. Autonomy-supportive teachers tend toward a more student-focus, as they adopt a curious, open, and flexible attitude toward their students and as they take an interest in students' emerging interests and preferences (Vansteenkiste et al., 2019). They keep an eye on the lesson plan, the quality of their instruction, and the time remaining on the clock (i.e., a teacher-focus), but mostly they pay attention to the rise and fall of their students' interests, preferences, emotions, engagement, and progress.

Understanding teachers let their students know that they (a) care about how their students are feeling, (b) are listening, (c) are paying attention to students' concerns, (d) are "on their side," (e) are working to understand why students are fussing, and (f) are working to find ways to adjust their instruction so that it better aligns with what students need and prefer. When they make an engagement request (e.g., "open your book") and when they react to students' difficulties and problems (e.g., misbehavior, poor performance), understanding teachers never get into a "me vs. my students" interaction to force students' compliance or obedience. This is not giving in to students but, instead, is working with students to help them successfully accomplish important classroom tasks.

Together, a student focus and an understanding tone set the stage for and enable the teacher's forthcoming autonomy-supportive instructional behaviors, as illustrated in Figure 4.2 and as defined in Table 4.1. Collectively, the seven instructional behaviors shown in the figure and table represent the day-to-day practice of autonomy-supportive teaching. These individual acts of autonomy-supportive teaching typically co-occur (Cheon, Reeve, & Ntoumanis, 2018), presumably because they all emanate out of the same underlying source (student focus, understanding tone) and because they serve similar instructional purposes (i.e., support intrinsic motivation, support volitional internalizations). These individual acts of instruction tend to coalesce together into a single coherent *autonomy-supportive motivating style* (Reeve & Cheon, 2021). While students see teachers display these individual acts of autonomy-supportive instruction, what students mostly perceive, respond to,

TABLE 4.1 Seven Autonomy-Supportive Instructional Behaviors, Each with a Definition and Example

Autonomy-supportive Instructional Behavior	Definition and Example
PERSPECTIVE TAKING	
Take the Students' Perspective (Chapter 6)	*Definition*: The teacher sees and experiences classroom events and activities as if he or she were the students (rather than the teacher). *Example*: Conduct formative assessments, such as starting a class (or activity) by soliciting students' input into the forthcoming lesson and then integrating those suggestions into the lesson plan.
SUPPORT INTRINSIC MOTIVATION	
Invite Students to Pursue Their Personal Interests (Chapter 7)	*Definition*: Invite and encourage students to pursue their own personal interests and goals. *Example*: Begin a lesson on the Inca period in history by asking, "What would you like to know about the Incas?" Students might then take the lesson in a personally interesting direction, "How did Inca children play?"
Present Learning Activities in Need-Satisfying Ways (Chapter 8)	*Definition*: Present a learning activity in a way that creates an opportunity for students not only to learn new information but also to experience autonomy, competence, or relatedness satisfaction while doing so. *Example*: Offer students a choice: "Here is a list of several different topics you may write your essay on."
SUPPORT INTERNALIZATION	
Provide Explanatory Rationales (Chapter 9)	*Definition*: Introduce teacher requests, procedures, and rules by explaining their usefulness so that students will see each request's personal benefits, be more open to accept it, and be more willing to engage it. *Example*: "Let's use respectful language, *because* we want a classroom that is welcoming, safe, and supportive for everyone."
Acknowledge and Accept Negative Feelings (Chapter 10)	*Definition*: First, acknowledge that a teacher request may be at odds with students' preferences; then, accept that any aroused negative feelings may have potential legitimacy. *Example*: "I see that everyone looks bored about today's lesson (i.e., acknowledge negative feelings). "Yes, we have practiced this same routine many times, haven't we?" (i.e., accept negative feelings as understandable reactions).

(*Continued*)

TABLE 4.1 Seven Autonomy-Supportive Instructional Behaviors, Each with a Definition and Example (*Continued*)

Autonomy-supportive Instructional Behavior	Definition and Example
Rely on Invitational Language (Chapter 11)	*Definition*: When making an engagement request and when helping students diagnose a problem, use a tone of voice (higher, softer pitch) and word choice that communicates understanding and support. Minimize pressure ("you must," "you have to") while conveying choice and volition. *Example*: "You *may* want to conduct a Google search. You *might* find it helpful."
Display Patience (Chapter 12)	*Definition*: Show an optimistic calmness as students struggle to start and adjust their behavior. *Example*: Watch, listen, be responsive to students' initiatives, communicate your willingness to help, and await a student-generated signal that your help would be welcomed and appreciated.

and benefit from is the teacher's larger, overall, gestalt autonomy-supportive motivating style that says, "I'm here to help. I'm here to support you and your strivings."

Take the students' perspective

Perspective taking is the active consideration of students' mental states and subjective experiences. For the teacher, this means seeing and experiencing classroom events as if he or she were the students (rather than the teacher). To do this, the teacher needs to partially set aside or deprioritize his or her own perspective to make room to attend to the students' perspective and concerns (i.e., adopt a student-focus). By adopting the students' frame of reference, teachers become both more willing (because of greater empathy) and more able (because of greater perspective taking) to create classroom conditions in which students' needs, interests, and goals can energize and direct their classroom activity. Once achieved, perspective taking enables teachers to provide instruction in ways that support students' intrinsic motivation and internalization of external regulations.

Support intrinsic motivation

Intrinsic motivation is the motivation to engage in an activity out of interest and enjoyment. Perspective taking allows the teacher to become aware of what students find interesting and enjoyable, so "support intrinsic motivation" is the instructional effort to create classroom opportunities for students to pursue and satisfy these interests, needs, and goals. One way teachers can do this is to create opportunities for students to pursue their personal interests (e.g., "What are you most interested in about this lesson?"). Another way is to present classroom activities in ways that can involve and satisfy students' psychological needs for autonomy (i.e., offer choices), competence (i.e., provide optimal challenges paired with guidance and feedback), and relatedness (i.e., have students pursue a prosocial goal together). As teachers present learning activities in these ways, students become increasingly able to experience not only psychological need satisfaction but intrinsic motivation too (Jang, Reeve, & Halusic, 2016; Patall, Dent, Oyer, & Wynn, 2013; Vansteenkiste, Simons, Lens, Sheldon, & Deci, 2004). When teachers are able to do this, students begin to feel that:

1. They are the origins of their behavior.
2. Their behavior is self-authored and self-directed (rather than teacher mandated or externally pressured).
3. They have a sense of ownership during their behavior.
4. They have engaged in the lesson with an authentic and volitional sense of "wanting to" (i.e., with interest and intrinsic motivation), rather than with a sense of "having to" (i.e., with obligation and pressure).

Support internalization

Internalization is the process of taking in values, beliefs, and ways of behaving from other people to then transform them into one's own values, beliefs, and ways of behaving (Ryan & Deci, 2017). Many teachers consider the instructional effort to facilitate students' internalization to be one of the most difficult challenges in teaching (Vasconcellos et al., 2020), and this is mostly because teachers are in the position of asking students to do what students view as uninteresting, not worth their time and effort, or even a source of negative feelings (e.g., completing homework, cleaning up, or revising a paper that the student thinks is already good enough). Understandably, when teachers request students to embrace such unappealing activities, students tend to complain, express negative emotions, and tilt toward a "me vs. you" conflict (Aelterman, Vansteenkiste, & Haerens, 2019). Such "motivational resistance" requires a highly skilled teacher response, including all of the following: Explain why the request is truly useful to the student; acknowledge and accept the negative feelings as a potentially valid reaction to the request; use invitational (rather than pressuring) language; and display patience to give students the time and space they need to work through the internalization experience.

PREPARING ONESELF TO SUPPORT STUDENTS' INTEREST AND VALUE

Most teachers agree that the subject matter they teach and the learning activities they provide are (1) interesting and (2) important/of value. Most teachers further agree that it is a worthy goal to provide instruction in ways that promote their students' intrinsic motivation (interest) and internalization (value). But this is easier said than

BOX 4.1

Is what I teach interesting? Important?

Is what I teach interesting? Why? In what way?
Is what I teach important? Why? In what way?

Before a teacher is ready to go into the classroom and teach a particular subject matter, it helps to first reflect on the two questions above. If the teacher can identify and articulate what makes the subject matter interesting, then he or she is ready to go to the classroom. The teacher just needs some instructional strategies to communicate and share that subject matter interest with students, so we suggest two:

- Invite students to pursue their personal interests
- Present learning activities in need-satisfying ways

Similarly, if the teacher can identify and articulate what makes the subject matter important, beneficial, and worth one's attention and effort, then he or she is ready to go to the classroom. The teacher just needs some instructional strategies to communicate and share that subject matter value with students, so we suggest four:

- Provide explanatory rationales
- Acknowledge negative feelings
- Rely on invitational language
- Display patience

If the teacher stumbles a bit to generate convincing and satisfying answers to these questions, then there is some important preparatory work to do. The teacher might, for instance, ask fellow teachers why the subject matter is interesting and valuable. Or the teacher might consult educators from all around the world by conducting a Google search (e.g., Is learning a foreign language important? Why?). Overall, the two essential tasks are (1) to appreciate what makes the learning activity of the day interesting and (2) to appreciate what makes the learning activity of the day worthwhile—and then communicate that interest and value to one's students.

done. In our experience, teachers benefit from working through the reflective activity shown in Box 4.1.

The activity in Box 4.1 is designed to create a state of teaching readiness to support students' interest and value. To begin, we ask teachers to reflect on and answer two questions. The first is, "Is what I teach interesting?" Once answered, we ask the follow-up question, "Why? In what way is your subject matter interesting?" We encourage teachers to write down, reflect on, and revise their answers until they gain a sense of clarity about what makes their subject matter interesting. We understand that there is still a gap between why the teacher finds the subject matter interesting and why students might find that same subject matter interesting, but generating these answers is an excellent way to prepare oneself to support students' intrinsic motivation during classroom instruction.

We continue the exercise by asking a second question, "Is what I teach important?" We explain that "important" means all of the following: valuable, beneficial, worthwhile, and of personal use. As before, we continue with the follow-up question, "Why? In what way is your subject matter important?" We again encourage teachers to write down their answers and revise them until they reach a point of satisfaction, as in "Yes, this is why what I teach is important." Again, there is a gap between why the teacher finds the subject matter important and why students might find that same subject matter important, but generating these answers is an excellent way to prepare oneself to support students' internalization during classroom instruction.

Once teachers make it clear to themselves why their subject matter is both interesting and important, we explain what we will do during the workshop. We will recommend (1) two instructional strategies teachers can use to translate what they know is interesting about their subject matter into classroom activities that can promote students' interest and (2) four instructional strategies teachers can use to translate what they know is important about their subject matter into classroom activities that can promote students' value (as listed in Box 4.1).

TEACHER CONTROL

Autonomy support is only one possible motivating style. Another frequently occurring classroom motivating style is interpersonal control (Assor, Kaplan, Kanat-Maymon, & Roth, 2005; Bartholomew, Ntoumanis, Mouratidis, & Katartzi, 2018). *Controlling teaching is the adoption of a teacher-focused authoritarian attitude and an interpersonal tone of pressure in which the teacher prescribes what students should think, feel, and do, irrespective of what students prefer* (Aelterman et al., 2019; Reeve, 2009; Soenens, Sierens, Vansteenkiste, Dochy, & Goossens, 2012). When controlling, the teacher first prescribes what students should think, feel, and do ("Open your book. Page 12. Read it.") and second applies an increasing amount of pressure ("If you don't, then you won't get your break. So, hurry, let's go; get it done!") until students forgo their own needs, interests, preferences, and goals to instead think, feel, and do as they are told.

Controlling instructional behaviors include behavioral control and psychological control (Soenens & Vansteenkiste, 2010). Behavioral control is the teacher's effort to gain control over students' behaviors, as exemplified by pressuring-inducing behaviors such as yelling, scolding, intimidating, bribing (i.e., offering contingent rewards), and various intrusive and manipulative socialization practices, such as punishing and denying rights (Assor et al., 2005). Psychological control is the teacher's effort to gain control over students' thoughts and feelings so that students will pressure themselves into doing what they are told, as exemplified by positive conditional regard (i.e., the teacher gives attention and love only following the student's compliance), negative conditional regard (the teacher withdraws attention and love following the student's noncompliance), personal attacks of the student's self-worth, expressions of disappointment, guilt inductions, and shaming (Kaplan, 2018; Roth, Assor, Niemiec, Ryan, & Deci, 2009; Soenens & Vansteenkiste, 2010).

Behavioral control

Teachers use behavioral control to pressure and coerce students to perform prescribed behaviors. They do this by uttering directives/commands, applying pressure (e.g., yelling, invoking a deadline), and by the giving and taking away of environmental contingencies, such as incentives, rewards, punishers, and many varieties of token economies and point systems. The teacher makes it clear that his or her giving or taking away of a particular consequence depends on whether or not the student complies with the teacher's request. Here is a definition of behavioral control (De Meyer, Soenens, Aelterman, De Bourdeaudhuij, & Haerens, 2016, p. 652):

> ... is characteristic of teachers who want to pressure students explicitly and from the outside, that is, using strategies external to the individual. The finality of this style is that students feel obliged from the outside to participate in an activity: There are external contingencies that either need to be avoided (punishment and negative consequences) or achieved (deadlines, privileges, and rewards). The strategies used are usually clearly visible to others.

Psychological control

Teachers use psychological control to manipulate students' thoughts and feeling so that students will then pressure and coerce themselves into performing teacher-prescribed behaviors. Controlling teachers do this by invoking in students feelings of guilt, shame, anxiety, or self-worth concern. The teacher makes it clear that his or her approval (or "positive regard") depends on whether or not the student complies with the teacher's request (e.g., "My teacher is less friendly with me when I do not do the things his/her way"; De Meyer et al., 2016, p. 640). Here is a definition of psychological control (De Meyer et al., 2016, p. 652):

> ... is characteristic of teachers who want to pressure students by appealing to students' self-worth. Their aim is to let students pressure themselves from within. The finality of this style is that students feel obliged from the inside to participate in an activity, for example to avoid feelings of guilt, shame, inferiority, and disappointment or to prove their worth to themselves or to the teacher. The strategies are sometimes subtle and difficult to observe directly because, for example, they are shown in a non-verbal way.

Behaviorally controlling teaching practices produce many harms, including (1) suppressing students' own personal motivations (needs, interests, preferences, and goals), (2) enflaming students' negative emotions (e.g., anger) and feelings of resistance and defiance, and (3) damaging the future quality of the teacher-student relationship. Psychologically controlling teaching practices produce many of these same harms, but they primarily produce internalizing, rather than externalizing, problems, such as anxiety and self-inflicted attacks on self-worth (De Meyer et al., 2016). What the two categories of teacher control have in common is that they both diminish the student to make him or her feel small, as through shaming, criticizing, humiliating, and by attacking their social status and self-worth. Once students are made to feel small, it then becomes relatively easy for the teacher to gain power, influence, and control over them. Unfortunately, this same controlling style can be seen in some parents and principals too.

TWO MOTIVATING STYLES

In early research, a teacher's motivating style was conceptualized along a bipolar continuum that ranged from a highly autonomy-supportive style on one end to a highly controlling style on the other (Deci, Schwartz, Sheinman, & Ryan, 1981). Teachers were either autonomy supportive or controlling. As empirical research progressed, however, several interesting findings emerged to suggest that the two aspects of motivating style existed mostly as separate (rather than as opposite) dimensions (Bartholomew, Ntoumanis, Ryan, Bosch, & Thøgersen-Ntoumani, 2011; De Meyer et al., 2014; Haerens, Aelterman, Vansteenkiste, Soenens, & Van Petegem, 2015), including the following four findings:

1. The two styles were only modestly negatively correlated with each other.
2. A low level in one style did not imply a high level in the other.
3. Autonomy support strongly predicted high autonomy satisfaction and effective functioning but only weakly predicted low autonomy frustration and maladaptive functioning; and
4. Teacher control strongly predicted high autonomy frustration and maladaptive functioning but only weakly predicted low autonomy satisfaction and effective functioning.

What this means is that teachers generally have two, rather than just one, motivating styles. This led researchers to conceptualize autonomy support as the "bright side" of motivating style and teacher control as the "dark side" of motivating style (Bartholomew et al., 2011).

As researchers watched teachers in action, they further noticed that the same teacher could be autonomy supportive in one moment but then switch over to be controlling in the next (Haerens et al., 2015). To illustrate this point, the motivational strategies used by nine different 6th grade teachers in the Netherlands appear

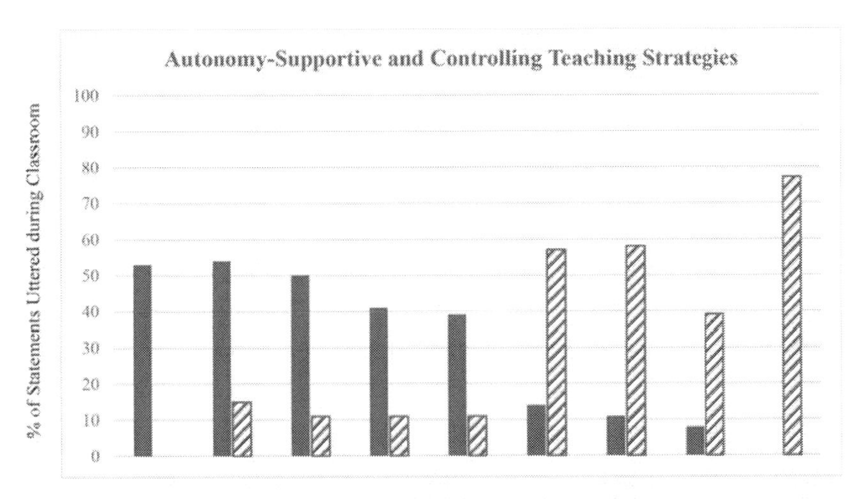

Teacher	Sam	Ella	Gemma	Tom	Anne	Rachel	Cathy	Jane	Bert
Autonomy-Supportive	53%	54%	50%	41%	39%	14%	11%	8%	0%
Controlling	0%	14%	11%	11%	11%	57%	58%	39%	77%
Other	47%	29%	39%	48%	50%	29%	32%	54%	23%

FIGURE 4.3 Sixth-Graders' Reports of the Percentage of Autonomy-Supportive, Controlling, and "Other" Motivational Strategies Their Teacher Used During Class Instruction

Solid bars = autonomy-supportive strategies; striped bars = controlling strategies

Source: Adapted from Hornstra, Mansfield, van der Veen, Peetsma, and Volman (2015).

in Figure 4.3. Of the nine teachers, one is clearly and consistently only autonomy supportive (Sam; see solid bar), one is clearly and consistently only controlling (Bert; see dashed bar), while the other seven teachers are both autonomy supportive and controlling (from Ella to Jane), even during the same class period (Hornstra, Mansfield, van der Veen, Peetsma, & Volman, 2015).

In terms of professional development, it is an important finding that teachers have within them both the autonomy-supportive and controlling styles. This means that a teacher who desires to upgrade the quality of his or her classroom motivating style needs to focus on and develop two skills (rather than just one)—namely, learn how to become both more supportive *and* less controlling.

CONCLUSION

A teacher's motivating style is an important classroom phenomenon, and research shows that some styles are better than others. The autonomy-supportive style represents motivating style's "bright side," because it catalyzes students' motivational satisfactions and effective functioning. The controlling style represents motivating style's "dark side," because it galvanizes students' motivational frustrations and maladaptive functioning. The teacher's challenge is to learn how to become increasingly autonomy supportive and decreasingly controlling.

Measuring motivating style

How does a teacher know if they are autonomy supportive? To answer this question requires a way to measure motivating style. Such an assessment can be done in one of three ways. First, trained observers can visit the teacher's classroom to make behavioral ratings of that teacher's actual instructional behaviors. This assessment is referred to as objectively scored motivating style. Second, students can complete a questionnaire to report their perceptions of their teacher's motivating style. This assessment is referred to as students' perceived motivating style. An example of this approach appears in the chapter's opening box Box 5.1, which shows nine items to measure three core features of autonomy-supportive teaching from the Student Evaluation of Educational Quality survey (SEEQ; Marsh, Dicke, & Pfeiffer, 2019). Third, the teacher can use a questionnaire to self-report his or her own motivating style. This assessment is referred to as teacher-reported motivating style. The purpose of this chapter is to describe and provide examples of each of these three assessment strategies.

BOX 5.1

Measuring autonomy-supportive teaching (SEEQ)

Perspective taking

1. My teacher listens to how students would like to do things.
2. My teacher wants to know what we are feeling during class.
3. My teacher asks what we want to do.

Interest support

1. My teacher allows us to pursue our own interests.
2. My teacher gives us a lot of choices about how to do our schoolwork.
3. My teacher provides interesting in-class activities.

Value support

1. My teacher explains why what we do in school is important.
2. My teacher talks with us about how we can use the things we learn in school.
3. My teacher explains to us why we need to learn the materials presented in this class.

DOI: 10.4324/9781003091738-7

OBJECTIVELY SCORED MOTIVATING STYLE

The most objective way to assess motivating style is to ask trained experts to make behavioral ratings of teachers' actual in-class instruction. To do this, the trained observer visits the classroom to rate the teacher in action (or, perhaps, views a videoclip or listens to an audio recording of the class.) The rater scores the extent to which the teacher does or does not engage in instructional behaviors known to represent a particular motivating style. One such rating sheet to score autonomy-supportive teaching is the Behavior Rating Scale (BRS; Cheon, Reeve, & Ntoumanis, 2018), as shown in Figure 5.1. To complete the BRS, the rater observes the teacher for a full class period (e.g., 50 minutes) and uses a 1-7 unipolar rating scale to score the frequency and intensity of each of the seven aforementioned autonomy-supportive instructional behaviors. After the class is over, the seven ratings are averaged into a single overall score to represent the teacher's autonomy-supportive motivating style. Objectively scored rating sheets can also be used to score teachers' actual, in-class controlling instructional behaviors (e.g., see Reeve, 2016, p. 132; De Meyer et al., 2014, p. 554). If you have a video recording of one of your own classes, you might want to use these rating sheets to score your own tendencies toward autonomy-supportive and controlling teaching

	Never, Not at All			*Occasionally Sometimes yes, Sometimes no*		*Frequently, Always*	
Takes the Students' Perspective • Invites, Asks for, Welcomes, and Incorporates Students' Input • Is Aware of Students' Needs, Wants, Goals, Priorities, Preferences, and Emotions	1	2	3	4	5	6	7
Invites Students to Pursue their Personal Interests • Asks Students What They Are Interested in/What They Want to Do • Provides Interesting Learning Activities	1	2	3	4	5	6	7
Presents Learning Activities in Need-Satisfying Ways • Autonomy: Offers Choices and Options; Introduces Intrinsic Instructional Goals • Competence: Offers Optimal Challenges Paired with How-to Guidance and Feedback • Relatedness: Creates Opportunities for Students to Pursue Prosocial Goals Together	1	2	3	4	5	6	7
Provides Explanatory Rationales for Requests, Rules, Procedures, and Uninteresting Activities • Explains Why; Says, "Because,…", "The reason is…" • Identifies the Value, Importance, Benefit, Use, Utility of a Request	1	2	3	4	5	6	7
Uses Invitational Language • Non-Pressuring, Flexible, Responsive Communication • Verbally and Nonverbally says, "You may…", "You might…"	1	2	3	4	5	6	7
Acknowledges Negative Feelings • Acknowledges Students' Negative Affect ("Yes"; "I understand") • Accepts Complaints as Reasonable, as Valid ("Okay"; "You make a good point.")	1	2	3	4	5	6	7
Displays Patience • Calmly Waits for Signals of Students' Willingness & Initiative • Allows Students to Work at their Own Pace, in their Own Way	1	2	3	4	5	6	7

FIGURE 5.1 The Behavior Rating Scale to Score Autonomy-Supportive Teaching

STUDENTS' PERCEIVED MOTIVATING STYLE

A second way to assess a teacher's motivating style is to ask the students (Kaplan, 2018). Separate questionnaires are used to assess perceived autonomy-supportive teaching and perceived controlling teaching.

Perceived autonomy-supportive teaching

Learning climate questionnaire

The questionnaire most often used to assess students' perceptions of their teachers' autonomy-supportive motivating style is the 6-item short-version of the Learning Climate Questionnaire (LCQ; Williams & Deci, 1996). Table 5.1 shows the six items from the LCQ. The individual items ask the student to what extent he or she perceives that the teacher provides choices, understands the student, conveys confidence in the student, provides encouragement, listens to what the student wants, and takes the student's perspective. Importantly, the LCQ (like most of the questionnaires in this chapter) has been translated into several different languages.

Perceived controlling teaching

Controlling teaching includes both behavioral and psychological control. For this reason, educators and researchers generally use two different questionnaires to assess

TABLE 5.1 The Six Items from the Learning Climate Questionnaire

Instructions. This questionnaire asks about your experience with your teacher during this particular class. Teachers have different styles in helping students learn, and we would like to know more about how you feel about interactions with your teacher in this class. Use the 7-point scale to communicate your extent of agreement vs. disagreement that your teacher relates to you during class in this way.

	Strongly Disagree			Agree & Disagree Equally		Strongly Agree	
1. My teacher provides me with choices and options.	1	2	3	4	5	6	7
2. I feel understood by my teacher.	1	2	3	4	5	6	7
3. My teacher conveys confidence in my ability to do well in this course.	1	2	3	4	5	6	7
4. My teacher encourages me to ask questions.	1	2	3	4	5	6	7
5. My teacher listens to how I would like to do things.	1	2	3	4	5	6	7
6. My teacher tries to understand how I see things before suggesting a new way to do things.	1	2	3	4	5	6	7

TABLE 5.2 The Four Items from the Controlling Teacher Questionnaire

Instructions. This questionnaire asks about your experience with your teacher during this particular class. Teachers have different styles in helping students learn, and we would like to know more about how you feel about interactions with your teacher in this class. Use the 7-point scale to communicate your extent of agreement vs. disagreement you're your teacher relates to your during class in this way.

	Strongly Disagree			Agree & Disagree Equally			Strongly Agree
1. My teacher tries to control everything I do.	1	2	3	4	5	6	7
2. My teacher is inflexible.	1	2	3	4	5	6	7
3. My teacher uses forceful language.	1	2	3	4	5	6	7
4. My teacher puts a lot of pressure on me.	1	2	3	4	5	6	7

perceived controlling teaching. To assess behavioral control, researchers often use the Controlling Teacher Questionnaire. To assess psychological control, researchers often use the Psychologically Controlling Questionnaire.

Controlling teacher questionnaire

The behaviorally-oriented 4-item Controlling Teacher Questionnaire (CTQ; Jang, Reeve, Ryan, & Kim, 2009) shown in Table 5.2 assesses the directly controlling and pressure-inducing dimension of perceived teacher control. The individual items ask the student to what extent he or she perceives that the teacher uses pressure and forceful language to control the student's classroom activity.

Psychologically controlling teaching questionnaire

The 7-item Psychologically Controlling Teaching questionnaire (Soenens, Sierens, Vansteenkiste, Dochy, & Goossens, 2012) shown in Table 5.3 assesses the psychologically intrusive dimension of perceived teacher control. The individual items ask the student to what extent he or she perceives that the teacher tries to control his or her thoughts and feelings, as through the teaching practices of guilt-induction, shaming, expressions of disappointment, blaming, personal attacks, and conditional regard.

TEACHER-REPORTED MOTIVATING STYLE

A third way to assess a teacher's motivating style is simply to ask the teacher himself or herself. The two most widely used questionnaires for this purpose include the *Situations in School* questionnaire (Aelterman, Vansteenkiste, Haerens, Soenens, Fontaine, & Reeve, 2019) and the *Teaching Scenarios* measure (Reeve & Cheon, 2016). Each questionnaire features both an autonomy-supportive and a controlling motivating style scale.

TABLE 5.3 The Seven Items from the Psychologically Controlling Teaching Questionnaire

	Strongly Disagree		Agree & Disagree Equally			Strongly Agree	
1. My teacher is always trying to change me.	1	2	3	4	5	6	7
2. My teacher clearly shows that I have hurt his or her feelings when I have failed to live up to his or her expectations.	1	2	3	4	5	6	7
3. My teacher is less friendly with me, if I do not see things his or her way.	1	2	3	4	5	6	7
4. My teacher reacts harshly if I have disappointed him or her.	1	2	3	4	5	6	7
5. My teacher makes me feel guilty when I dissatisfy him or her.	1	2	3	4	5	6	7
6. My teacher avoids talking with me when I have disappointed him or her.	1	2	3	4	5	6	7
7. My teacher often interrupts me.	1	2	3	4	5	6	7

Situations in schools questionnaire

The Situations in School questionnaire (SIS) was developed in collaboration with self-determination theory experts to assess four dimensions of teachers' motivating styles—autonomy support, control, structure, and chaos (Aelterman et al., 2019). Here, we describe only the autonomy support and controlling scales. The SIS presents 15 common classroom situations in which the teacher requests some type of student engagement. One situation is, "It is time for students to practice what they have learned. You...". A second situation is, "At a difficult point in the lesson students begin to complain. In response, you..." For each teaching situation, the SIS offers four different ways that a teacher can make that engagement request—in a way that is autonomy supportive, controlling, structured, or chaotic. For each of the four response options, the teacher indicates the degree to which that teaching behavior describes his or her own style.

SIS Situation #1 appears in Table 5.4, in which the teaching situation is how a teacher might introduce *classroom rules*. The first response option describes an autonomy-supportive approach to this teaching situation, as the teacher invites students' input and takes their perspective. The second response option describes a controlling approach to this same teaching situation, as the teacher tells students what they are to do and imposes consequences ("sanctions") to pressure students into following the rule. Response options 3 and 4 describe a structured and chaotic approach to the teaching situation, respectively. Additional illustrative situations from the SIS questionnaire will appear at the beginning of Chapters 6–12.

TABLE 5.4 Teaching Situation #1 from the Situations in Schools Questionnaire

1. Classroom Rules
You are thinking about classroom rules.
So, you:

Does not Describe Me at All			Somewhat Describes Me		Describes Me Extremely Well		
1	2	3	4	5	6	7	Invite students to suggest a set of guidelines that will help them to feel comfortable in class.
1	2	3	4	5	6	7	Post your rules. Tell students they have to follow all the rules. Post the sanctions for disobeying the rules.
1	2	3	4	5	6	7	Make an announcement about your expectations and standards for being a cooperative classmate.
1	2	3	4	5	6	7	Don't worry too much about the rules and regulations.

Teaching scenarios measure

The teaching scenarios measure first presents a paragraph-long description of highly autonomy-supportive teaching (see Table 5.5)—one that includes all the essential features of autonomy-supportive teaching, such as perspective taking, supporting intrinsic motivation, and encouraging volitional internalization (Reeve & Cheon, 2016). The paragraph is followed by four questions to assess the extent to which the teacher personally endorses (agrees with) that approach to instruction (i.e., the autonomy-supportive teaching scenario). These four scores are averaged to create the self-reported autonomy-supportive motivating style score. [The teaching scenarios measure also presents a second teaching scenario, which includes all the essential features of controlling teaching and then asks the same four questions shown in the lower part of Table 5.5 to assess how much the teacher personally endorses that approach to instruction—one in which the teacher directs what students are (and are not) to do and applies pressure to make sure they do as they are told.]

The teaching scenarios measure includes 12 additional follow-up items to understand why a teacher does (or does not) personally endorse autonomy-supportive teaching. Following items 1-4, items 5-16 assess the teacher's beliefs about autonomy-supportive teaching (see Table 5.6). Items 5–8 assess the easy-to-do belief, items 9–12 assess the effectiveness belief, and items 13–16 assess the normative belief. The easy-to-implement belief reflects the teacher's judgment that autonomy-supportive teaching is a relatively easy, feasible (plausible), time-efficient, and practical (not just idealistic) way to motivate and engage students. The effectiveness belief reflects the teacher's judgment that students benefit from autonomy-supportive teaching in terms of their motivation, engagement, learning, and achievement. The normative belief reflects the teacher's judgment that autonomy-supportive teaching represents

TABLE 5.5 Autonomy-Supportive Scenario from the Teaching Scenarios Measure

Teaching Scenario #1: As you plan and prepare for an upcoming lesson, you think about what your students want and need. You wonder if students will find the lesson interesting and relevant to their lives. To support their interest and valuing of the lesson, you prepare some resources in advance so that they can see how interesting and how important the lesson truly is. To better engage students in the lesson, you create a challenging activity for students to do, and you create some engaging questions to piqué their interest. As the class period begins, you invite your students' input and suggestions before finalizing the day's lesson plan, letting your students know that you welcome and value their initiative, ideas, and suggestions.

To motivate students, you take the time to explain why the lesson is important, how it aligns with their personal goals, and why it is a truly worthwhile thing to do. When students encounter difficulties and setbacks, you display patience—giving them the time and space they need to figure out the problem for themselves. When students complain and show little or no initiative, you acknowledge and accept their negative feelings, telling them that you understand why they might feel that way, given the difficulty and complexity of the lesson. As you talk with your students, you resist any pressuring language such as "you should," "you must," and "you have to." Instead, you communicate your understanding and encouragement. Overall, you take your students' perspective, welcome their thoughts, feelings, and actions into the flow of the lesson, and support their developing capacity for autonomous self-regulation.

Please answer the following questions in reference to Teaching Scenario #1.

	No, Not at All				Yes, Very Much So		
1. This approach to teaching describes how I teach my students on a daily basis.	1	2	3	4	5	6	7
2. This approach to teaching nicely describes what I do during class.	1	2	3	4	5	6	7
3. This is an accurate and true description of what I do during my teaching.	1	2	3	4	5	6	7
4. I do ***not*** teach this way.	1	2	3	4	5	6	7

a culturally expected, accepted, and commonplace way that one's peer teachers motivate and engage students. Overall, the Teaching Scenarios measure produces four key scores—personal endorsement of autonomy-supportive teaching and the beliefs that autonomy-supportive teaching is easy to do, effective, and normative. (The same items 5–16 are repeated following the controlling teaching scenario, except this time to assess the easy-to-do, effectiveness, and normative beliefs in reference to controlling teaching.)

CONCLUSION

Using one, two, or all three assessment strategies (behavioral ratings, student perceptions, or teacher reports), teachers can put a number on the quality of their autonomy-supportive and controlling motivating styles. The scores produced by

TABLE 5.6 The Three Beliefs about Motivating Style from the Teaching Scenarios Measure

My Impressions of Teaching Scenario #1							
	No, Not at All				**Yes, Very Much So**		
5. This approach to teaching is ***easy*** to do.	1	2	3	4	5	6	7
6. Most teachers can teach in this way. (It is *not* asking or demanding too much from teachers.)	1	2	3	4	5	6	7
7. This approach to teaching is ***easy*** and ***simple*** to do. (It is *not* hard and difficult to do.)	1	2	3	4	5	6	7
8. This approach to teaching is ***effortless*** and ***manageable*** (It is *not* too demanding and unmanageable.)	1	2	3	4	5	6	7
9. This approach to teaching is ***effective*** in terms of motivating and engaging students.	1	2	3	4	5	6	7
10. This approach to teaching would ***benefit*** my students in terms of their performance and achievement.	1	2	3	4	5	6	7
11. I ***like*** and think ***positively*** about this approach to teaching.	1	2	3	4	5	6	7
12. This approach to teaching will produce ***good*** and ***desirable*** results. It works!	1	2	3	4	5	6	7
13. Most teachers teach this way.	1	2	3	4	5	6	7
14. Where I work, this approach to teaching is the ***norm***. Most teachers I know and work with teach this way.	1	2	3	4	5	6	7
15. This approach to teaching is very ***typical***. Every teacher I know teaches this way.	1	2	3	4	5	6	7
16. This approach to teaching is ***common*** among the teachers I know and work with.	1	2	3	4	5	6	7

Note: Items 5–8 assess the easy-to-do belief, items 9–12 assess the effectiveness belief, and items 13–16 assess the normative belief. Items 1–4 (see Table 5.5) assess personal endorsement of that approach to teaching.

raters, students, and teachers positively intercorrelate with one another, yet provide three different perspectives to tell essentially the same story about that teacher's motivating style (Cheon et al., 2018; Reeve & Cheon, 2016). With these scores in hand, teachers have the information they need to engage in personal reflection, to understand why their students might be thriving or suffering, and to track their ongoing personal progress to upgrade the quality of their motivating style.

Part 3

"How to"

Take the students' perspective

BOX 6.1

How would you respond to teaching situation #3 from the situations in school questionnaire?

Starting Class
The class period begins.
You:

Does not Describe Me at All		Somewhat Describes Me			Describes Me Extremely Well		
1	2	3	4	5	6	7	Provide a clear, step-by-step schedule and overview for the class period.
1	2	3	4	5	6	7	Don't plan too much. Instead, take things as they come.
1	2	3	4	5	6	7	Insist firmly that students must learn what they are taught—your duty is to teach, their duty is to learn.
1	2	3	4	5	6	7	**Ask students what they are interested to know about the learning topic**.

Notes: The above is teaching situation #3 from the Situations in Schools Questionnaire (Aelterman, Vansteenkiste, Haerens, Soenens, Fontaine, & Reeve, 2019). The four response options represent, in order, structure, chaos, control, and autonomy support. The boldfaced autonomy-supportive response illustrates "Take the students' perspective."

To view several brief video clips (20 seconds each) of teachers demonstrating the autonomy-supportive instructional behavior of ***Take the Students' Perspective***, go to this online link: https://vimeo.com/518006247.

DOI: 10.4324/9781003091738-9

"You can't understand someone until you've walked a mile in their shoes." This famous proverb offers counsel as to how teachers might better understand their students.

Motivationally speaking, perspective taking starts with this question: "What do my students want?" To the extent that teachers can answer this question in a way that students will say is right and true (i.e., "Yes, you understand what I want."), then teachers will be well positioned to deliver classroom experiences that align with students' preferences and priorities. To gain this sort of understanding, teachers can ask:

- What do you think of this material—how do you feel about it?
- How interesting is this material to you?
- Does this information relate to your life in some important way?

Consider a high school teacher who is in the middle of planning a week-long lesson on "the scientific method." Being an experienced professional, she will have excellent notes on what the scientific method is, a step-by-step plan of instruction on how to put the scientific method into practice, interesting stories prepared about how famous scientists have successfully used this method, and a ready-to-go YouTube video demonstration (there are many of these). She is ready to provide excellent instruction. Still, the science teacher may have overlooked something crucial to her students' learning and engagement—the students' perspective.

Without some intentional effort, coming to know what your students want, think, and feel can be both harder and rarer than you might think (Tettegah & Anderson, 2007). It turns out to be difficult to infer correctly the private motivation and the subjective experience of another person. This is particularly true in those classrooms where students do not typically speak up to express their thoughts, feelings, and needs.

Perspective taking is seeing and experiencing an event as if one were that other person. Formally defined, perspective taking is the cognitive capacity to consider the world from another's viewpoint (Galinsky, Ku, & Wang, 2005). For a middle-school teacher, perspective taking is knowing and understanding what it is like to think like a 14-year-old, to sit in a plastic chair for 50 uninterrupted minutes, to wish the teacher would slow down (or speed up), to wish the teacher would provide a clear example of a confusing topic, to have one's mind wander off to the things 14-year-olds think about, and to want to ask a question but refrain from doing so out of a fear of looking dumb.

Among the seven recommended autonomy-supportive instructional behaviors, perspective taking has a special status. Every journey has a beginning, and the journey to autonomy-supportive teaching begins with perspective taking. Adding this skill to one's repertoire lays the groundwork to develop the other six instructional behaviors. It is difficult, for instance, to "Acknowledge Negative Feelings" without first taking and appreciating the student's perspective on that experience of negative emotion.

Perspective taking is not "mind reading." Mind reading is too difficult and unreliable. Instead, perspective taking is "data collecting." For instance, the most direct way teachers can understand and appreciate their students' perspective is to ask. The teacher can ask, "What would you like to do?" Or the teacher can ask students to complete anonymous index cards or sticky notes. Teachers can also use technology to collect such data, such as by having students enter their input on an "exit card" (via Google Forms) or by using interactive software such as menti, both of which will be described later in the chapter. Such student input will give the teacher the information he or she needs to adjust, adapt, bend, tailor, and personalize the content and the delivery of the upcoming lesson so that it becomes more aligned with students' needs, interests, and goals. Perspective taking produces benefits once the teacher actually begins to adjust the lesson to better reflect students' preferences. The more teachers do this, the more students get the message that the teacher cares about (and will be responsive to) their input. Teacher responsiveness is a central feature of what autonomy-supportive teaching is, as it represents much of the "support" part of "autonomy support."

THE "HOW TO" OF PERSPECTIVE TAKING

Perspective taking originates in and grows out of the teacher's willingness to embrace a student focus and an understanding tone. From this starting point, teachers can begin to appreciate their students' perspective by taking the following three steps:

Step 1: Ask the students what they think, want, and feel.
Step 2: Provide an opportunity for students to voice their perspective (i.e., to say aloud what they think, want, and feel).
Step 3: Adjust the lesson accordingly (to integrate students' preferences).

Perspective-taking skill begins with the teacher soliciting the students' perspective, which means giving students an opportunity to communicate what they are thinking, feeling, and wanting. Once done, the teacher needs to listen to and understand that student input. Sometimes students are willing to tell the teacher what they are thinking, feeling, and wanting, but often students just remain silent. In these cases, teachers can invite students to provide their perspective anonymously, as by asking students to complete anonymous index cards or exit tickets, as will be discussed later. Once the teacher understands the students' perspective, he or she can then bend the upcoming or ongoing lesson in a direction that more aligns with the students' preferences. Teachers can carry out this 3-step process at multiple points in the flow of instruction, including before the lesson, in the first minute of instruction, during instruction, and after instruction.

Before the lesson

Lesson plans are malleable and open to improvement. Even when the teacher sits back in his chair to look over a well-prepared lesson plan, there are always unseen opportunities for improvement. One such opportunity is to shift one's perspective from the teacher's to the students'. The teacher who is preparing a lesson may pause, look over the day's lesson plan, and ask:

> "If I were the students, would I find this interesting?
> Is this something I would want to do?
> Will students see this information and these activities as important and useful?
> What would my students say to improve this lesson plan?
> Would they change anything?"

Similar pre-lesson introspection may take the following form:

> "Okay, I've finished my lesson plan for tomorrow on photosynthesis.
> If I were to show this lesson plan to some of my students, what would they say about it?
> Would they want to add (or remove) something?"

These questions will be difficult (or at least ambiguous) for the teacher to answer without corresponding student input. Nevertheless, these are important questions to ask. For tentative answers, teachers can use their reservoir of teaching experience. Teachers can recall what students in the past have said about their preferences in similar situations. For more confident answers, teachers can ask students directly—either in the first moment of instruction, during the delivery of instruction, or at the end of instruction to prepare for tomorrow's new-and-improved instruction.

First moment of instruction

A critical opportunity for perspective taking occurs during the first moment of instruction. To capitalize on this potential turning point in any lesson, the teacher might initiate a learning activity with the following:

> It is time for us to engage in group work. But before we do, I would like to know if you like working in groups or not. So, if you do like working in groups, then please raise your hand to let me know.

Similarly, teacher talk in the first moment of instruction might be as follows:

> Today, we are going to learn about the Pythagorean theorem. We are going to work with this worksheet, your ruler, and your calculator. So, how does this sound? Does anyone have a suggestion how we might make today's lesson more interesting?

It takes courage to stand in front of 30 teenagers and ask, "How does this sound?" After all, students may say, "Yuck! It sounds terrible." But this one-minute conversation puts a spotlight on a crucial motivational issue—do students *want* to engage in the lesson? If students do not actually want to engage in the lesson, then it probably will not go well. Thus, it makes sense for the teacher to consider bending or adjusting the lesson to better reflect what students want and prefer to do. If the teacher cannot go in the direction of students' interests and requests, they can provide a rationale to explain why (as per Chapter 9). This does not mean compromising one's instruction and it does not mean "dumbing down" the lesson; rather, it means presenting the lesson in a way that students prefer, will get excited about, and will respond favorable to.

The risk of starting a lesson with, "How does this sound?," helps explain why some teachers prefer a controlling motivating style. It is easier to maintain a position of "I am the teacher" and hence "I already planned out the class, and I know what is best for you" if one avoids taking the students' perspective. After all, if you ask for their perspective, students might ask for a big change. If so, the (controlling) teacher might wonder why he or she is "just asking for trouble."

There is also the very real risk that students will respond to "How does this sound?" with stone silence. This is actually a common student response. If students stay quiet, then the teacher understandably wonders why he or she should ask for their input in the first place. When students stay quiet, however, it does not mean that they do not have a perspective on the lesson. It probably means that students would prefer to communicate their preferences either anonymously or at a later time (e.g., after they see how the lesson is going).

Even if students react with stone silence, there are still important benefits in asking for students' input. If the teacher asks what students are thinking and feeling day after day, then students will begin to build up an expectation that the teacher might ask for their input tomorrow: "The teacher asked what I thought about the lesson today; maybe she will ask what I think about the lesson tomorrow too." It may take some time before students are comfortable in offering their input and suggestions, so teachers need to be patient in giving students the time and opportunities they need to ready themselves to speak up. Before they speak up, students need to know that the teacher will treat them and their input with understanding and empathy (Noddings, 2012). Then, once they have spoken up and given voice to their perspective, students wait on the edge of their seats to see how responsive the teacher will be to their input. It can be a powerful experience for students, motivationally speaking, when the teacher responds to their input with, "Okay, yes; let's start there..."

During instruction

As instruction proceeds, teachers can keep the perspective taking going, as in the following:

> "Okay, it is time to practice what we have learned today. But before we do so, I would like to know what you think. Does anyone have any advice or input to help make our practice time more interesting or more helpful?"

In-lesson perspective-taking questions are opportunities for teachers to hear and to acknowledge the students' perspective on what is happening in the moment. During the learning, one student might want and need a real-life example. A second student may be confused or stuck. When students are unable to see how the lesson applies to their life and when students are confused or overwhelmed, they are at-risk of a landslide of negative emotions (e.g., frustration). In-lesson perspective taking allows teachers to become aware of these threats to students' classroom motivation and engagement and nip them in the bud.

A similar example in which the teacher uses student input to adapt the delivery of instruction might look like the following:

TEACHER: "We are going to learn 10 new Spanish vocabulary words. I've prepared these flash cards, and we will learn them together. How does that sound? Would something different be more helpful?"
STUDENT: "I have some words I want to learn, can we add them to the list of words for today?"
TEACHER: "Okay."

Sometimes what is best is to simply ask how students are feeling at the moment:

TEACHER: "Are you okay? What do you need?"

A more extended example of in-lesson perspective taking is an autonomy-supportive dialogue (Kaplan & Assor, 2012). An autonomy-supportive dialogue is a teacher-student conversation in which students collectively express how they perceive and feel about classroom issues. To initiate such a dialogue, the teacher invites students to enter into an open-ended conversation about:

1. How students feel and perceive the issues that concern them.
2. The choices students want to have in their studies.
3. The extent to which they feel that their studies and assignments are relevant to their lives and interests.
4. Students' views on what they are learning, including those aspects they feel need to be improved.

When teachers include autonomy-supportive dialogues within the classroom flow, students tend to feel that the teacher listens to and understands them. Students of teachers who use autonomy-supportive dialogues tend to agree with statements such as (Kaplan & Assor, 2012):

- The teacher listens to our ideas and opinions in class.
- The teacher lets us talk about things that bother us in class.
- The teacher asks us which subject we want to study more and which to study less.
- We talk with our teacher about the connection between learning and the real world.

Before and during instruction

Menti is an interactive technology tool that allows for teacher-student communication. The teacher enters www.mentimeter.com, while the students enter www.menti.com (and a code or link). The teacher asks an open-ended question, such as "How are you feeling as we start class?," "What did you like best from today's class?," or the earlier-mentioned query of "Does anyone have any advice or input to help make our practice time more interesting or more helpful?" Students type their answers using technology, such as a laptop computer, iPad, or smartphone. Typing answers into an iPad can be less threatening to students than speaking aloud in class as an individual voice. Everyone—the teacher and all the students—can see the students' answers in real time. Students can see that some of their classmates, for instance, prefer a slower (or faster) pace while others would prefer to work in small groups. The same software can also be used in the workshop itself so that the research team and participating teachers can be in constant communication, as the research team can benefit from taking the perspectives of the participating teachers much in the same way that a teacher can benefit from taking the perspective of their students.

End of instruction

A formative assessment is student-provided feedback that allows the teacher to evaluate what impact his or her instruction is having on students. Formally defined, *formative assessment* refers to "the collaborative process engaged in by teachers and students for the purpose of understanding students' learning and conceptual organization, identification of strengths, diagnosis of weaknesses, areas for improvement, and as a source of information that teachers can use in instructional planning, and that their students can use in deepening their understand and improving their achievement" (Cizek, 2010, pp. 6–7). Formative assessments provide teachers with the data they need to answer questions such as, "Do students understand the key points in the lesson?" and "Does my instruction need to change?" The information gained from a formative assessment can then be used to better "form" future instruction.

Formative assessments can be given at any point in the flow of a lesson (e.g., a pretest, a teacher-student conversation, an in-lesson question or brief quiz), but they are often used in the interval between two periods of instruction (i.e., at the end of instruction). That is, the students have one learning experience, the teacher conducts a formative assessment, and the students then have a second follow-up or next-day learning experience that is informed and improved on by the data collected during the earlier formative assessment. One such example might be the following:

"Tomorrow is our review day.
Please write down on a piece of paper at least 1 question you want clarified.
We'll make sure we clarify that question in tomorrow's review."

Another example is the "index card" activity, as follows:

> "That is the end of today's lesson. But before the bell rings, I would like to take these last 3 minutes of class to ask you to fill out this index card. At the top of the index card is a single question, 'Any suggestions?'
>
> This is an optional activity, and your input is anonymous. So, please don't write your name on the card. This is only for me to know how you feel about today's class. Please write about what went through your mind during today's class—what went well, what went poorly, what you would like to do differently in the next class. If nothing comes to mind, that's fine—you can just leave the card blank.
>
> When you are done with your index card, please drop your card into this shoe box as you leave—even if your card is blank. I will take the box and all its cards back to my office, read them, and see what we need to do to make this class better."

The "index card" activity provides the teacher with a stack of index cards (or a group of sticky notes that students attach to the whiteboard as they leave the class). The teacher can expect about half of the index cards to be blank or very brief statements, which seem to say, "Class is fine." The teacher can also expect about a third of the cards to offer a constructive suggestion that the teacher might have overlooked or might not have been aware of. Reading these suggestions ("I would like more class discussion.") serves the essential purpose of the formative assessment—to help the teacher tweak or gently restructure tomorrow's lesson so that it more aligns with students' preferences. And the teacher can expect a few cards to be truly eye-opening (e.g., "Whoa! I had no idea that this is what they were thinking and wanting."). These comments might be hard for the teacher to hear. Some may be both hard-hitting and upsetting, at least at first. For an autonomy-supportive teacher, however, these eye-opening comments are exactly what the teacher needs to hear, as they show a path forward to improved instruction, at least from the students' point of view.

Index cards and sticky notes are low-tech (but very easy to use). Their electronic version is to use exit cards (or exit slips or exit tickets). With exit cards, the teacher takes the last few minutes of class to ask students a single, key question using Google Forms or Microsoft Forms, such as: "Any suggestions?" or "What made you curious or interested today?" or "Did you value the group activity today, or do you think the activity would have been better done alone?" Using some type of electronic device (e.g., a laptop computer), students simultaneously type in their responses to the teacher's question. Exit card responses provide an equitable way for all students to share their voice, and they can open up opportunities both for future teacher-student dialogue and for improved future instruction. Once entered electronically, these responses can be either (a) shown publicly to the whole class on a projected screen or (b) collected as privately communicated messages that students send only to the teacher.

CULTURALLY RESPONSIVE TEACHING

Culturally responsive teaching is an approach to instruction that recognizes the importance of including students' cultural references in all aspects of their learning (Ladson-Billings, 1994). When teachers work with students from a different culture or socio-economic status, teachers need a deep appreciation and respect for their students' values, goals, perspective, worldview, obstacles, and preferred instructional methods. In practice, this means a good deal of teacher adaptation and accommodation.

Perspective taking can play a key role in helping teachers deliver culturally responsive teaching. This is because teachers—especially teachers new to the profession or new to the school district—simply do not have the experience and background to deeply understand their students. What perspective taking provides is greater understanding, and greater understanding lies at the center of both autonomy-supportive teaching and culturally responsive teaching. A teacher can even make a game of it. The teacher might put a line on the floor (using masking tape) and ask students to take a step forward if they, say, are from another city, speak a second language at home, play a musical instrument, and so forth.

The more teachers ask about students' values, goals, perspective, worldview, obstacles, and preferred instructional methods, and the more teachers try to adapt and accommodate their lessons to align with that student input, the more they will understand students and the more able they will be to deliver instruction in ways that are culturally informed, culturally relevant, and culturally sensitive (Aronson & Laughter, 2016; Patall & Zambrano, 2019).

IS PERSPECTIVE TAKING "GIVING IN" TO STUDENTS?

Upon learning the benefits of perspective taking, some teachers will protest, "Why should I take my students' perspective? They should take my perspective! They should listen to me!" The teacher's perspective is clearly important, as is the teacher's subject matter expertise and the teacher's leadership role in the classroom. Perspective taking does not mean that teachers should give up that leadership role or that "students get whatever they want" (i.e., permissiveness or student independence). It does not mean, "Doing only what students want or like." Instead, what autonomy-supportive teachers do is partially set aside or de-centralize their own perspective and agenda. In doing so, they make room—cognitively and emotionally—for students' input. In this way, perspective taking allows teachers to integrate their own perspective with that of their students.

When done well, teachers and students both benefit. Teachers and students become more in sync and less distant from one another. For instance, one student who had a teacher who used autonomy-supportive dialogues was asked, "What is a meaningful dialogue for you in school?" This student's answer was as follows (Kaplan & Assor, 2012, p. 265):

> For me, a meaningful dialogue is a dialogue where both sides are willing to change their point of view or to compromise. When you can speak freely without fear.... Usually we [the students] don't feel that way at school, but it's different with David [the homeroom teacher who participated in the program]. He really listens and I can really express myself.

Perspective taking bears three crucial fruits. First, it gives teachers the insight they need to better support their students' motivation during classroom instruction. Second, perspective taking helps build a high-quality teacher-student relationship (i.e., more in-sync, less in-conflict). When one person in a relationship takes the initiative to better understand the other, to show empathy and concern, and to work cooperatively, the quality of that relationship is bound to improve. Third, perspective taking is the starting point to autonomy-supportive teaching. After perspective taking, it becomes almost easy to enact the other six autonomy-supportive instructional behaviors that are the subject of Chapters 7–12.

CONCLUSION

Perspective taking allows teachers to better understand what students want. This understanding then helps teachers restructure their lesson plans to align with students' needs, interests, and goals. Perspective taking also helps build a positive teacher-student relationship, and it sets the stage for teachers to enact the other six recommended autonomy-supportive instructional behaviors to which we now turn.

Invite students to pursue their personal interests

BOX 7.1

How would you respond to teaching situation #2 from the situations in schools questionnaire?

Lesson Plan
As you prepare for class, you create a lesson plan.
Your top priority would be to:

Does not Describe Me at All			Somewhat Describes Me		Describes Me Extremely Well		
1	2	3	4	5	6	7	Communicate which learning goals you expect students to accomplish by the end of the lesson.
1	2	3	4	5	6	7	Don't plan or organize too much. The lesson will unfold itself.
1	2	3	4	5	6	7	**Offer a very interesting, highly engaging lesson.**
1	2	3	4	5	6	7	Insist that students have to finish all their required work—no exceptions, no excuses.

Notes: The above is teaching situation #2 from the Situations in Schools Questionnaire (Aelterman, Vansteenkiste, Haerens, Soenens, Fontaine, & Reeve, 2019). The four response options represent, in order, structure, chaos, autonomy support, and control. The boldfaced autonomy-supportive response illustrates "Invite students to pursue their interests."

To view several brief video clips (20 seconds each) of teachers demonstrating the autonomy-supportive instructional behavior of ***Invite Students to Pursue their Personal Interests***, go to this online link: https://vimeo.com/518008570.

DOI: 10.4324/9781003091738-10

A teacher sets up an art-themed interest area for her elementary-grade students to explore. On a tabletop, she organizes materials she thinks her students might find interesting—white and colored paper, markers, crayons, paints, stamps, sponges, glitter, rollers, safe scissors, tape, and so forth. Nearby lay some clay and felt-coated wires for sculpting. On the room divider she pins displays of famous artwork and children's own past creations. A sink for cleaning is nearby, and a posted sign explains the type of play and exploration that is to occur here—"Quiet voice; solitary and social play are both welcome." As the children return from lunch, the teacher announces the interest area. She invites students to use the art materials as an opportunity to pursue their personal interests. Eagerly, the children begin to choose among and manipulate the materials. As the students bring their art to life, they show initiative, creativity, and they deeply enjoy themselves.

INTRINSIC MOTIVATION

Intrinsic motivation is the motivation to engage in an activity out of interest and enjoyment. It is the inherent desire to seek out novelty and challenge, to explore, to take interests in activities, to learn, and to exercise and stretch one's skills and abilities (Ryan & Deci, 2017). When intrinsically motivated (i.e., when students pursue their personal interests), they explore their surroundings, process information deeply, think creatively, engage themselves fully, strive to learn something new, and seek out optimal challenges as opportunities to develop their skills and extend their capacities. All this intrinsically motivated energy pays off for students in terms of greater achievement, learning, school attendance, and various indicators of academic success and well-being (Boncquet et al., 2020; Froiland & Oros, 2014; Gottfried, 1985; Vallerand, Fortier, & Guay, 1997; Vansteenkiste, Timmermans, Lens, Soenens, & Van den Broeck, 2008).

The basic motivational process of how intrinsic motivation fuels classroom engagement and academic achievement (measured by GPA) appears in Figure 7.1.

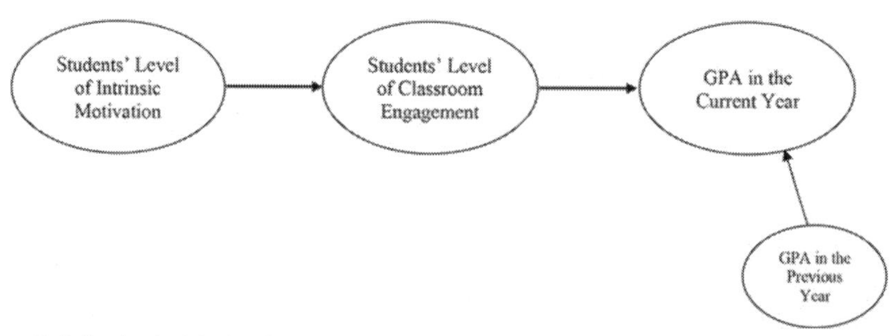

FIGURE 7.1 Intrinsic Motivation Explains Gains in Students' Engagement and Achievement

Researchers (Froiland & Worrell, 2016) assessed thousands of ethnically-diverse high school students' intrinsic motivation (i.e., "Class is fun"; "When we work on something in class, I feel interested.") to predict how engaged they were during classroom learning activities (i.e., "In class, I work hard.") and subsequent gains in their GPAs (grade point averages). The researchers statistically controlled for students' GPA in the previous year, so the study's dependent measure was year-over-year growth in student achievement. The point of Figure 7.1 is to highlight that intrinsic motivation is one of the main motivational roots that contribute positively to educationally-important outcomes, such as engagement and achievement.

Origins of intrinsic motivation

All students have intrinsic motivation because all students possess psychological needs. As shown in Figure 7.2, intrinsic motivation is literally the motivation that arises out of autonomy, competence, and relatedness need satisfaction. When students feel personal ownership over their behavior (autonomy), effective in what they are doing (competence), and accepted and loved by those around them (relatedness), they experience and display high intrinsic motivation. As shown in the lower part of Figure 7.2, when the teacher and when the classroom activity generate in students feelings of autonomy, competence, and relatedness, then students experience psychological need satisfaction and, hence, intrinsic motivation.

What this means for classroom teachers is twofold. First, students' intrinsic motivation rises and falls with the satisfaction vs. frustration of their psychological

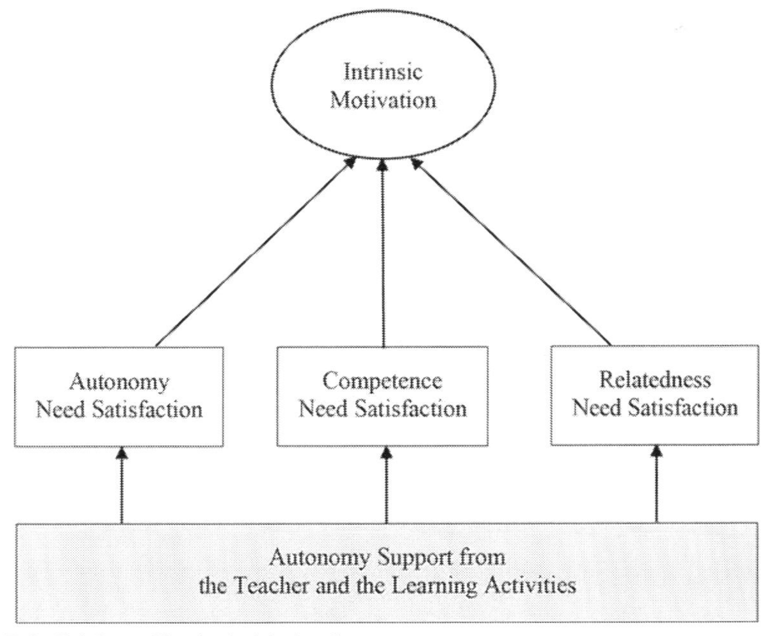

FIGURE 7.2 Origins of Intrinsic Motivation

needs. Second, when teachers provide classroom experiences that support students' need satisfaction, teachers are in effect supporting students' intrinsic motivation.

Autonomy as a psychological need

Autonomy is the need to feel personal ownership during one's behavior. It is the psychological need to experience self-direction and personal endorsement in the initiation and regulation of one's behavior (Ryan & Deci, 2017). Its hallmarks are feelings of willingness and volitional self-endorsement of one's action, as in "Yes, I want to do this."

Teachers do not need to create autonomy for students. Autonomy is not something that students need to learn, acquire through experience, or increase through training or socialization. Instead, autonomy is an inherent (inborn) motivation that is to be appreciated, encouraged, and supported, which means that autonomy-supportive teaching revolves around finding ways to support the need for autonomy that students already have.

Students need autonomy

Just as healthy physical growth and development depends on the availability of food, water, and sleep, healthy psychological growth and development depends on opportunities for personal ownership during one's behavior. Autonomy is a need in that it is an essential nutriment required for effective functioning, healthy development, personal thriving, and psychological well-being. One signal that students are experiencing autonomy (and thus thriving psychologically) is to look for the tell-tale sign of autonomy satisfaction—namely, students' classroom vitality. Vitality is the energy available to the self. Autonomy satisfaction creates the psychological energy (vitality) students need to interact with their surroundings with enthusiasm and excitement (Ryan & Frederick, 1997). Without autonomy satisfactions, however, the feeling is one of stagnation, not vitality. Worse, autonomy frustration leads to apathy and amotivation (feeling motivationally empty) and to compromised behavioral functioning (e.g., defensiveness, challenge avoidance).

Students benefit from autonomy

A feeling of autonomy is a potent source of engagement and well-being. If supported during instruction, autonomy satisfaction is fully capable of energizing, directing, and sustaining students' classroom activity in productive and beneficial ways. For instance, the ups and downs of students' classroom engagement and disengagement reflect students' ongoing experiences of autonomy satisfaction vs. frustration (Jang, Kim, & Reeve, 2012, 2016). When students are in classrooms that provide autonomy satisfaction then their engagement rises, but when students are in classrooms that fail to provide these same autonomy satisfactions then their engagement falls (Patall, Vasquez, Steingut, Trimble, & Pituch, 2016). Autonomy also provides the motivation to learn new information, develop new skills, and be prosocial with classmates (Cheon, Reeve, & Moon, 2012; Cheon, Reeve, & Vansteenkiste, 2020; Vansteenkiste, Simons, Lens, Sheldon, & Deci, 2004). Autonomy satisfaction generates enjoyment, such as "I enjoyed today's class," which represents the "satisfaction" part of "autonomy satisfaction" (Lee & Reeve, 2017).

Autonomy and interest

When teachers support students' autonomy during a lesson, interest rises; when teachers suppress students' autonomy during a lesson, interest falls (Tsai, Kunter, Ludtke, Trautwein, & Ryan, 2008). This close relation between autonomy and interest generalizes across different courses/subject matters, and it remains after considering students' dispositional interest in the subject matter, grade in the course, and gender. In other words, autonomy and interest are closely intertwined—more autonomy means more interest.

Interest is a powerful source of motivation, one that plays a major role in students' learning and development (Ainley, Hidi, & Berndorff, 2002; Renninger & Hidi, 2016). When a student pursues a personal interest, the quality of their attention rises, as concentration deepens and he or she becomes immersed in the activity. Thinking and problem solving become more flexible and creative. Understanding deepens, knowledge accumulates, imagination is stirred, plans are made, and goals are set. Initiative and agency rise, as the student begins to explore what is new and to manipulate available objects and sources of information. Books get read, websites are explored, role models are sought, and journal entries and diaries are written. Learning occurs, as new knowledge is gained and existing knowledge structures are enriched. Emotions turn positive, as the student shows a sense of excitement, spontaneity, enjoyment, and delight. Skills and talents are developed. When an interest is shared with a classmate, a new friendship may develop. Perhaps most important of all, when students are allowed to pursue their personal interests, they learn how to initiate and to take responsibility for their own learning.

INVITE STUDENTS TO PURSUE THEIR PERSONAL INTERESTS

When students are free to pursue their interests, they feel a sense of autonomy satisfaction (Sheldon, Elliot, Kim, & Kasser, 2001). To invite students to pursue their personal interests, teachers can offer invitations such as:

- "What are you interested in?"
- "What would you like to do?"

The teacher can offer these interest invitations casually, especially at the beginning of the class or at the beginning of a learning activity. A more formal interest invitation appears in Box 7.2.

BOX 7.2

A classroom activity to invite students to pursue their personal interests

Science

One example of an everyday invitation to pursue one's personal interests appears on the Google homepage. This page presents a rectangle that awaits the user to type in an interest query. In the classroom, the teacher can draw a rectangle on the whiteboard, write the course subject matter above the search box (e.g., Science, History, Speaking Spanish), and invite students to ask questions that represent what is most interesting to them (e.g., "Where did the moon come from?" or "Why are bumblebees disappearing?"). The teacher either answers the question or, if unsure of a quality answer, simply types the student's query into an actual Google search to show the search results on the classroom projector.

If students seem hesitant to volunteer questions aloud, the teacher might invite students to write down their interest queries on a piece of paper, ask students to send their written questions forward, and select those questions that are both relevant to the course material and of wide interest to the class.

Teachers who have put this activity into classroom practice (for 10-minutes or for the whole class) typically find that it creates one of their best classroom experiences—because students show such strong interest, initiative, and leave the class saying, "that was a fun class today."

A structured way to invite students to pursue their personal interests

Sometimes teachers think that the teaching practice of inviting students to pursue their personal interests is too unstructured and open-ended. "What would you like to do?" seems like an invitation for students to go off-task. This is because, for many lessons, teachers ask students to produce a specific end-of-class product (e.g., learn 20 new vocabulary words) or performance (e.g., write a paragraph that includes these 4 key features). In these more structured cases, teachers can still offer students a meaningful opportunity for self-direction by creating an opportunity for students to pursue their own way of completing the lesson and their own way of producing the product. After announcing the need for students to produce a specific product, the teacher can add an opportunity for self-direction by saying:

- "What do you want to focus on?"
- "Where would you like to begin?"

Ask students what is most interesting about the lesson

Teachers can invite students to pursue their personal interests, even while keeping students' attention and engagement focused on a particular learning activity that the teacher has prepared in advance. In this common situation, teachers can ask students what they find to be most interesting about the teacher-selected learning activity, such as the following:

- "Here is the home page of the website for today's topic (roalddahl.com)
  Take a look around this home page and tell me what looks most interesting to you."

Within the boundaries of almost any lesson, teachers can ask students:

- "What are you most interested in *about this lesson*?
  Is there anything about this topic that you are especially curious about?"

When teachers ask students what is most interesting about the lesson, the teacher is inviting students to pursue their personal interest. But for students to actually experience autonomy satisfaction, the teacher needs to be responsive to the student's expression of interest, as in:

TEACHER: "Today, we are going to learn about the solar system and outer space.
Is there something that you find interesting about outer space?"
STUDENT: "Mars. What about Mars? Can we talk about that?"
TEACHER: "Yes, we can talk about Mars.
In fact, that makes a good place to start. Here is a question:
Is Mars closer to the sun than is the Earth, or is it farther away?"

In this example, both the interest invitation and the interest support are important. The invitation opens students up to anticipate a forthcoming experience of autonomy satisfaction ["Hey, this might be interesting (satisfying)..."]. When teachers are responsive to and supportive of the student's expression of interest, then teachers are supporting students' as origins of their own learning and behavior (Reeve & Jang, 2006). It is this experience of being able to self-author and self-direct one's own learning and behavior that provides the student with an experience of autonomy satisfaction. Thus, teachers can (1) invite students to pursue their personal interests and (2) be responsive to and supportive of those expressed interests. Box 7.3 explains this teacher-student dynamic more fully.

Interesting activities are autonomy supports

Just as a teacher can be autonomy supportive, so can an interesting activity. A student who feels free and volitional while playing the guitar or while creating art will likely experience autonomy satisfaction. Thus, an interesting activity becomes an environmental source of autonomy support.

BOX 7.3

The instructional challenge of "invite students to pursue their personal interests"

It is not difficult for teachers to learn the following skill:

> The teacher introduces the topic of the day and, in doing so, invites students to pursue their personal interests. The teacher asks, "What about this topic are you most interested in?" Is there anything about this topic you are especially curious about?'

The difficulty begins with the teacher's fear that students will respond to such interest invitations with stone silence. The teacher asks, "What are you interested in?," and students stay silent, look at the floor, and simply maintain a state of passivity. Worse, students may be unresponsive on Monday, and continue to be unresponsive on Tuesday, Wednesday, Thursday, and Friday as well. After a week of silence and passivity, the teacher may understandably wonder, "What's the point?"

The above teacher-student dynamic often takes one or two weeks to unwind—for students to leave behind their passivity to instead give voice to their interests and preferences. Before they speak up, students need to build up an expectation that the teacher will invite them to speak up and, when they do, be responsive to their input, suggestions, and inquiries. The good news is that students do typically make this transition from passive recipients to active agents—if the teacher will persist in inviting students to pursue their personal interests despite the initial blank faces and silent voices. Helping students find greater agency within themselves is a terrific way for teachers to support students' motivation (e.g., see Chapter 21).

Two weeks of blank faces and silent voices can be daunting. To bridge this transition period, teachers can supplement their interest invitations with interest-fishing expeditions. If the topic of the day is genetics, the teacher might begin with, "What is interesting to you about genetics?" Given silence, the teacher might fish for pockets of students' interests with follow-up questions such as,

> "Did you know there is no such thing as a gene for music or basketball talent?"
> "Did you know that, at a genetic level, all humans are 99% identical?"
> "Did you know that genes put a cap on human life expectancy of about 125 years?"

The idea is to identify points of interest *before* providing information about genetics (so that an experience of interest can then energize students' learning of that information).

In addition, through clubs, organizations, programs, places to go, and technology, the student can find additional sources of autonomy support (that are not necessarily provided by the teacher) (Mynard & Shelton-Strong, 2021). The student who is interested in learning a foreign language can find many autonomy need-supportive places to go (e.g., conversational lounges, writing centers, and community events) and technology-rich resources and tools to interact with (e.g., smartphone apps, websites, "how to" software programs). When these environmental resources allow the student to feel interested and volitional, they are autonomy supports. The role that the teacher can play in this process is not only to provide students with interesting activities but also to suggest where students might find such environmental autonomy supports to explore and engage.

Intrinsic goal pursuits are autonomy supports

Just as teachers and interesting activities are autonomy supports, so are intrinsic goal pursuits. As discussed in Chapter 2, a goal is an "intrinsic goal" if it puts the goal-striver on an inwardly oriented pathway of activity toward recurring opportunities for autonomy satisfaction. Many goals can do this, but examples of prototypical intrinsic goals are those for personal growth, and close relationships, (Niemiec, Ryan, & Deci, 2009). Thus, a personal growth goal such as "I want to join a club that allows me to pursue my interests" puts the goal-striver on an autonomy-satisfying pathway of activity. The reason why intrinsic goal pursuits are especially beneficial is because the autonomy satisfaction they produce provides extra motivational support for the learner to display greater effort, make more goal progress, and experience greater well-being (Koestner, 2008).

Overall, students have three opportunities to experience autonomy satisfaction. First, the teacher can invite the student to pursue his or her personal interest within the context of the teacher-presented learning activity. Second, the student can seek out and engage in an interesting activity. Third, the student can set and pursue an intrinsic goal.

TEACH IN STUDENTS' PREFERRED WAYS

Teaching in students' preferred ways is a two-step approach to interest-enhancing instruction (Jang, Reeve, & Halusic, 2016). The teacher first becomes aware of students' preferred ways of learning. This can be done by soliciting students' input, as by conducting a formative assessment in which students report their preferred vs. non-preferred ways of learning. Once the teacher becomes aware of students' preferences, the teacher can act on that input to deliver the lesson in a way that aligns with students' preferred ways and avoids nonpreferred ways of learning.

In one experimental demonstration of this two-step approach, teachers first asked students to rate (on a questionnaire) how interesting and enjoyable they found

TABLE 7.1 Students' Preference Ratings for 10 Different Ways of Learning

Rank	Way of Learning	Mean Preference Rating (1–7 scale)
1.	Listen to a Guest Speaker	5.86
2.	Watch a Video Clip	5.66
3.	Participate in a Whole-Group Discussion	5.26
4.	Listen to an Audio Clip	5.11
5.	Participate in Cooperative Learning	4.63
6.	Engage in Independent Seatwork	4.21
7.	Listen to a Lecture	4.08
8.	Complete a Drill-and-Practice Session	3.57
9.	Complete a Prepared Worksheet	3.38
10.	Listen to a Student Presentation	3.37

each of ten possible ways of learning (using a 1–7 rating scale). Table 7.1 shows these student ratings listed in rank order from most to least preferred.

With this student input in hand, researchers prepared two different versions of the same 30-minute lesson. The left side of Table 7.2 shows the Preferred Way of Learning, which integrated students' second and third ranked preferences (i.e., watch video clip, whole-group discussion). The right side of Table 7.2 shows the parallel Nonpreferred Way of Learning, which integrated students' sixth and ninth ranked preferences (i.e., engage in independent seatwork, complete a prepared worksheet). The content of the two lessons was identical, so the only thing that varied was the way the lesson was delivered during minutes 13–28. After the lesson, students took a test to assess their conceptual understanding of the learning material and completed a questionnaire to report their felt autonomy satisfaction. In addition, classroom observers surreptitiously rated how engaged each student was during the lesson. Results showed that teaching in students' preferred ways increased students' engagement and learning. Further, the reason why students showed higher engagement and

TABLE 7.2 Scripts to Create the Preferred and Non-Preferred Ways of Learning Lesson Plans

Minutes	Preferred Ways of Learning	Nonpreferred Ways of Learning
0–3	Introduction	Introduction
4–12	PowerPoint-based Lecture	PowerPoint-based Lecture
13–16	Watch Video Clip	Engage in Independent Seatwork
17–28	Whole-Group Discussion	Complete Prepared Worksheet
29–30	Wrap-up	Wrap-up

learning was because the instructional strategy allowed students to first experience a high level of autonomy satisfaction (Jang, Reeve, & Halusic, 2016).

Three-minute version (of teach in students' preferred ways)

The above approach to instruction requires preparation time. For instance, the teacher might conduct the paper-and-pencil formative assessment or ask students to enter data using some technology platform on day 1, analyze and interpret the student input on day 2, and then on day 3 prepare to deliver a lesson in its student-preferred way. For instance, students might express a strong preference for "listen to a guest speaker" and "watch a videoclip," as in Table 7.1. If so, on day 2, the teacher could spend some time looking on YouTube for a brief videoclip of an interesting, highly relevant, and well-known guest speaker to represent a guest speaker for the next day's class (e.g., Neil deGrasse Tyson explains the earth's rotation in science class; Roald Dahl explains his writing technique in language class).

But it is also possible to deliver a 3-minute (instead of a 3-day) version of this same teaching strategy. For instance, teachers could begin any lesson by asking, "What would you like to do?" and then on the spot (to the extent possible) adapt the delivery of that lesson so that it more aligned with students' preferred ways of learning. Students may, in fact, nominate an interesting, highly relevant, and well-known video clip that the teacher might consider showing (e.g., students really like "The photosynthesis song" videoclip for their science learning).

What preferred ways of learning is not

As a practical concern, teaching in students' preferred ways is not slapping "bells and whistles" onto a lesson. Bells and whistles (e.g., videos, stories, jokes, cartoons, games, gifts, holding class outdoors) might be interesting and entertaining, but they might also be distracting. So, a teacher's accommodation to students' preferences needs to be done within a context of what constitutes good pedagogical practice. Teachers need not accommodate to all student preferences. Instead, teaching in students' preferred ways opens up a two-way dialogue to merge together students' preferences and teachers' knowledge of what constitutes best practices.

TWO WAYS TO SUPPORT INTRINSIC MOTIVATION

Teachers have two ways to support intrinsic motivation. The first way (covered in this chapter) is to appreciate that students come into class with their own personal interests, so the recommended instructional strategy is to invite students to pursue those interests by (1) extending an invitation for students to pursue their personal interests, (2) introducing a learning activity and then asking students what they find to be most interesting about that particular lesson, (3) suggesting where students might find interesting activities and resources to explore and engage, (4) encouraging students to pursue intrinsic goals, and (5) teaching in students' preferred ways. This first way of supporting intrinsic motivation is, essentially, to invite students to pursue their preexisting interests.

The second way (covered in the next chapter) is to appreciate that students come into class possessing psychological needs, but also that these needs may lay dormant until they are brought to life by a needs-supportive environment. So, the recommended instructional strategy is to present the day's learning activity in a way that will satisfy (rather than neglect or frustrate) students' psychological needs. This can be done by presenting the learning activity in a(n) (1) autonomy-satisfying way, as by providing choices, (2) competence-satisfying way, as by providing optimal challenges with guidance and scaffolding, and (3) relatedness-satisfying way, as by asking students to pursue a prosocial goal together. This second way of supporting students' intrinsic motivation is, essentially, to provide learning activities in need-satisfying ways.

CONCLUSION

It sounds so simple and easy for a teacher to ask, "What would you like to do?" or "What is most interesting to you about this topic?" But such an interest invitation is uncommon teacher talk. In some schools, such words are never spoken. Despite its rarity, such teacher talk is as direct and reliable a route to supporting students' intrinsic motivation as there is.

CHAPTER 8 Present learning activities in need-satisfying ways

BOX 8.1

How would you respond to teaching situation #15 from the situations in schools questionnaire?

Homework
When assigning homework you …

Does not Describe Me at All		Somewhat Describes Me		Describes Me Extremely Well			
1	2	3	4	5	6	7	Make it clear that the homework has to be done well; if not, bad consequences will follow.
1	2	3	4	5	6	7	Communicate what it involves to competently do the homework. Check that everyone understands what is required to successfully accomplish the homework.
1	2	3	4	5	6	7	**Offer a number of different homework exercises (e.g., three) and you ask students to pick a few of them (e.g., two).**
1	2	3	4	5	6	7	Let the homework speak for itself rather than over-explaining everything.

Notes: The above is teaching situation #15 from the Situations in Schools Questionnaire (Aelterman, Vansteenkiste, Haerens, Soenens, Fontaine, & Reeve, 2019). The four response options represent, in order, control, structure, autonomy support, and chaos. The boldfaced autonomy-supportive response illustrates "Offer choice."

DOI: 10.4324/9781003091738-11

To view several brief video clips (20 seconds each) of teachers demonstrating the autonomy-supportive instructional behavior of ***Present Learning Activities in Need-Satisfying Ways***, go to this online link: http://vimeo.com/518009334.

Activities vary in how interesting students find them to be. This observation raises an important question: What makes an activity interesting?

In a self-determination theory analysis, a student will experience a classroom activity as interesting and enjoyable to the extent that it enables an experience of psychological need satisfaction (Deci, 1992; Krapp, 2005). When a student is participating in a group discussion, or playing a musical instrument, or working on the computer, that student will say to himself or herself, "This is interesting," to the extent that the activity allows the student to feel:

1. Personal ownership while acting (high autonomy);
2. Effective and capable (high competence); or
3. Accepted and close to those in the class (high relatedness).

It is the experience of need satisfaction that creates the interest and enjoyment. If the activity was unable to generate these feelings of autonomy, competence, or relatedness satisfaction, then it would not be experienced as interesting and enjoyable.

It is not the activity itself that is interesting. Playing basketball and creating art with an iPad are not inherently interesting things to do. Instead, they are conduits to need satisfaction. In a PE class, if one student feels competent and effective during a basketball game, he or she will say that basketball is interesting and enjoyable; but if a second student feels incompetent and ineffective during that same game of basketball, he or she will likely say that basketball is not interesting and not enjoyable. Similarly, in an art class, if a student draws anime and feels free to create the art in her own way, she will likely say that drawing is interesting and enjoyable, while another student who draws the same anime but feels forced and obligated to create the art (because of an assignment or deadline) will likely say that drawing is not interesting. Hence, the interest lies in the experience of need satisfaction, rather than in the task itself.

Some activities do possess features that tend to make them relatively interesting to most people, such as novelty and new information, suspense about what will happen next, a puzzle or mystery to solve—as well as humor, fantasy, and esthetic appeal (Reeve, Lee, & Won, 2015). This is generally why some movies, YouTube videos, and classroom lectures are more interesting than others. The practical point for the teacher, however, is that almost any educational activity (e.g., playing music, solving math problems, and taking a field trip) can be made to be more interesting and enjoyable by presenting it in a need-satisfying way.

WHAT IS "SATISFYING" ABOUT A SATISFYING LEARNING EXPERIENCE?

Several motivation researchers have asked, "What explains a satisfying learning experience?" (Jang, Reeve, Ryan, & Kim, 2009; Sheldon, Elliot, Kim, & Kasser, 2001). To answer this question, 9th grade students in South Korea were asked to recall a recent highly satisfying classroom learning experience and then rate the felt presence vs. absence of eight different types of motivational satisfaction during that experience. Specifically, students were asked the following (Jang, Reeve, Ryan, & Kim, 2009, p. 646):

> Consider a recent classroom learning experience. What we want you to do is bring to mind the single most personally satisfying learning experience you had during class last week. We are being vague about the definition of a satisfying learning experience on purpose because we want you to use your own definition. Think of satisfying in whatever way makes sense to you. Take a couple of minutes to be sure that you come up with a very satisfying learning experience.

Each student briefly described his or her satisfying experience and then rated how prevalent was each of the eight motivational satisfactions. Table 8.1 shows the students' ratings.

What the table shows is that experiences of competence, autonomy, and relatedness were the "active ingredients" underlying students' experiences of satisfaction. When these Korean students brought to mind a particularly satisfying classroom learning experience, what came to mind were classroom episodes of high autonomy, high competence, and high relatedness, though students also recalled experiences of feeling high self-esteem and high stimulation. A follow-up study showed that when

TABLE 8.1 Presence of Eight Motivational Satisfactions during a Satisfying Classroom Experience

Psychological Need	Importance
High competence	4.34_{a}
High autonomy	$4.11_{a,b}$
High self-esteem	4.09_{b}
High relatedness	$4.07_{a,b}$
High stimulation	4.00_{b}
High self-actualization	3.72_{c}
High safety–security	3.38_{d}
High popularity–influence	3.17_{e}

Notes: N = 144 9th grade Korean students. Scores could range from 1 to 7. Means not sharing a subscript are significantly different from each other, $p < 0.01$.

another sample of Korean students experienced high levels of autonomy, competence, and relatedness during their regular classroom instruction, they then displayed high engagement, high intrinsic motivation, high achievement, and little negative emotionality, showing that these three motivations were not only sources of satisfaction but were academically productive as well (Jang, Reeve, Ryan, & Kim, 2009).

These findings suggest that it makes sense for teachers to think about how they might present their learning activities in need-satisfying ways. Accordingly, the rest of this chapter explains how teachers can do this.

HOW TO PRESENT A LEARNING ACTIVITY IN AN AUTONOMY-SATISFYING WAY

The surest way to signal to students that autonomy satisfaction may be forthcoming is to offer choice (Patall, 2013). Teachers cannot make students choose but, when students seek choices and options, teachers can offer choice to create classroom opportunities for autonomy need satisfaction. With choice, the teacher allows students to decide for themselves to engage in one activity rather than another, in one course of action rather than another, or to put themselves in one situation rather than another. In practice, teachers can offer many types of choices (Mouratidis, Vansteenkiste, Sideridis, & Lens, 2011; Patall, Cooper, & Robinson, 2008), including a choice of

- Activities ("Select your favorite art activity—painting, drawing, sculpting...").
- Methods ("You may work by yourself, with a partner, or in a small group.").
- Topics ("Here is a list of topics to write on; select the one that is most interesting to you.").
- How to Interact with a Task ("You can start at any level—easy, moderately difficult, or advanced.").
- Work Pace ("Do you want to keep going—or pause and take a break?").
- Participation ("Who would like to volunteer to be the teaching assistant today?").

The reason why choice is a pathway to autonomy satisfaction is because, to make a choice, students first need to look inside themselves to consider their interests, goals, priorities, preferences, values, and needs. When students' behaviors and decision-making are guided by their interests, goals, and so forth, then students have the sense that their behaviors and decisions originate from within themselves. When students rely on their inner motivational resources to make a choice, they are likely to experience self-direction, volition, and personal endorsement while acting on that choice, which is the essence of what autonomy is. Choices allow students to experience personal ownership during their behavior—and hence to experience autonomy satisfaction.

Most teachers agree that "offer choice" is an effective motivational strategy (Flowerday & Schraw, 2000). Still, it is a controversial teaching practice. This is because not all teacher-provided choices successfully produce in students an experience of autonomy satisfaction (Katz & Assor, 2007). Some ways of offering choice are autonomy satisfying, while many others are not (Reeve, Nix, & Hamm, 2003). Three aspects of choice explain this differentiation (Patall, Linnenbrink-Garcia, Liu, Zambrano, & Yates, 2021).

First, before a choice can translate into autonomy satisfaction, it needs to be backed-up by the other autonomy-supportive instructional behaviors (i.e., take the students' perspective). Choice offered in a context of other autonomy supports will generate autonomy satisfaction, while choice offered in a context void of other autonomy supports will not. In practice, many choices teachers offer actually come across to students as quite controlling, such as "Do you want to apologize to your classmate, or be banned from the playground for a week?" and "Are you going to finish the assignment, or take an F?" If the choice simply pushes the student into a particular course of action, it is pressure-inducing and emerges mostly out of the teacher's impatience.

Second, before a choice can translate into autonomy satisfaction, it needs to be meaningful (Williams, 1998). "Meaningful" means that students care about the alternatives being offered to them. The choices students care about are those that are relevant to their interests, identities, and goals (Katz & Assor, 2007). When a choice is an opportunity to explore an interest, express an identity, or pursue a personal goal, it will be both meaningful and autonomy satisfying. Even seemingly trivial choices can be meaningful to the student—so long as they are interest, identity, or goal relevant, such as "Select a character-icon to represent you" or "Choose a name for your group" (Cordova & Lepper, 1996; Patall et al., 2008).

Third, before a choice can translate into autonomy satisfaction, students need to feel competent and informed enough to make that choice (Flowerday & Schraw, 2000; Patall et al., 2021). When students (a) are overwhelmed by the sheer number of alternatives, (b) lack the experience or information they need to make the choice, (c) feel exhausted from all the effort to make the choice, or (d) see little or no difference between the alternatives, they tend to feel indecisive and therefore do not want to make that choice. Under these circumstances, students sometimes prefer to defer the choice to a trusted other, such as a parent (Bao & Lam, 2008). For instance, for some high school seniors, the school counselor's choice of, "Which university do you want to go to?," may come across as overwhelming, as guesswork, and as too many alternatives with too little difference among them. Such choices tend to breed anxiety rather than autonomy. To avoid choice-overload, offering students 2 to 5 options best allows for autonomy-enhancing effects (Schneider, Nebel, Beege, & Rey, 2018).

What this all means is that "offer choice" (what teachers do) does not automatically translate to "satisfy autonomy" (what students experience). To bridge the two, the teacher's choice needs to encourage students *to look inside themselves* to find the means to self-initiate and self-regulate their own behavior (Waterschoot, Vansteenkiste, & Soenens, 2019). These choices offer students authentic invitations (choices) to act on their interests, goals, and identities (Patall, 2013; Patall et al., 2018; Patall, Vasquez, Steingut, Trimble, & Pituch, 2016; Waterschoot et al., 2019).

HOW TO PRESENT A LEARNING ACTIVITY IN A COMPETENCE-SATISFYING WAY

The surest way to signal to students that competence satisfaction may be forthcoming is to offer an optimal challenge. With an optimal challenge, the essential question is, "Can you do this? Do you have the skill, ability, and know-how to master the challenge built into this activity?" Teachers can build an optimal challenge into a learning activity by offering students (1) a clear goal to strive for or (2) a standard of excellence to meet. Both provide students with a vision for what competent functioning looks like for that particular task. Here are some examples:

Offer Students a Clear Goal to Strive for

- Learn all 20 vocabulary words.
- Identify, spell, and pronounce the eight major parts of a cell.
- Try to pronounce the French letter "u" like a native French speaker.
- Here is your performance from yesterday—can you do better today?

Offer Students a Standard of Excellence to Meet

- Here is a model of great writing—see if you can write sentences as good as these.
- Watch this role model perform—see if you can perform as well as the role model.
- Here is a difficult problem to solve; see if you can solve it.
- Here is a rubric scoring system—can you earn 20 points?

Here is one specific example:

"Take the next 15 minutes to revise your paragraph.
Even if you improve it by only 1%, it is important.
The goal is to get better and better."

There is pleasure in an optimal challenge (Harter, 1978). But there is also anxiety and doubt. This is because optimal challenges are defined as those performances in which the student has an equal chance of success and failure. Optimal challenges are particularly motivating because it is often the students' effort and determination that is the tipping point between success and failure. With an optimal challenge, students concentrate deeply and show impressive engagement (Keller & Bless, 2008). Still, asking students to take on and try to master a 50/50 outcome is a motivationally risky thing to do. This is because there is a good chance that the student will fail and become discouraged or frustrated. Recognizing this, teachers need to offer not only optimal challenges but also the step-by-step guidance and mentoring students need to raise the quality of their performance up to the goal level or standard of excellence.

Guidance and mentoring come in many forms, such as modeling, coaching, scaffolding, helping, offering hints, suggesting strategies, providing resources, providing worked-out examples, and providing "how to" instruction. In addition, students who are trying to raise their performance benefit from feedback. Constructive feedback comes in many forms, such as letting students know what they are doing well, what they need to work on the most, what they might do differently the next time, and what a path to future progress looks like. The key point is that an optimal challenge raises the possibility for competence satisfaction, but before students actually experience that competence satisfaction, they first need to make progress to attain the goal and meet the standard, which becomes a more likely outcome when teachers provide constructive guidance and mentoring.

Here is an example of optimal challenge and guidance together. The teacher first offers students a clear goal to strive for, such as "Write a topic sentence in 10 words or less that comprehensively foreshadows the paragraph to come." Helpful guidance might be, "Generate a title for your paragraph; then make sure your topic sentence covers that title really well." When students struggle, the teacher could offer commentary and feedback, as in "Let's look closely at your sentence—Is every word really needed? Does every word and phrase serve a purpose? If you deleted this phrase, would any meaning be lost?" When students are able to capitalize on the teacher's guidance, feedback, and support, they are likely to improve and, in doing so, begin to feel more effective and more capable, which is the essence of competence satisfaction.

But even optimal challenge, helpful guidance, and insightful commentary may not be enough for students to experience competence satisfaction. This is because a teacher's challenge, guidance, and commentary need to be provided in an autonomy-supportive way (Cheon, Reeve, & Song, 2019). Therefore, before the teacher introduces a standard of excellence or a goal to strive for, it represents best practices if she will first:

- Ask perspective-taking questions
  (e.g., "What are your goals? What do you want to work on the most?")
- Listen and respond to students' input
- Acknowledge the negative feelings associated with high standards
  (e.g., "Yes, this will be difficult; it will take a lot of work.").

Similarly, before the teacher provides guidance, she can:

- Ask perspective-taking questions
  (e.g., "Do you think you can do this? Are you stuck anywhere?")
- Be responsive to students' initiatives
- Display patience and understanding.

And, before the teacher offers a performance commentary, she can:

- Ask further perspective-taking questions (e.g., "Do you think that was a good performance? What do you think you did well, and what did you do poorly? What do you think it will take to improve?")

- Acknowledge negative feelings with a lack of progress (e.g., "Yes, progress is slow, isn't it? It must be frustrating to work so hard for every little gain.")
- Provide a rationale to explain why making progress is important.

In the same way that choice needs to be backed-up by the other autonomy-supportive instructional behaviors (e.g., perspective taking) to support an experience of autonomy satisfaction, the same is true for optimal challenge and guidance. When the teacher offers a challenge and provides progress-enabling guidance, she needs to also take the student's perspective, be responsive to students' initiatives, acknowledge negative feelings, etc. to help support the student's journey toward an experience of competence satisfaction.

HOW TO PRESENT A LEARNING ACTIVITY IN A RELATEDNESS-SATISFYING WAY

The surest way to signal to students that relatedness satisfaction may be forthcoming is to bring two people face to face. But, of course, bringing two people together can produce a social interaction that might devolve into conflict and strife just as easily as it might develop toward closeness and harmony. The type of face-to-face interaction that moves a pair toward relatedness satisfaction is "promotive interaction" (Johnson & Johnson, 2002, p. 97), which involves students promoting each other's learning (e.g., one student explains to the other how to solve a problem).

Promotive interaction can get students working collaboratively with each other, but for a genuine experience of relatedness need satisfaction to emerge, that social interaction needs to be characterized by acceptance, warmth, care, and mutual concern. Teachers can tip the social interaction toward relatedness satisfaction (and away from relatedness frustration) by asking the pair (or small group) to pursue a prosocial goal together. Typical prosocial goals the teacher might suggest include the following:

- Help each other improve.
- Give meaningful feedback to each other.
- Share your understanding of the information with the other person.
- Work together to produce a joint product—a consensus answer to a question.
- Work together to produce a joint product—a consensus solution to a problem.

The two active ingredients that generate relatedness satisfaction are: (1) face-to-face promotive social interaction and (2) pursuing a prosocial goal together. How teachers can integrate these two essential features into an everyday lesson plan is nicely illustrated by a "Turn-To-Your-Partner Discussion" (Johnson & Johnson, 2002). Here is how Johnson and Johnson (2002, p. 100) describe this teaching practice:

> Divide the lecture into 10-to-15-minute segments. Plan a short discussion task to be given to pairs of students after each segment. The task needs to be short

enough so students can complete it within three or four minutes. Its purpose is to ensure that students are actively thinking about the material being presented.

To start the class period, the teacher presents information on a topic, such as a 10-minute lecture or video presentation. A high school sociology teacher might present a brief video on the causes of crime. The teacher then pauses the delivery of information to put a reflective question on the whiteboard or a PowerPoint slide. The reflective question is always both interesting and central to the subject matter, such as "What is the primary cause of crime? Pick one: Poverty; unequal society; drug abuse; population density; low self-esteem; other." The teacher then asks students to take 1 minute to write down their own answer. In the next minute, the student turns to a partner (classmate). The two pair up, exchange answers, and read or listen to the other's answer. The pair then creates a new answer that is superior to each member's initial answer, as both partners build on the thoughts of the other. This group-based answer represents the pair's consensus answer (thereby achieving the prosocial goal). The teacher might then call on two or three pairs to provide their consensus answer. Next, the teacher presents the second segment of information that is then followed by a second reflective question and a second "Turn-To-Your-Partner Discussion" cooperative learning episode. A full example of how a teacher might integrate a relatedness-satisfying Turn-to-Your-Partner Discussion into a typical lesson plan appears in Box 8.2.

What is so impressive about this activity is how interesting and enjoyable students find it to be, as the turn-to-your-partner discussions are usually quite lively. Students almost always say that the small group discussion was their favorite part of the class. From a self-determination theory point of view, a lot of students' interest and intrinsic motivation can be explained by students' experiences of relatedness satisfaction during the face-to-face promotive interaction. The teacher's lecture is generally a relatedness-neglecting classroom event, while the face-to-face promoting interactions are relatedness-satisfying classroom events. It is simply a satisfying experience to open up and tell another person what you are thinking and then have that person listen and respect your answer and point of view and then to work collaboratively (prosocially) with a responsive partner to reach a consensus.

The above activity offers students an opportunity to experience relatedness satisfaction via student-to-student interactions, but students can also experience relatedness satisfaction via student-to-teacher interactions. Teachers promote relatedness-satisfying interactions by offering students individualized conversations, task-related support, promoting cooperation and teamwork, showing enthusiasm, showing awareness of students' concerns, providing care and help when it is needed, and engaging in generally friendly conversation (Sparks, Dimmock, Whipp, Lonsdale, & Jackson, 2015, 2016).

REFLECTIONS ON "SUPPORT INTRINSIC MOTIVATION"

Many involved in education—teachers, principals, parents, and media commentators—sometimes throw up a flag of caution about the instructional practice to support intrinsic motivation. They have no problem with allowing students to pursue

BOX 8.2

Full example of how a teacher might implement a "turn-to-your-partner discussion"

The Lesson: A biology teacher prepares the following lesson plan on the heart and circulatory system. While doing so, the teacher integrates the learning material with three episodes of a "Turn-To-Your-Partner Discussion."

Segment 1: (15 minutes)	1. Teacher explains an anatomical diagram of the human heart for 10 minutes. 2. Teacher posts a reflective question on the white board: "Put the cardiac cycle in its proper order: Right atrium, left atrium, right ventricle, left ventricle, lungs, body." 3. Each student writes down an individual answer, partners exchange answers, and together the two generate a consensus answer. 4. The teacher calls on two pairs to share their answers with the class.
Segment 2: (15 minutes)	1. Teacher shows a 10-minute YouTube video on the structure of the human heart. 2. Teacher posts a reflective question on the white board: "Why does the heart have separate right and left sides?" 3. Students answer the question for themselves, exchange answers with their partner, and listen to the reasons behind the partner's answer. Together, the pair generates a final answer that is better than either individual answer. 4. The teacher calls on two pairs to share their answers with the class.
Segment 3: (15 minutes)	1. Teacher provides a lecture on the circulatory system for 10 minutes. 2. Teacher posts a reflective question on the white board: "When you hear a heartbeat's 'Lub-dub,' what cardiac event are you hearing?" 3. Students individually answer the question, exchange answers, and the pair generates a final, best, consensus answer. 4. The teacher calls on two pairs to share their answers with the class.

their personal interests and need satisfactions during their leisure time, but they suggest that intrinsic motivation needs to be dialed back a bit in the classroom. The fear is that if students spend all their time pursuing only interesting activities, then they will not be able to do what educators, parents, and potential employers judge to be more important for their learning and social adjustment (e.g., homework, following rules, learning how to code, and speak a foreign language). The worry is that students will not be prepared to become productive members of society, which means being willing and able to work through uninteresting activities that are nevertheless socially valued and necessary.

Interest and intrinsic motivation are powerful motivators. Their importance should not be underestimated. But it is also important for students to willingly roll up their sleeves and work on uninteresting but educationally and culturally valued activities (Isen & Reeve, 2005). Here, the motivational issue is not intrinsic motivation but, rather, internalization. What teachers need is the dual skill of being able to support intrinsic motivation *and* support internalization of societal regulations. Recognizing this, we used Chapters 7 and 8 to recommend instructional strategies that support students' intrinsic motivation. It is now time to recommend instructional strategies on how teachers can support students' volitional internalization of societal values and ways of behaving. We do this in Chapters 9–12.

CONCLUSION

Intrinsic motivation arises out of the students' psychological needs for autonomy, competence, and relatedness. Thus, for teachers to support students' intrinsic motivation, they can learn how to present their learning activities in ways that students will find to be autonomy-satisfying (offer choice), competence-satisfying (offer optimal challenge and guidance), and relatedness-satisfying (encourage students to pursue a prosocial goal together).

Provide explanatory rationales

BOX 9.1

How would you respond to teaching situation #10 from the situations in schools questionnaire?

Student Misbehavior
A couple of students have been rude and disruptive.
To cope, you:

Does not Describe Me at All			Somewhat Describes Me		Describes Me Extremely Well		
1	2	3	4	5	6	7	Command that they get back on task immediately; otherwise, there will be bad consequences.
1	2	3	4	5	6	7	**Explain why you want them to behave properly.** **Later talk to them individually; listen carefully to how they see things**.
1	2	3	4	5	6	7	Communicate the classroom expectations for cooperation and prosocial skill.
1	2	3	4	5	6	7	Let it go, because it is too much of a pain to intervene.

Notes: The above is teaching situation #10 from the Situations in Schools Questionnaire (Aelterman, Vansteenkiste, Haerens, Soenens, Fontaine, & Reeve, 2019). The four response options represent, in order, control, autonomy support, structure, and chaos. The boldfaced autonomy-supportive response illustrates "Provide an explanatory rationale."

To view several brief video clips (20 seconds each) of teachers demonstrating the autonomy-supportive instructional behavior of ***Provide Explanatory Rationales***, go to this online link: https://vimeo.com/518009762.

DOI: 10.4324/9781003091738-12

"Teacher, why do we have to do this?" This student-generated question creates a motivational tipping point in any classroom (see Box 9.1). Once voiced, class wide engagement hangs in the balance as students wait eagerly to see if the teacher can justify the just-uttered engagement request.

If the teacher is unable to answer this question in a satisfying way, then students will likely shut down. They think, "What the teacher is asking us to do is bogus; it's just busywork." When the teacher is able to provide a student-satisfying answer, however, something motivationally important and empowering begins to occur—an internalization experience.

INTERNALIZATION

Internalization is the process of taking in values, beliefs, and ways of behaving from societal sources (e.g., the teacher) and transforming them into one's own (Ryan & Deci, 2000). Stated less formally, internalization is discovering the value in an activity or in a way of behaving.

Imagine the situation in which the teacher says, "I am going to ask you to follow the class rule." For the student, the motivational question is one of value and volition. As to value, the student asks, "Does this rule have value?" Is that value "low," "high," or "something in between?" Student engagement occurs in proportion to that judgment of value. As to volition, the student asks, "Is this something I want to do?" and "Do I accept this rule as my own?" Again, student engagement occurs in proportion to the student's sense of personal ownership and volition.

Ground zero for internalization is the quality of the teacher-student relationship—the student feels close to the teacher (Grolnick, Deci, & Ryan, 1997; Ryan, Stiller, & Lynch, 1994). Generally speaking, students will accept and take in the requests, values, beliefs, and behaviors of those they trust ("I know you only want what is best for me"), while they tend to reject and push away the values, beliefs, and behaviors of those they do not ("You are just trying to get me to do and believe what you want").

Relatedness with the teacher makes internalization possible, but it does not guarantee it. For an internalization experience to occur, the student also needs to understand and agree with whatever it is he or she is being asked to internalize (e.g., "Okay, I trust you, but please explain why homework is important"). Providing explanatory rationales helps students see and understand why the teacher-recommended activity or behavior has value, is important, and can be personally useful to the student. The teacher's explanatory rationale is the answer to the most basic question in all of motivation: "Why should I do this?"

EXPLANATORY RATIONALES HELP SOLVE TWO MOTIVATIONAL PROBLEMS

Teachers can offer students' explanatory rationales to solve two common motivational problems. The first is to help students develop the motivational resources they need to undertake and successfully complete a behavior change. The second is to help students develop the motivational resources they need to engage in and benefit from an uninteresting (but important) activity. These represent two different domains for internalization, but the motivational challenge is the same: Increase value. The challenge is to increase value enough to warrant the effort necessary for behavior change and increase value enough to warrant engaging in an activity that otherwise tends to generate negative feelings.

Behavior change

Teachers often communicate what they, the school, and the society consider to be effective behavior. During such communications, teachers may add a rationale to explain why the teacher, school, and society consider that way of behaving to be effective and healthy. For instance, an elementary school teacher might be concerned about students' problematic behavior of running and yelling wildly in the hallways as they transition from classroom to lunchroom. Students behave this way, they say, because it is fun and because it gets them to lunch faster. The teacher, however, can explain why a behavior change would be useful. In explaining the rule (i.e., "No running and yelling in the hallway"), the teacher can explain why the rule exists and why it represents a useful and effective way of behaving, as in "When our class is loud and noisy, it distracts all the other classes you pass by on your run to lunch. So, we have this rule because we want to help out the students in all the other classes."

The motivational problem the children face is "run and have fun" vs. "walk quietly and help out the students in all the other classes." This is a difficult motivational problem, but teachers can help students better understand why the teacher, school, and society value the latter way of behaving. The behavior change may take time to occur, because the internalization process will take time to occur, but the teacher's rationale is an excellent starting point to help students begin to work through the motivational challenge of behavior change.

Teachers make many behavior change requests, but it is surprising how rarely they use an explanatory rationale while doing so. Much more commonly, teachers will try to generate motivation to support the behavior change request by offering some type of reward, such as a token (elementary school) or points (middle school). We ask teachers why they give out these coins and points. They say, "Look, I just need class to be quiet, students in their seats, and students to quit throwing those paper balls at each other." At best, extrinsic rewards will gain students' temporary compliance, but temporary compliance should never be miss-interpreted as enduring behavior change. Explanatory rationales help teachers actually solve this motivational problem because they help students take in (internalize) a sense of value for being quiet, in their seats and resisting the paper ball entertainment. With an internalized value, students can begin to volitionally self-initiate their own behavior change.

Uninteresting activities

How can a teacher motivate students to engage in an unappealing, uninteresting activity? Not all lessons, classroom procedures, and behavioral requests can be intrinsically motivating things to do, at least from the students' point of view. So, in the course of instruction, teachers often ask students to do things that students may perceive to be uninteresting and unimportant (e.g., follow safety procedures, double-check their work). In those instances, their motivation is fragile. When faced with an activity that is uninteresting and unappealing, a student reaction of apathy and disengagement is quite understandable. If students show only a half-hearted effort of just going through the motions, this is also understandable. However, if teachers press the issue (e.g., "Let's go, get to work"), students may transition from apathy to something worse—defiance and rebellion (Haerens, Aelterman, Vansteenkiste, Soenens, & Van Petegem, 2015; Van Petegem et al., 2017).

Sometimes an uninteresting lesson can be restructured into an interesting one (see Box 9.2, "Motivating a Young Einstein"). For instance, teachers can add an

BOX 9.2

Motivating a young Einstein

As a young boy, Albert Einstein attended an elementary school that had installed military rules and regulations. As the story is told in the *Albert Einstein* biography (Beckhard, 1959), young Albert motivationally protested, "They make us memorize the day's lesson. They don't tell us what it says or what it means, but we must learn every single word. And I can't. Unless I know what a thing means, I just can't remember it (p. 14)."

One day, young Albert's uncle was visiting the Einstein home and heard the young Albert scream out, "I hate school." His uncle asked, "What subject do you hate the most?" Young Albert said it was a tie between algebra and geometry. His uncle suggested, "I want you to try something—an experiment."

"Try playing detective for a change. You're looking for a villain. You don't know whether he's a thief or a pickpocket. You don't even know his name. All you're sure of is that he's somewhere around and you've got to find him to keep him from doing any more harm. First thing you do is give him a name for your files. Right?"

"You call him 'X'."

"Then you tail him. You follow him into one formula and out of it and into another or you slide down the hypotenuse of a triangle after him and chase him up the side wall of a parallelogram. Finally, you catch up with him. You find out what he is and who he is. Now you've got him! You put the cuffs on him and take him in. That's all algebra is. Or geometry. Like to give it a try?"

"Yes, I would" young Albert said earnestly, "I think that would help a lot." (Beckhard, 1959, pp. 17–18).

optimal challenge onto the activity, and the striving to improve and make progress can involve students' competence need in a way that the task per se cannot. We have seen teachers do this, for instance, during a review session for the next day's exam. The teacher will "gamify" the review by putting students in teams and asking questions in a way that their team can score points to try to win the game. The teacher might also place students into teams and ask those teams to pursue a prosocial goal together (e.g., help each other), which supports interest and intrinsic motivation via relatedness satisfaction. The theme of the preceding chapter (Chapter 8) was that any activity that creates a feeling of autonomy, competence, or relatedness is going to be fun, or at least more fun. Still, not all activities can be re-engineered from "boring and uninteresting" to "interesting and enjoyable."

Consider three possible strategies a middle-school language teacher might try to motivate her students to "read the book":

> Option 1: **No strategy**.
> "Read the book."
>
> Option 2: **Introduce a consequence**.
> "Read the book, because there will be a test on this material on Friday."
>
> Option 3: **Provide an explanatory rationale.**
> "Read the book, because it will expose you to what good writing is. It is also a good opportunity to learn some new vocabulary and to stir your curiosity."

Option 1 (No motivational strategy) does not energize students' effort or engagement, so it is not a viable motivational strategy. Option 2 (Introduce a consequence, or "promote external regulation") can energize students' short-term effort and engagement, but that effort represents only behavioral compliance rather than learning-fostering engagement. It is also a controlling strategy, so it will produce motivational side-effects, such as undermining students' autonomous self-regulation. Option 3 (Provide an explanatory rationale, or "promote internalization") can energize students' effort and engagement, and it can energize the type of engagement that promotes learning (Savard, Joussemet, Pelletier, & Mageau, 2013; Steingut, Patall, & Trimble, 2017).

When researchers have conducted experiments to test the effectiveness of these three teaching strategies, they have assessed students': (1) effort; (2) task value; and (3) perceived autonomy while doing the task (Jang, 2008; Reeve, Jang, Hardre, & Omura, 2002). Effort was lowest with no strategy, moderate with consequences, and highest with an explanatory rationale. Perceived value and perceived autonomy were both low when teachers used either of the first two strategies, while they were both high when teachers offered an explanatory rationale. So, the only teaching strategy that produced high effort, a sense of valuing, and perceived autonomy (and did so without any troubling side effects) was providing an explanatory rationale. This leads to the recommendation to use only strategy 3.

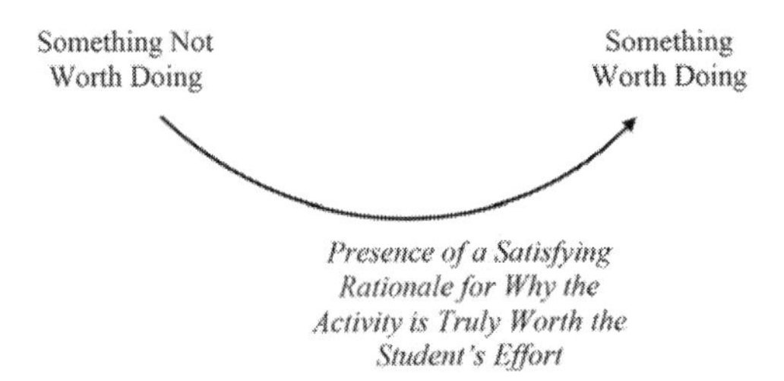

FIGURE 9.1 The Essence of the Motivational Challenge to Transform an Unvalued into a Valued Activity

Figure 9.1 boils the teacher's challenge of trying to motivate students to engage in an unappealing, uninteresting activity down to its basics. The motivational challenge is to convert or transition students' perception that the task is "something not worth doing" into a perception that it is actually "something worth doing." Because this can be such a difficult motivational problem for students to solve on their own, they need to hear a teacher's explanatory rationale as to why the activity is "something worth doing."

RATIONALES

A rationale is a verbal explanation as to why putting forth effort during the activity might be a personally useful thing to do (Reeve et al., 2002). Such rationales are typically communicated with a phrase such as, "Doing this activity has been shown to be useful" (Deci, Eghrari, Patrick, & Leone, 1994, p. 127), with the teacher then proceeding to explain what that personal utility is. Rationales often feature an explanatory "because...," as in "the reason why this activity is worth your time and effort is *because*..."

To students, teacher-provided rationales can feel satisfying or unsatisfying. So, teachers need to provide more than "just a rationale," because students need a "convincing and satisfying rationale." A satisfying rationale explains clearly and convincingly why the activity has personal utility for the student. The most satisfying rationales often serve one of the following four purposes (Vansteenkiste et al., 2018):

- Doing this activity can help you *build skill*
- Doing this activity can help you *improve performance*
- Doing this activity can help you *build a friendship*
- Doing this activity can *help others*

Most students value greater skill, better performance, deeper friendships, and helping others. If a teacher can show how the current classroom activity is a clear pathway to one of these uses, then students will tend to see the requested activity as "something worth doing." It is worth doing because it can help the student build a skill, improve a performance, build a friendship, or help others. Of course, there are many additional rationales that students will find to be satisfying, but these four provide the teacher with a good starting point.

Here are three examples. In the first, the teacher explains how following a class rule can build friendships.

> "In this class, we will work on using respectful language. That means that we are not saying things that put others down or hurt their feelings. Why is using respectful language important? First, it keeps conflict out of class. Second, it helps maintain friendships. Don't you think that is important—friendships?"

Students tend to have a positive reaction to this teacher talk because they understand that the teacher is trying to help them build their friendships. The teacher is not trying to force a rule on students but, rather, the rule is just a pathway to something the students really do want and value (i.e., friendships).

In a second example, the teacher explains why deliberate practice is useful to help students build a valued skill.

TEACHER: "Today, I am going to ask you to revise your book reports. Revising means making your writing better than before."

STUDENTS: "Ugh! Do we have to?"

TEACHER: "Revising your book report is a useful thing to do, because all good writing is re-writing. Actually, you may be surprised at how much better your second draft will be than was your first draft. Let's try it and see."

In a third example, the teacher explains how attending to a video clip offers students an opportunity to build a new skill.

> "Here is a demonstrational video to watch. It is a how-to video.
> By watching this video, you have an opportunity to build a new skill."

To support students' motivation on uninteresting activities, the teacher needs to identify and then communicate the activity's value, worth, importance, and personal benefit to the student. Additional qualities of effective, satisfying, and internalization-catalyzing explanatory rationales include the following (Vansteenkiste et al., 2018):

- Clear
- New Information
- Personal Relevance

Clear

"Clear" means that the benefit gained from the teacher-provided rationale is specific and concrete, rather than general and vague (Vansteenkiste, Simons, Soenens, &

Lens, 2004). A physical education teacher can encourage students to participate in a beginning-of-class stretching routine either because "stretching is good for you" (general, vague) or because "stretching increases your flexibility and will prevent any injury during today's jump roping" (specific, concrete).

New information

"New Information" means that the teacher provides some special insight about the activity's usefulness that the student is not yet aware of. When teachers make engagement requests, they have good reasons for why they are asking students to engage in that particular task, though students are often not aware of what those good reasons are. To students, it is just an uninteresting activity. So, teachers need to reveal this "hidden value" to students (Reeve, 2016). A biology teacher, for instance, can explain why students should wear safety goggles during a laboratory exercise either "because it is required" (old, familiar information) or "because, last year, a girl was working on this same lab exercise and some formaldehyde accidently splashed into and burned her eye. We don't want anything like that to happen to you. Goggles will prevent such injuries, so it is important to wear these safety goggles" (new, unfamiliar information).

Personal relevance

Satisfying rationales are those that students find to be personally relevant to their concerns, rather than relevant only to the teacher's concerns. While common, a teacher-centric rationale ("because I said so" or "because it is the rule") leaves students unable to see the personal relevance of the activity. In contrast, when teachers connect the activity in some way to student's interests, needs, values, goals, and personal aspirations, that same activity can take on personal relevance. One of the authors witnessed a student asking a literature teacher, "Teacher, why do we study Greek mythology?" This question seemed to dumbfound the literature teacher, who muttered, "It's part of the curriculum." Understandably, the student walked away rather uninspired to read the Greek mythology he was holding in his hands. But what if the teacher instead replied with, "Studying Greek mythology helps you appreciate popular movies (Achilles, Wrath of the Titans), songs (Cupid), company names (Nike, Amazon, Pandora, and Oracle), life lessons (how to handle jealousy, how to triumph over obstacles by using perseverance to achieve your goals), and how to tell a good, audience-captivating story yourself." Such a rationale connects the activity to the students' life and self-functioning.

Providing a satisfying rationale requires skill

Providing a satisfying explanatory rationale requires a good deal of skill. To get a sense of how difficult it can be to generate a satisfying rationale that is clear, insightful, and personally relevant, try this exercise. Why should your students do the following (besides "because you have to")?

- Complete a homework assignment
- Revise an essay
- Participate in the class discussion
- Read a book over the weekend when there are so many other interesting things to do

Here is one teacher's attempt to provide a satisfying, convincing explanatory rationale. To create a satisfying rationale, the teacher frames his request as an opportunity for students to build greater skill and to improve their performance.

TEACHER: "I am going to ask you to do your homework. It is all the practice problems from pages 23 through 28."

STUDENTS: "Ugh. Ahh. Sigh."

TEACHER: "Okay. Let's think about athletes and dancers. How do they improve? They improve by practicing continuously. So, homework is basically the same thing. Homework is practice. So, the reason I am asking you to do your homework is because it is useful and helpful to you and your improvement in this class."

It can also be surprisingly fruitful to type "Why is it important for students to learn fractions?" into a Google search and see what other teachers, educators, and scholars have to say. If you try this activity yourself, you will indeed find many satisfying reasons to justify fractions in the curriculum. These "Why is it important to *x*?" queries apply to many educational activities and generally yield several satisfying rationales.

INTRINSIC GOAL PURSUITS

Another way teachers can support students' motivation for an uninteresting activity is to explain how that activity connects to a valued intrinsic goal the student already has, information that can be understood by taking the students' perspective and seeking their input. An internalization-facilitating teaching technique is to remind the student of an intrinsic goal they have and then explain how the educational activity helps the student attain that sought-after intrinsic goal. When students pursue an intrinsic goal, they tend to display higher levels of engagement, learning, and well-being—because the motivation comes not from the motivationally empty (uninteresting) activity but, instead, from the motivationally rich intrinsic goal (Koestner, 2008; Vansteenkiste, Simons, Lens, Soenens, & Matos, 2005).

Here is an example of how a drama teacher in Korea did this. She knew that some of her students were aspiring actors, so she suggested, "As you watch this videoclip, you might use it as an opportunity to learn some new skill-building techniques and strategies for yourself. Watch what these actors do. You may discover some new skills and techniques to help you become a better actor yourself."

Student-generated rationales

A third teaching strategy to support students' internalization is to ask students to generate their own rationales. The teacher might ask, "Why do you think this task is important?" Such a question can spark students' own self-reflection on why the activity or subject matter might be personally useful. As a caution, the time to ask this question is not while students are in the middle of complaining and suffering through the "Why do I have to do this?" struggle but, instead, prior to the engagement request, especially during a period of personal reflection.

Researchers have asked this question to first-year college students taking a math (Husman & Hilpert, 2007) or a STEM (Hulleman & Harackiewicz, 2009) course. Generally, after some reflection, most students are able to self-generate an explanatory rationale or two, which helps them build a sense of value for that particular course. Here are the instructions one group of researchers gave to students in a physics course to encourage them to self-generate a rationale (Hulleman & Harackiewicz, 2020):

> I would like you to think about how what we have been learning about in this class is important to your life in some way. What connection can you find between one of the topics we have been studying and something that is important in your life?

One student wrote the following:

> Playing hockey and friction are connected because in hockey while passing or shooting the puck it slides on the ice which causes friction, slowing down the puck. Friction could be important to my life because I can better understand how much more force I need to get the puck to move with the friction moving against it.

Such a rationale is personal, as the student used personal pronouns and referred to his interests, hobbies, and goals. Such a rationale was also relevant to what was being taught in the course. And such a rationale is probably not something the teacher would have thought to offer. Despite these positives, it is still the case that some students will find such an exercise to be overwhelming or too difficult (Hulleman, Godes, Hendricks, & Harackiewicz, 2010). In this case, it may be helpful for the teacher to come prepared to provide otherwise-overwhelmed students with a preexisting list of possible rationales for why the course might be important. In this case, the otherwise overwhelmed student can look through the teacher-prepared list and selectively find one (or a few) explanatory rationales to endorse as his or her own (Gaspard et al., 2015).

Counterargument

It is easier to just present a classroom learning activity and tell students to do it. Taking the time to explain why the learning activity (or classroom rule) is useful takes time. A teacher might understandably worry whether it is worth two minutes of class time. It is also possible that students might counter-argue against the teacher's rationale (e.g., "C'mon, is learning this foreign language really useful for me?"). But such a student-teacher discussion (or debate) is actually a crucial motivational turning point for students, as this teacher-student conversation provides the very guts of the internalization process. If students are going to be able to build a sense of value, they first need their teachers to take the time and effort to explain why a requested behavioral change or why a requested uninteresting activity might be accepted and internalized as their own.

CONCLUSION

Helping students find the value they need to change their behavior and to engage in uninteresting classroom activities is perhaps the most difficult motivational challenge teachers face. Facing an uninteresting activity, students are motivationally vulnerable. They need to hear their teacher's insight about why the activity is useful. When teachers are able to provide this motivational support, students discover the value they need to engage in and benefit from the requested activity.

Acknowledge and accept negative feelings

BOX 10.1

How would you respond to teaching situation #6 from the situations in schools questionnaire?

Students Complain
At a difficult point in the lesson, students begin to complain.
In response, you:

Does Not Describe Me at All			Somewhat Describes Me		Describes Me Extremely Well		
1	2	3	4	5	6	7	**Accept their negative feelings as okay. Assure them that you are open to their input and suggestions.**
1	2	3	4	5	6	7	Insist they pay attention. They must learn this material for their own good.
1	2	3	4	5	6	7	Show and teach them a helpful strategy for how to break down the problem to solve it step-by-step.
1	2	3	4	5	6	7	Just ignore the whining and complaining. They need to learn to get over the obstacles themselves.

Notes: The above is teaching situation #6 from the Situations in Schools Questionnaire (Aelterman, Vansteenkiste, Haerens, Soenens, Fontaine, & Reeve, 2019). The four response options represent, in order, autonomy support, control, structure, and chaos. The boldfaced autonomy-supportive response illustrates, Acknowledge and accept negative feelings.

DOI: 10.4324/9781003091738-13

To view several brief video clips (20 seconds each) of teachers demonstrating the autonomy-supportive instructional behavior of ***Acknowledge and Accept Negative Feelings***, go to this online link: https://vimeo.com/518011131.

Students sometimes complain, resist, and express negative feelings about having to engage in uninteresting and difficult activities (see Box 10.1). Students sometimes show a bad attitude when teachers ask them to clean their desks, complete their homework, follow the rules, or improve their performance. These negative feelings are tell-tale signs that the student is suffering some motivational problem. These feelings flash a warning signal: All is not well. Their presence suggests that whatever the student is doing at the moment is problematic and basically not working out. Negative feelings are a metaphorical red light to stop what one is doing (Carver & Scheier, 1998), which is pretty much the opposite of being a motivated and engaged student.

The concern is that such negative feelings, if unaddressed, will interfere with—and perhaps even poison—the student's engagement and learning. For instance, when overwhelmed by a difficult foreign language lesson, a student can quickly become frustrated and discouraged and, feeling so, simply shut down and quit trying. Quitting is seen as a strategy to stop the negative feelings. Soothing these negative feelings therefore becomes a prerequisite to motivationally readying students to engage in and benefit from the lesson.

HOW TEACHERS TYPICALLY REACT TO STUDENTS' NEGATIVE FEELINGS

When teachers see boredom, stress, anger, and confusion in the faces and voices of their students, they understandably want to whack down those feelings—to fix them, to change them into something better. A first reaction might be, No, don't be bored; you should be interested and enthusiastic; or Hush—quit your complaining. Teachers may also suggest some remedy, such as, Instead of complaining, you should be grateful and want to work hard; or Apologize right now, young man. Occasionally, the teacher will add a twist of pressure to make sure his or her remedy to jettison the negative feelings gets implemented: All your complaining is embarrassing, I thought you were better than this.

When the teacher (1) judges students' negative feelings as bad, (2) unilaterally diagnoses why the negative feelings occurred, (3) proposes a solution to eradicate them, and (4) insists that students' comply with the teacher's solution, things generally do not go well. Such a controlling approach to instruction rarely succeeds in dissipating the negative feelings and instead typically yields these results:

1. The teacher is frustrated—because the negative feelings persist or intensify.
2. The students are frustrated—because they have been judged negatively.

3. The negative emotion may intensify, spread to other students, and recur again tomorrow.
4. The teacher-student relationship slips toward conflict (i.e., me vs. them).

Such an approach to instruction is natural and understandable, but it is not skilled. It is natural and understandable because any message of class is not going well (i.e., students' negative feelings) can put the teacher on the defensive. In many cases, the teacher may not see students' complaining and drama as valid (You shouldn't feel that way.) or appropriate (You're being immature.). The teacher will likely try to counter and otherwise change the student's negative feelings (Don't be sad, cheer up) and resistance (e.g., Quit wasting your time; get back to work.). Instead of soothing, the teacher inadvertently throws fuel on the fire.

It is not skilled because it is ineffective. First, countering and trying to change students' negative feelings does not work because it fails to acknowledge or convey understanding of whatever has caused the negative feelings in the first place. This lack of empathy in turn can have harmful relational side effects (e.g., My teacher won't listen, My teacher doesn't understand me, or My teacher doesn't care about me). But perhaps as importantly, simply trying to alter feelings is losing an opportunity—because negative feelings provide *information* about the obstacles to inner motivation and engagement.

The goal to transform negative into positive feelings is laudable—that is what good friends often do by cheering us up. It becomes problematic, however, when the teacher fails to understand where the feelings are coming from. Negative emotionality has roots. If it is to be soothed, then the teacher needs to attend to its underlying cause. What represent skilled teaching in this situation is to acknowledge and accept students' expressions of negative feelings—to hear that there is a problem, to take it to heart that the student's reaction may be legitimate or warranted (from the student's point of view), and even, eventually, to welcome these expressions as opportunities to improve both the classroom environment and the teacher-student relationship.

ACKNOWLEDGE AND ACCEPT NEGATIVE FEELINGS

As an instructional strategy, acknowledge and accept negative feelings is like aspirin. Acknowledgment can quickly diminish negative emotion. It clears away a daunting obstacle (i.e., negative feelings) that would otherwise block out students' volition and internalizations and shut down their classroom engagement.

Acknowledge and accept negative feelings begins with listening carefully and nondefensively. It continues as the teacher accepts the students' negative feelings as a potentially valid reaction to being asked to do things that seem to the student to be uninteresting, overwhelming, or not worth the effort. With time and practice, it begins to bear fruit once the teacher works collaboratively with the student to resolve the underlying cause of the negative feelings. This is usually done by soliciting and incorporating the student's input into the redesign of the teacher's request or the uninteresting activity. The basic instructional script for a teacher to acknowledge and accept students' negative feelings is as follows:

1. *Acknowledge Negative Feelings*
   A good starting point is for the teacher to describe what they see. For example, "I hear some grumbling, and am guessing there are some negative feelings. Is that so?"
2. *Accept and Try to Understand the Negative Feelings*
   A good starting point is for the teacher to say: "I can imagine that this seems long (or hard; or boring, etc.); is that the issue?" And then it's important to listen to be sure you understand the obstacle as students see it.
3. *Work Collaboratively with Students to Dissipate the Negative Feelings*
   A good starting point is for the teacher to say: "Any suggestions for how we could go about doing this differently?"

Acknowledge negative feelings

The first step in addressing and solving any problematic classroom behavior is to acknowledge it. The negative feelings signal some underlying problem—usually one of a motivational nature (i.e., We don't want to do this). To acknowledge the negative feelings (e.g., You look bored, I see stress, and It appears that many people are finding this task to be unusually frustrating), teachers can:

- Listen carefully and non-defensively to hear what students are expressing
- Understand and name the source of the negative feelings

Some teachers also use technology to invite students to input their feelings into a word cloud, often at the beginning of class or after a performance. Student input into the word cloud is anonymous, and the collective cloud picture that emerges can give the teacher a good idea of how students are feeling—both in general (from the range of feelings nominated) and in specific (from the largest centralized feelings within the image).

The teaching skill is to be open, willing, and able (via empathy) to acknowledge that things are not going well at the moment. When teachers are able to do this, they might want to double-check with the students that all agree that things are not going well at the moment. The teacher might describe what she is seeing, You looked bored and uninterested in the lesson today. And then follow-up that behavioral description with a confirmation request, Do I have that right? If students agree with the teacher's description, then they can together begin to address the problem. If students do not agree with the teacher's description, then the conversation may take a different turn as the student might say, No, I'm not bored, I just didn't get much sleep last night. This phrase, Is that right? is meant to help the student label their feelings or describe their experience for themselves. It is also helpful to be patient until students are ready to open up in this way.

Teachers do not always agree with this recommended teaching practice. Sometimes teachers counter with, Yes, but where is the limit to all of this? Acknowledging negative feelings takes courage. It also takes a willingness to take some personal responsibility for why students feel bored, angry, or frustrated. And it takes a good deal of teaching efficacy to know that you have the knowledge, experience, and instructional strategies necessary to solve the problem that is being acknowledged. Without a deep sense of teaching efficacy (confidence that you have what it takes to solve the problem), it makes sense to avoid the problem. After all, teachers will say, Why acknowledge an unsolvable problem? The answer to this teacher query is that acknowledgement is the first step in dissipating the negative feelings, and such an acknowledgment then opens up possibilities for (1) teachers to facilitate students' internalizations and (2) the teacher-student relationship to improve and grow in trust (rather than deteriorate into conflict).

Accept negative feelings

It is one thing to acknowledge students' negative feelings, yet another to accept them as okay—as both valid and understandable, given the circumstances. Upon hearing, This is so boring! or I hate this!, teachers may evaluate and judge what they hear as wrong or bad, or the teacher might begin to blame the student (e.g., You're immature). Such self-protection, however, arises out of taking only the teacher's perspective. If the teacher takes the student's point of view, then he or she becomes increasingly able to listen to what the students are saying in a nonjudgmental way. The skill is to listen to the student and to do so without trying to judge or condemn.

To accept students' negative feelings, the teacher can say, Okay or Yes. The teacher might also supplement the Okay with an acknowledgement that the student's feelings are a potentially valid and legitimate reaction to the teacher's request. An I understand can serve this same purpose, as in Okay, I understand. Understanding can then lead to acceptance, as in Okay, I understand, the reason you did not come to class prepared today was because another student took your backpack. Such words are powerful because they not only let students know that the teacher understands their perspective but it also implies that the teacher accepts that some change in the instruction might be needed. This utterance does not mean, I agree with you, but it does mean, Now I understand why you feel the way you do—and perhaps things do need to change.

Here are some examples of teacher talk that combines both acceptance and understanding:

- Okay, I understand. You think this is unfair to you.
- Okay, I see. You think the amount of work (e.g., homework, reading list) is too much—and maybe even unreasonable.
- Okay; this material is new and difficult, isn't it?
- Yes, you make a good point. I am expecting a lot from you, aren't I?

Acceptance may bring empathy. The teacher might add, Yes. I understand. If I were in your position, I might feel the same way. When I have a huge workload, I sometimes get stressed out too. This sentiment expresses understanding—but not necessarily agreement.

Another way of validating (i.e., accepting) students' negative feelings is to acknowledge that the student is probably not alone in feeling that way, as in, I'm sure you are not alone in feeling this way, many of your classmates probably feel the same way.

Acceptance does not amount to giving in to students' complaining. Teachers can acknowledge and accept students' negative feelings while maintaining resolve in their original request, required classroom procedure, high standards, or required behavior. Teachers need not back down to students' fussing. Instead, the teacher maintains his or her request (e.g., complete the homework, participate in the group discussion, run the laps, read the 300-page book), but the teacher and students work collaboratively to dissolve the negative affect associated with the homework, class participation, physical exertion, or time-consuming assignment, all the while maintaining the importance and need for the engagement request (as by providing an explanatory rationale).

Dissipate negative feelings

Once a valid cause of the negative feelings has been identified and understood and once the student agrees that, yes, this is indeed what is causing the emotional upset, then the teacher gains an opportunity to actually resolve the problem (get rid of the negative feelings). As a starting point, teachers can use their professional knowledge and experience with similar situations in the past. Experienced teachers know that repetition can lead to boredom, a class presentation can be anxiety-provoking, unfamiliar equipment can be frustrating, and trying to learn all the nuances within a foreign language can be overwhelming and exhausting.

That said, nine times out of ten the student knows why he or she is bored, stressed, or just wants to give up and quit. Nevertheless, students might still say, I don't know or Whatever. Even if students know exactly why they feel the way they do, they might not want to say that out loud. As a student, it can be uncomfortable to have the spotlight put on you when feeling sad or angry or discouraged. Before they will speak up, students need to know that their teacher is sincere in the effort to alter the classroom circumstances. Hence, it is often necessary for teachers to take the first step and offer instruction-altering options for the students to consider, such as:

"Okay. So, I want to think about what would help you.
Would you like an example? Or, perhaps you need more practice time.
Or, I could show you a demonstration of how a problem like this is done."

While a student might not want to suggest a remedy, that same student might be responsive to the teacher's fishing expedition (e.g., Would you like an example? A demonstration?). The teacher's genuine curiosity can kick start a joint problem-solving effort to find a way to remove, modify, or remedy the source of the negative affect in a way that is acceptable to both student and teacher.

Putting it all together

Acknowledge and accept negative feelings is a three-part skill. It is one part acknowledge the negative feelings, one part accept the negative feelings, and one part work collaboratively to dissipate the negative feelings. Here are three examples that combine all of these elements into a motivationally-constructive teacher-student conversation.

Example 1: Students Look Bored

Acknowledge the Negative Affect
I see that you are not very enthusiastic about today's lesson. Do I have that right?
Accept the Validity of the Negative Affect
Yes, I understand; we have practiced this same skill many times before, haven't we?
Work Collaboratively to Remedy the Cause of the Negative Feelings
Okay. Let's see. What might we do differently this time? Any suggestions?

Example 2: Students Complain that the Lesson Is too Difficult

Acknowledge the Negative Affect
I am seeing some frustrated faces out there. Is that right?
Accept the Validity of the Negative Affect
Okay, I understand. This material is new and unfamiliar.
And it is a little harder than what we did last week.
(Teacher offers a yes head nod).
Work Collaboratively to Remedy the Cause of the Negative Feelings
Okay. So, I want to think about what would help you.
Would you like an example? Or, perhaps you need more practice time.
Or I could show you a demonstration of how to solve a problem like this.

Example 3: Students Show Stress Over an Upcoming Exam

Acknowledge the Negative Affect
Some of you look pretty anxious and stressed. Is that right? Is everyone okay?
Accept the Validity of the Negative Affect
Okay. That makes sense. You are worried about how you will do on the test, especially since the test will cover so much new material.
Work Collaboratively to Remedy the Cause of the Negative Feelings
Okay. Let's get rid of all this stress. What can we do about it? Any suggestions?

TWO BENEFITS

Acknowledge and accept negative feelings generates two benefits. The first is to dissipate or get rid of the negative feelings. Once done, student engagement and learning can proceed. But there is a second less obvious benefit. Acknowledge and accept negative feelings preserves and even enhances the quality of the teacher-student relationship. It is a very powerful interpersonal experience to know that *My teacher understands me* and *My teacher cares about me* (Rogers, 1969). Recall that My teacher cares about me is one of the cornerstone qualities students nominate when they describe My Best Teacher (Chapter 3).

Being accepted for who one is—even when expressing negative feelings, is a surprisingly potent catalyst to developing a high-quality relationship with another person. By acknowledging and accepting negative feelings, the teacher shows sensitivity to and an authentic concern for students' classroom experience and welfare. On the other hand, when teachers criticize, counter, and try to change (or fix) students' negative emotionality, they unintentionally slip into a controlling motivating style and, in doing so, put the teacher-student relationship at risk. When a teacher insists without listening that the student pay attention or apologize, then the student can be expected to think not only, She doesn't understand me but even She doesn't like me.

Is it worth the time and drama to acknowledge negative feelings?

There is only so much time available in a given class period, so it is a fair question to ask whether or not it is a good use of class time to pause instruction to acknowledge, accept, and dissipate students' negative feelings. From a motivational perspective, it will always represent best practices to pause the instructional flow—to put down the chalk, close the book, stop the lecture—to give students' negative feelings the teacher's full attention. In the end, it does not really make much sense to continue with instruction when students show boredom, become discouraged, and want to quit. Such negative, deactivating feelings block motivation and shut down engagement (Pekrun, Goetz, Titz, & Perry, 2002). So, even if the teacher needs to sacrifice 10 minutes of instruction time to acknowledge and address the negative feelings, it is still worth the effort in the long term, as 30 minutes of motivated learning is better than 45 minutes of boring, confusing, or frustrating instruction.

Just as important, attending to negative affect has instructional value. Negative feelings are information about what is interfering with engagement and performance. So even from a pedagogic point of view, listening to your learners helps you better design and pace instruction, as well as identify who is struggling.

ACKNOWLEDGE AND ACCEPT POSITIVE FEELINGS TOO

Although our chapter title is on negative emotions, we cannot leave this topic without addressing positive emotions too! Positive feelings are just as common and just as important in the classroom as are negative feelings. These positive feelings are to be acknowledged, accepted, celebrated, and shared. So just as we suggested acknowledging and giving voice to negative feelings, the same is true for positive feelings. Letting students share what interests or moves them in an activity helps them feel ownership, as well as lifting mood. Reflecting positively on feelings of accomplishment, celebrating minor victories, and appreciating moments of awe can all contribute to students' interest and engagement.

Positive feelings signal that all is well, and their presence reflects the involvement and successful satisfaction of students' needs and goals (Carver & Scheier, 1998). Positive feelings—interest, joy, gratitude, hope, curiosity, pride, amusement, inspiration, empathy, compassion, awe, and love—provide a metaphorical green light for continuing to pursue one's goals, need satisfactions, and interpersonal relationships.

To flourish, students need their classroom experiences of positive feelings to outweigh their classroom experiences of negative feelings. One researcher even suggested that this ratio needs to be 3:1 (Fredrickson, 2009). That is, to flourish, students need three classroom experiences of interest, joy, inspiration, and gratitude for every individual experience of frustration, boredom, and discouragement. The same likely holds true for an interpersonal relationship. Any relationship, such as teacher-student or student-student, needs to generate far more positive than negative feelings if it is to flourish and yield benefits such as well-being, learning, creativity, and staying power. Autonomy-supportive teachers provide such classroom environments and such interpersonal relationships better than anyone, but it is still a good idea to stop and smell the roses along the way with one's students—to acknowledge, accept, celebrate, and share these positive feelings, not as the occasional exception that sometimes pops up in the classroom but as the wonderful enduring emotionality that prevails every day, every week, and throughout the year in classrooms led by an autonomy-supportive teacher.

CONCLUSION

When students believe that the teacher's requests and assignments are unreasonable, unfair, boring, or asking too much of them, negative feelings arise. These negative feelings signal that students' motivation is at risk and, if left unattended, may shut down their learning and participation. While it may be a natural response for teachers to counter-argue and defend against such negative feelings, such a teacher reaction is a recipe for classroom disaster. The constructive path is to acknowledge and accept students' negative feelings and, using them as information to identify barriers to engagement, work collaborative with students to remove the cause of the negative emotionality. Once done, students' volitional motivation can be restored and the teacher-student relationship strengthened. Beyond attending to negative emotions, working to create and celebrating positive moments can be just as important, as the goal is to have an engaged *and* flourishing classroom.

CHAPTER 11

Rely on invitational language

BOX 11.1

How would you respond to teaching situation #11 from the situations in schools questionnaire?

Practice Time

It is time for students to practice what they have learned.
You ...

Does Not Describe Me at All			Somewhat Describes Me		Describes Me Extremely Well		
1	2	3	4	5	6	7	**Ask students which types of practice problems they may want to work on the most.**
1	2	3	4	5	6	7	Demand that now is the time to work, whether they like it or not. Tell them that they sometimes need to learn to do things against their will.
1	2	3	4	5	6	7	Not to plan too much and see how thing evolve.
1	2	3	4	5	6	7	Explain the solution to one problem step-by-step, then guide their progress and improvement on the follow-up problems.

Notes: The above is teaching situation #11 from the Situations in Schools Questionnaire (Aelterman, Vansteenkiste, Haerens, Soenens, Fontaine, & Reeve, 2019). The four response options represent, in order, autonomy support, control, chaos, and structure. The boldface autonomy-supportive response illustrates, "Use invitational language."

DOI: 10.4324/9781003091738-14

To view several brief video clips (20 seconds each) of teachers demonstrating the autonomy-supportive instructional behavior of ***Rely on Invitational Language***, go to this online link: https://vimeo.com/518011674.

Teachers tend to use two types of language to make their engagement requests (see Box 11.1). One way of speaking is to encourage students to explore the learning activity. This way of speaking uses a soft, mild tone of voice with relaxed body language to utter phrases such as, "You might want to consider doing this..." What the teacher is offering students is an invitation to action. A second way of speaking is to utter a directive. This way of speaking uses a harsher, louder tone of voice with no-nonsense body language to utter phrases such as, "Get started; let's get this done." What the teacher is offering students is a command. These two ways of speaking serve two different purposes (e.g., support volition vs. push for compliance) and, because of this, they rely on two different languages.

WHAT YOU SAY AND HOW YOU SAY IT: UNDERSTANDING SPEECH PROSODY

Motivational language is a person-to-person communication in which one person inspires the other into action (e.g., come to class, join the class discussion). The two key components of motivational language are speech content (what you say) and speech prosody (how you say it).

Speech content includes the words the teacher uses (e.g., "watch the video"), while speech prosody includes the tone of voice used while speaking those words (e.g., "watch the video?" vs. "watch the video!") (Zougkou, Weinstein, & Paulmann, 2017). As shown in Table 11.1, the invitational-based speech content and speech prosody used by autonomy-supportive teachers are very different from the pressure-inducing speech content and speech prosody used by controlling teachers (Hodgins, Brown, & Carver, 2007; Radel, Sarrazin, & Pelletier, 2009; Weinstein, Zougkou, & Paulmann, 2018).

Speech content

Autonomy-supportive teachers rely on invitational language. The words they use inspire students to action by promoting choice, self-direction, and autonomous self-regulation. Their speech includes sentences such as, "You might want to..." and "You may want to try this..." Key words and phrases include "You may," "You

TABLE 11.1 Speech Content and Speech Prosody that Differentiate Invitational from Pressuring Language

	Invitational Language	Pressuring Language
Speech Content	You may...	You have to...
(Words)	It's your decision...	You should...
	It's your choice...	You must...
	If you want to...	You ought to...
	May I suggest...	You've got to...
	You might consider...	You are required to...
	If you are willing...	You have to do this now.
	This may be a good opportunity to...	You must obey...
	When you are ready...	I demand that you...
	It is your option to continue.	You have to do it correctly.
	Maybe you can try...	If you don't, then...
Speech Prosody		
(Tone)		
Pitch:	High	Low
Volume:	n/a	Loud (Intense)
Speed:	Slow	Fast
Quality:	Mild	Harsh

might consider," and "I suggest that." Such speech content communicates teacher flexibility, as in the following:

> "You *may* want to conduct a Google search. You *might* find that helpful."
>
> "There are many different materials here that are available to you. *You might* find some of them to be helpful. *You may* want to look through these materials for some ideas."
>
> "*If you are willing, this may be a good opportunity to* get started."

Controlling teachers rely on pressuring language. The words they use urge students into action by grabbing their attention. Their speech includes commanding language such as, "You have to hurry up and finish..." and "You've got to get this done." Key words and phrases include "You should," "You must," and "You have to" (Ryan, 1982). All of these phrases are prescriptive, meaning that the teacher tells the student what he or she has to do. Such phrases are typically accompanied by pressure-packed gestures, such as the teacher pointing a finger at the student or showing a stern "I won't budge" facial expression. When controlling teachers push even harder, they take the next step to use pressure-inducing words and language to shame and induce guilt (Barber, 1996), to offer conditional regard (Roth, Assor, Niemiec, Ryan, & Deci, 2009), and to invoke perfectionistic standards (Soenens et al., 2005). Such language might succeed in producing students' short-term compliance, but that compliance will likely be both short-lived and a catalyst for all sorts of problematic side effects, such as negative feelings, poor internalization, superficial performance, and a low-quality teacher-student relationship.

Speech prosody

Speech prosody is essentially the teacher's *tone of voice*. Tone of voice can be measured by its pitch, volume, speed, and quality (Weinstein et al., 2018; Zougkou et al., 2017).

- **Pitch**: Pitch is how low vs. high a person's voice is perceived to be. Technically, pitch is the number (or frequency) of vibrations per second in a sound wave, measured in Hertz. Women and children have higher pitched voices than do men, but what matters motivationally are those occasions in which the same person's pitch is raised or lowered from its natural baseline level. To illustrate the point, one can repeat the word "Yes" over and over, first with a baseline voice, then with an intentionally higher pitch, and then with an intentionally lower pitch (like moving up and down the musical scale). A raised pitch sounds like asking a question (e.g., "Watch the video?"); a lower pitch sounds like conveying authority (e.g., "Watch the video!").
- **Volume**: Volume is just loudness. Technically, voice volume refers to its amplitude or intensity, measured in decibels (dB). During a typical conversation, the human voice is spoken at about 60 dBs. As with pitch, what matters most (motivationally speaking) is when volume is raised or lowered from its natural baseline level. When volume rises (from 60 to 65 dBs), the voice becomes increasingly forceful—it grabs the other person's attention. When volume rises even higher, it demands the other's attention. When shouting (85 dBs), volume can be so intense as to be painful—painful enough that the student becomes increasingly willing to do whatever it takes to escape from or end it. The teacher's words then tell the student what needs to be done to escape or end the volume-induced pain ("Sit. Now!").
- **Speed** (Speech Rate): Speech rate is how many seconds it takes the person to speak a syllable (i.e., "tempo"). The sentence, "Who would like to ask a question?" can take 1 second (fast), 2 seconds (medium), or 3 seconds (slow) to say. When words are slower than usual, speech rate communicates patience and confidence that the student can self-generate their own behavior. When words are faster than usual, speech rate communicates a need for urgent behavior change.
- **Quality** (Voice Quality): Voice quality ranges from *soft and relaxed* to *sharp and stern*. When milder than usual, voice quality communicates choice, interpersonal support and reassurance. When sharper than usual, voice quality communicates an energetic, urgent, no-nonsense call to immediate action. A harsh voice suppresses choice and demands compliance.

These four aspects of speech prosody tend to intercorrelate positively with each other. That is, a high pitch also tends to be a slower, milder voice, just as a low pitch tends to be louder, faster, and harsher. It can be overwhelming to try to change four aspects of your voice all at the same time, but pitch is the place to start. For teachers who want to communicate to students using more invitational language, a good practice activity is to, first, say "yes, yes, yes, yes, yes" in your regular tone of voice and then, second, to repeat "yes, yes, yes, yes, yes" but this time with an intentionally higher pitch (e.g., up one key on a piano keyboard). Once you can do that, insert an actual sentence in place of "yes, yes, yes, yes, yes" and say that sentence with both a normal and a higher pitch, as in the following:

"Would you like to get started?"	(start with your regular pitch)
"Would you like to get started?"	(now use a higher pitch)
"You may want to try this."	(start with you regular pitch)
"You may want to try this."	(now use a higher pitch)

Using milder speech prosody can become an acquired skill. With practice, teachers can intentionally manage (manipulate) their tone of voice to communicate support for student initiative (rather than pressure for compliance). The reader can do this by trying the exercise above, but also by using the software *Audacity* (though researchers generally use the more sophisticated software *Praat*).

Content and prosody together

Invitational language pairs together "You might want to consider…" content that is spoken with a higher pitched, slower, and milder voice prosody. This blend does not command the students' immediate attention and behavior change. Instead, it invites students to initiate and self-regulate their own behavior.

Pressuring language pairs together "You have to…" content that is spoken with a lower pitched, louder, faster, and harsher voice prosody. This blend does command students' immediate attention and behavior change. It has the effect of overwhelming students' personal motivations to replace them with a teacher prescription ("Do this.") or proscription ("Don't do that."). The lower the pitch, the louder the volume, the faster the speech, and the harsher the voice quality, the more urgent the teacher's demand that the student abandon their personal motivations and comply with the teacher's prescription or proscription.

Words and tone are usually consistent. When both the words and the prosody are consistent ("You may…" + high pitch with a mild quality), students receive a reinforced communication of support and self-direction. However, if either the words or the prosody is mixed ("You may…" + a harsh tone), then the communication sends a mixed or ambiguous message. So, the skill of invitational language requires mastering the words, the tone, and the coordinated pairing of words and tone.

INVITATIONAL, INFORMATIONAL, AND NON-PRESSURING LANGUAGE

Invitational language is an overarching name for autonomy-supportive teacher talk that encourages ("invites") students to initiate and self-regulate their own behavior. Sometimes, however, students struggle with difficult and overwhelming problems. A student who becomes confused and overwhelmed in a music or math class may become so discouraged and frustrated as to want to quit and give up. During these times, what students need from their teachers (motivationally speaking) is informational language to help them see a viable path forward. Together, invitational language and informational language coalesce into autonomy-supportive language.

Invitational language

Invitational language means using phrases such as "You may...," "You might consider...," "May I can suggest...," and "You might want to try..." to support students' volition during behavioral initiatives. Through invitational language, the teacher supports the students' initiative, exploration, participation, engagement, self-direction, choice making, and goal pursuits. Invitational language is especially timely in helping students overcome the inertia of inactivity or procrastination on a project, as in the following two examples:

> "There are many different ways you might complete this project.
> You might want to consider working with a partner."
>
> "May I suggest that everyone in the group take turns. Would that work?"

What is absent from such teacher talk is any reliance on directives, pressure, and the teacher's external regulation of the student's behavior or decision-making.

Informational language

Informational language means providing students with the special insights, tips, and strategies they need to better diagnose, understand, and solve the problems they face. Sometimes students struggle to make progress and solve problems. In these instances, they may become stuck because they do not know what to do next. Students are often motivationally vulnerable in this situation, as frustration and discouragement might be high and rising. Teachers can provide students with new, insightful, and hope-inspiring information about possible problem-solving strategies that the student may not be aware of—yet have the potential to get the student unstuck and back on track. Here are two examples in which the teacher helps the student self-diagnose why he or she is struggling to make progress or behave effectively:

> "I noticed that you made a low score on the test.
> Do you know why that happened?"

TEACHER: "You seem to be having some difficulty with this lesson. Do I understand that correctly?"
STUDENT: "Um. Yes."
TEACHER: "Do you know why that might be?"

Often, the struggling student knows why they are struggling. By asking the student to diagnose their own problem (assuming the student thinks there is a problem), the teacher is better able to (1) understand the student and his or her personal motivations and (2) preserve the student's sense of ownership and personal responsibility for regulating their own behavior and for solving their own problems.

Sometimes, however, students face a problem or skill challenge and they simply do not know what to do. They do not know what an effective course of action might be. In this situation, the student may be on the verge of giving up. At this point, the teacher might suggest a new problem-solving strategy, such as the following:

TEACHER: "So, what do you think you could do to make more friends?"
STUDENT: "I don't know."
TEACHER: "Last semester, I had a student who had a similar problem. She liked to play soccer. So, she played soccer with some of her classmates after school. After that, she was able to make a lot of friends. I think this strategy worked very well for her. Maybe something like this might work for you too. Do you have a fun activity that you can share with others?"

The "information" in informational language is the teacher's special insight that can help the student discover new, constructive answers to "Why is this problem occurring?" and "What can I do about it?" Sometimes, students can answer these questions for themselves, and what they need from their teacher is someone who will listen to them, understand what they are trying to do, and support their problem diagnosis and problem-solving initiatives. Other times, students need new information. Because the teacher is likely to possess a rich reservoir of experience in which students from past years have worked successfully through these same problems, the teacher might share some of that new, insightful information. In doing so, the teacher tries to get the student unstuck. To do this, what the teacher offers the student is new information, not pressure.

Change-oriented feedback

Students sometimes behave poorly and even irresponsibly, and teachers need to provide corrective feedback. For instance, a student might perform very poorly or behave very inappropriately. Change-oriented feedback (i.e., corrective feedback) is an autonomy-supportive way to tell students what they are doing is problematic and in need of change.

Telling students what they are doing wrong and what they need to change generally produces two contrasting effects: (1) performance improvement and

TABLE 11.2 Six Defining Characteristics of Autonomy-Supportive Change-Oriented Feedback

1. Empathic
   The teacher acknowledges that the task is difficult and the obstacles are many.
2. Accompanied by Choices of Solutions to Correct the Problem
   The teacher offers two or three problem-solving solutions and then lets the student choose the one he or she most prefers.
3. Linked to a Clear Objective
   What the teacher suggests is linked to a clear objective or goal.
4. Paired with Tips
   The feedback is accompanied by tips in how to improve future performances.
5. Free of Student-Related Statements
   The feedback describes the behavior and what is happening. It is free from all personal attacks on the student as a person.
6. Considerate Tone of Voice
   The teacher avoids yelling and a disrespectful tone.
   The teacher is careful not to ridicule the student in any way.

(2) negative after-effects, such as high anxiety, lower self-esteem, and a riff in the quality of the teacher-student relationship. When self-determination theory researchers investigated how teachers might best provide such corrective feedback, they suggested that teachers integrate change-oriented feedback with invitational-informational language (Carpentier & Mageau, 2013, 2016).

Feedback is information. It is post-behavior or post-performance information about how well or how poorly the student's behavior or performance corresponds to the teacher's expectations and standards (Hein & Koka, 2007). Such feedback often includes what it is about the students' behavior or performance that needs to be modified so to meet the teacher's expectations. For such feedback to be constructive and to produce desired rather than harmful after-effects, it needs to be communicated in an autonomy-supportive way, as shown in Table 11.2 (Carpentier & Mageau, 2013, 2016).

Collectively, what these six defining characteristics of autonomy-supportive change-oriented feedback do is allow the teacher's corrective feedback to be experienced by the student as emphatic, informational (descriptive, rather than evaluative), and choice-promoting. When teachers provide change-oriented feedback in this way, students tend to react by experiencing higher need satisfaction (not higher need frustration), greater (not lower) self-confidence, and a better (not an impaired) teacher-student relationship (Carpentier & Mageau, 2013, 2016). Because of the invitational-informational language, the student hears support and sees a path to progress, rather than criticism and forthcoming punishment.

Here is an example of what autonomy-supportive change-oriented feedback might sound like in the classroom. After a student performs poorly on a test, the teacher might say:

"How do you think you did on the test?
[Using a high pitched soften tone of voice. The teacher pauses to hear the student's self-evaluation. The teacher then continues...]
Your performance was below expectations—below where it needs to be at this point in the class.
I realize that the test covered new and difficult material.
Do you also think this was the case?
Perhaps I can suggest a few strategies that might improve your future performances.

> You might consider using the language lab more than you have in the past.
> Or, you might pair up with a classmate so that you can help and encourage each other.
> Or, you might try something different—such as flash cards or a personal tutor.

Perhaps one of these strategies might be helpful to you.
It would be great to see you make progress and become proficient."

Replace pressuring language with invitational language

Autonomy support blends together invitational language, informational language, and constructively communicated change-oriented feedback. But autonomy-supportive language still necessitates one more skill—namely, to replace pressuring language with invitational language. One skill is to use invitational language more, a second skill is to use pressuring language less, but a final skill is to replace existing pressuring language with new invitational language.

Skill 1 is to use invitational language more, especially to help students overcome problems of inertia. This requires the teacher to gain awareness of the words, phrases, and sentences that best encourage students' self-generated action (see Table 11.1). It also involves learning how to pair these words, phrases, and sentences with higher pitched, slower, and milder speech prosody.

Skill 2 is to use pressuring language less, especially when students perform poorly and behave inappropriately. This requires the teacher to forego any habitual tendency to utter words and harsh prosody to push for behavior change and immediate compliance. Pressuring language often includes no-nonsense gestures and body language that need to be jettisoned.

Skill 3 is the compound skill of replacing pressuring language with substitute invitational language. This is more easily said than done. The phrase "got to" is probably the most frequently occurring phrase in all of teacher talk (e.g., "You've *got to* pay attention. You've *got to* finish up. You've *got to* take this more seriously. You've *got to* try harder. You've *got to* get this done. You've *got to* be nicer to each other."). Developing this skill means becoming mindful of and intentionally removing language such as, "Look up here. Pay attention!," and replacing it with, "You may find this next topic interesting." It also involves transforming a low, harsh tone of voice into one that is higher, slower, and milder.

CONCLUSION

Language can inspire action. Through content and prosody, language carries a motivational message. Sometimes that message is prescriptive and pressure-packed. Other times it supports and encourages initiative and volition. The latter—invitational, informational, and nonpressuring language—supports both students' volitional task engagements and the quality of the teacher-student relationship.

Display patience

BOX 12.1

How would you respond to teaching simulation #13 from the situations in schools questionnaire?

Test Results

You have finished scoring a test. Several students scored low again, even though you paid extra attention to this material last week. You...

Does Not Describe Me at All		Somewhat Describes Me		Describes Me Extremely Well			
1	2	3	4	5	6	7	Insist that low scores are unacceptable to you. Tell students that they must score higher for their own good.
1	2	3	4	5	6	7	Help students revise their wrong answers so that they understand what went wrong and how to improve.
1	2	3	4	5	6	7	**Listen with patience and understanding to what the students say about their test performance**.
1	2	3	4	5	6	7	Don't spend class time on the low scoring students.

Notes: The above is teaching situation #13 from the Situations in Schools Questionnaire (Aelterman, Vansteenkiste, Haerens, Soenens, Fontaine, & Reeve, 2019). The four response options represent, in order, control, structure, autonomy support, and chaos. The boldfaced autonomy-supportive response illustrates, "Display patience."

To view several brief video clips (20 seconds each) of teachers demonstrating the autonomy-supportive instructional behavior of ***Display Patience***, go to this online link: https://vimeo.com/518012533.

DOI: 10.4324/9781003091738-15

When a student falls asleep in class, the teacher might walk to the student's desk, wake the student, and say, "Pay attention." To reverse this problematic behavior, the teacher might next introduce some motivational event (e.g., a stern facial expression) to quicken the desired behavioral change. Similarly, when a student makes the same mistake over and over again, the teacher may intervene to right the wrong, such as by giving the student the correct answer or by doing the work for the student. And, when an art student paints carelessly, the teacher may take the brush out of the student's hand and say, "Here, give me the brush. This is how you hold it. See? Now, hold the brush just like I showed you." In each of these three situations, the teacher's striving for immediate behavior change represents impatience.

A key question is whether or not these brief teacher interventions produce helpful, lasting behavioral change. You may notice that each follows the same script in that the teacher takes action to: (1) diagnose that the behavior is problematic; (2) propose a remedy; and (3) apply some consequence to spur the behavior change. While common, such teaching practices are ineffective (Baldwin & Baldwin, 1986; Koestner, Powers, Milyavskaya, Carbonneau, & Hope, 2015). Each does generally succeed in gaining the student's immediate attention and apparent behavior change, but that behavioral change lasts only minutes—or at least until the teacher's surveillance abates (Prendergast, Podus, Pinney, Greenwell, & Roll, 2006). The sleeping, the struggling, and the carelessness will likely return tomorrow. And, with these problematic ways of behaving will come some troubling side effects, such as upset feelings and poor internalization of the value for the behavior change.

Of course, doing nothing in these situations is also problematic. Being permissive, neglectful, lax, and "anything goes" are also ineffective—even irresponsible. So, what is a teacher to do (see Box 12.1)?

There is wisdom in the old adage that "Prevention works better than remediation." Once maladaptive behavior has taken root (e.g., disengagement, serious misconduct, and poor performance), it is difficult to reverse or undo, partly because one also needs to undo its underlying cause. In contrast, prevention means taking action to keep something from happening in the first place. This applies to both the maladaptive behavior and its motivational cause. Prevention works because students are not going to fall asleep in class (especially repeatedly) if they are deeply interested in what they are doing, and they will not behave carelessly if they value painting and desire to improve.

PATIENCE

Patience is the optimistic calmness teachers show as students struggle to start, adjust, and change their behavior. It is showing optimism and calmness, and it is giving students your attention and support as they attempt to work through the process of adjusting their thinking and behaving from something that is ineffective, passive, and irresponsible into some future way of thinking and behaving that is more effective, energized, and responsible.

Patience is not "doing nothing." Instead, patience means waiting calmly for students' readiness and willingness to change. When patient, teachers take the time to

1. Listen and understand where students' maladaptive way of thinking or behaving is coming from.
2. Postpone their advice until first receiving a signal or invitation from the student that the teacher's help would be welcomed and appreciated.

Listening, understanding

Displaying patience—even as students engage in maladaptive behavior or fail to engage in adaptive behavior—is important because it creates the opportunity for the teacher to really understand the student. Why is this student disengaged? Why is this student acting irresponsibly? Why is this student performing so poorly? Of course, teachers can usually (and quickly) generate their own hypotheses (e.g., "He didn't complete his homework because he thinks geography is boring."). Most of the time, however, the teacher's initial explanation is only a hypothesis—it might be true, partly true, or false. It seems helpful for teachers to first test out their hypotheses before taking action, and the most direct way to do this is to ask the student. A good first question is, Does the student see the behavior as problematic? If so, a second good question is, Why does the student believe the maladaptive behavior is occurring?

Patience involves a lot of listening. It is not refusing to give advice, but it is waiting to give advice until first understanding what the problem is, what its cause might be, and even if a problem exists at all. Here is an example of empathic listening, which features the teacher's actively listening to the student's words, feelings, and gestures:

TEACHER: "So, how is class going for you? I would like to hear about that."
STUDENT: "Class is fine. I'm a little behind on my work. Procrastinating a bit."
TEACHER: "Okay. Can you say anything more about the procrastination? What is the feeling behind the procrastination?"

From this point, the conversation might take any number of possible turns. However, the key point lies in the teacher's listening empathically to what the student has to say. Through empathic listening, the teacher offers the gist of autonomy support—namely, a student focus paired with an understanding tone. In terms of understanding, what reason (or reasons) does the student offer to explain the procrastination? Does the student think the procrastination is a problem? Of course, a teacher could simply judge the procrastination as problematic (e.g., "Procrastination is wrong. You should work harder and show a good work ethic."), but a teacher who responds in this way has probably not really actively listened to the students' thoughts, feelings, and intentions. This tendency to judge and to correct tends to interfere with the teacher's capacity to understand. It is a symptom of the absence of both patience and perspective taking.

To develop the skill of empathic listening, the renowned psychologist Carl Rogers suggested the following exercise (paraphrased to apply to teachers; from Rogers, 1961, p. 332):

> The next time you get in an argument with a student, try this before you present your own point of view. First, restate the ideas and feelings of the student accurately, and do so to the satisfaction of the student. Thus, before you speak, you would understand this student's frame of reference and what you would say next would qualify as communication (rather than as argumentation or interpersonal control).

Understanding also means recognizing how difficult behavior change really is. To change behavior (e.g., from disrespectful to respectful language, from procrastination to conscientiousness), teachers need to give students the time, space, and resources they need to achieve all of the following:

- Overcome the inertia of inactivity
- Explore and find new information and new role models
- Ask questions
- Formulate and test new hypotheses as to what might work, or work best
- Make new plans and set new goals
- Collect new data
- Process feedback
- Try out new strategies
- Reflect on how the attempted behavior change is going
- Revise one's thinking
- Try something new and different and, if necessary,
- Start all over again

All of this takes time. Because students need time to work through the process of behavior change, teachers need patience.

Postponing advice

For lasting behavior change to occur, it needs to be initiated and owned by the student. The teacher can certainly help the process along, but patiently so. Postponing advice means waiting for the right moment to provide encouragement, suggestions, and hints. The "right moment" is when the student is open to and ready to hear the teacher's input. As the student works to make personal progress, the teacher can wait for a student-initiated signal (even a subtle one) that the teacher's advice is needed and would be welcomed:

STUDENT: "This is hard. It is kind of complicated."
TEACHER: "Yes, can I help?"

[The teacher monitors the student for verbal and nonverbal signals as to whether the student would like and welcome the teacher's advice.]

STUDENT: "No, I would like to see if I can figure this out for myself."

TEACHER: "Okay."

[The teacher affirms the student's sense of autonomy ("Okay" with a soft smile and nod of the head), sits back in her chair, puts her hands in her lap, and waits patiently for the student's signal that help is wanted.]

Impatience

The value of patience is best seen in its absence. The opposite of patience is the teacher taking charge and rushing in to diagnose and solve the student's problem. The impatient teacher tries to solve the problem for the student and make it go away—by rushing in, taking over, and showing or telling the student what to do, as in "Here, let me show you how to do it" or "Give me the keyboard. I'll do it for you. Now, do it like I showed you."

Impatience refers to explicit attempts to change the behaviors students are presently engaged in or the opinions they express, and it includes intrusive behaviors such as not letting students work at their preferred pace, uttering directives, and not allowing students to voice opinions that differ from those expressed by the teacher (Assor, Kaplan, Kanat-Maymon, & Roth, 2005). Instead of successful behavior change, what impatience mostly leads to is negative emotionality (anger, anxiety), motivational apathy, doing only what is required, and less (rather than more) engagement.

PATIENCE = 100% AUTONOMY SUPPORT + 0% DIRECTIVE SUPPORT

As students struggle to attain their goals and change their behavior, autonomy support from the teacher involves listening, being open to students sharing their (negative) feelings, understanding how the student sees things, conveying confidence in the student, and accepting the student whether or not he or she attains the goal or changes the behavior.

More common than autonomy support in these situations is directive support. Directive support is not the same as pressure-inducing teacher control. Instead, directive support is more instrumental. The teacher offers guidance, actively helps the student's problem solving, and offers reminders about how important it is that the student attain the goal or change the behavior (Holding & Koestner, 2021). Directive support is reminding the student of his or her goals, reminding the student what they need to be doing, encouraging the student to persist, problem-solving, and making sure the student understands how important it is to attain one's goals and to change one's behavior. Directive support is a type of support, but research consistently shows that autonomy support is more helpful than is directive support

(Gorin, Powers, Koestner, Wing, & Raynor, 2014; Koestner, Powers, Carbonneau, Milyavskaya, & Chua, 2012, 2015). The problem with directive support is that, while it does offer potentially helpful guidance, it too often slips into what comes across to students as an interfering, meddling type of support.

It can be surprising (even very surprising!) to hear that listening and understanding can be a more effective teacher response to a struggling student than is directive support, but research consistently shows that this is the case. For example, one study asked a group of students what their goals were for the semester and then asked these students to identify three people who were providing support for their goal pursuit (e.g., a teacher, a friend, a parent) (Koestner et al., 2015). The researchers then asked students to report on each person's autonomy support and directive support. What the researchers wanted to know was, once the semester was over, to what extent had the student internalized the value of the goal, whether the student had attained the goal or not, how resilient (vs. fragile) the student's goal striving was over time, what direction the relationship with the support-provider had taken, and how the whole experience affected the student's well-being. When the student received autonomy support from others, the goal striving went very well—goal internalization, goal attainment, goal resilience, relationship satisfaction, and well-being. When the student received directive support, however, the goal striving did not go so well, as none of these positive outcomes occurred and both goal internalization and well-being took a turn for the worse.

The overall lesson for teachers who want to help a struggling student is this: Autonomy support is always helpful while directive support occasionally backfires to produce more harm than good (Gorin et al., 2014). This result seems counter-intuitive as it appears that what the struggling, frustrated student needs is problem-solving help. What actually helps, however, is listening, understanding, and supporting autonomy.

Learning vs. relearning

Much of classroom teaching is for initial learning, as the teacher introduces students to new information, a new skill, a new way of doing something, and new learning materials. When it comes to helping students make progress beyond an initial understanding and an initial performance, however, much of classroom teaching is for revising and relearning. Relearning occurs slowly, and it may occur at a pace that seems too slow for the teacher (e.g., "You learned this yesterday; let's move on to what is new"). Re-learning involves trying new things, revising one's thinking and problem-solving strategies, switching from one thing to another, and being willing to start all over, if necessary. Answers, solutions, and new insights do not come quickly or easily. While it makes sense for initial learning to be teacher-focused, it makes sense that re-learning is best when it is student-focused and teacher-supported.

As students work through the difficult and challenging processes of developing skill and re-learning what was not learned or mastered on the first try, what they need (and benefit from; Koestner et al., 2012, 2015) is for the teacher to understand how they see things, to accept them whether or not they make progress or attain the sought-after goal, and to simply offer that optimistic calmness that conveys the teacher's confidence in student's capacity to make the needed change and progress. From this point of view, patience can be boiled down to a simple formula: Patience = 100% autonomy support + 0% directive support.

PATIENCE + SUPPORT

As a teacher, it can be unsatisfying to hear advice such as, "Be patient." Waiting around for students' behavior to change all by itself seems fanciful—even irresponsible. But it is helpful to remember that patience does not mean "do nothing." As a motivating style, "awaiting" means taking a laissez-faire approach where the initiative to act lies fully with the student. The teacher tends to wait to see how things evolve, does not plan too much, and just lets things take their course (Aelterman, Vansteenkiste, Haerens, Soenens, Fontaine, & Reeve, 2019). Awaiting reflects a chaotic motivating style ("do nothing") more than it reflects an autonomy-supportive one. The reader can see this is the "chaotic" response options featured in the series of *Situations in Schools* questionnaire items that opened Chapters 6–12 (e.g., in this chapter: "Don't spend class time on the low scoring students").

Chaos and laissez-faire are terrible motivating styles (Aelterman, Vansteenkiste, Haerens, Soenens, Fontaine, & Reeve, 2019), and one reason teachers might be hesitant to accept a recommendation for autonomy-supportive teaching is that they worry that autonomy-support's next-door neighbors are chaos and laissez-faire.

To address this teacher concern, we highlight that "support" is just as important a word in the phrase "autonomy support" as is "autonomy." Thus, while teachers exercise their patience, they also need to provide their support. Teachers can pair their patience with several types of support, including interest support, competence support, and relatedness support. Support generally involves listening, understanding, taking the student's perspective, and being responsive to the student's signals, input, and initiative (i.e., "patience + support"). More specifically, though, the patient teacher can provide "patience + interest support," as in the following:

STUDENT: "I'm having a hard time getting started on this paper."
TEACHER: "Okay. Is this topic interesting? Perhaps you could write the paper on something that really interests you."

Teachers can also practice "patience + competence support." Patient teachers can support students' need for competence by scaffolding what students are currently trying to do, assuming the student has sent out a signal suggesting that such competence support might be appreciated. This is not directive support, because teachers are not directing students' behavior or offering explicit recommendations for what they should do. Instead, patience + competence support looks more like the following:

STUDENT: "It is difficult to know how to do this."
TEACHER: "For those of you who are struggling to get started, I have provided a couple of worked-out sample paragraphs you can use. Perhaps you will see something in these sample paragraphs that will help you get started."

Competence support can also come in the form of simply affirming that students are on the right track in their efforts to change behavior or improve performance, as in the following:

STUDENT: "I've been working on my project. It took a while, but I finally came up with a plan I think will work. My idea is to use a wide canvas and paint a picture of an island and the sea around it. I want to contrast the blue of the sky against the blue of the ocean."
TEACHER: Listens attentively. Nods and softly smiles to convey confidence in the student's plan of action.

Teachers can also practice "patience + relatedness support." Patient teachers can support students' need for relatedness by communicating acceptance and unconditional positive regard as the student works through the behavior change process, such as the following:

STUDENT: "I'm having a hard time getting started on the paper."
TEACHER: "Okay. I know you can do it.
It will be hard, but in the end, I know you can do it."

CONCLUSION

Teachers agonize when students think and behave in maladaptive ways. In response, teachers often rush in, take control, and tell or show students what they need to do (thinking that this is the best way to help students). Instead of trying to fix what is wrong, teachers can take an alternative, patient approach to support students' internalizations. When teachers are both supportive and patient (listen empathically, postpone advice), students generally but gradually figure out how to reorganize their maladaptive thinking and behaving in a more effective direction, though the teacher may need to supplement his or her patience with interest support, competence support, and relatedness support.

CHAPTER 13

Discipline, structure, and behavior change

Every school has a formal discipline policy. There is a good reason for this. Schools want to create an environment in which effective teaching and learning can take place. They want every student who walks on the school grounds to experience security, acceptance, support, and multiple opportunities for wellness and achievement. If you were to flip through the pages of any school's discipline policy, you would find a socially engineered framework designed to (a) communicate values and priorities, (b) establish rules and norms, (c) foster learning, (d) identify inappropriate behavior and its consequences, and (e) recognize and celebrate appropriate behavior.

A discipline policy typically begins with a list of core values, such as those for safety (physical, social, emotional), tolerance (acceptance of diversity), respect (treat others as you would like them to treat you), and excellence (work to fulfill one's potential). It continues with a list of rules designed to discriminate appropriate from inappropriate behavior. As students walk down the hallway of almost any school, they will likely see a poster or two that identify both what these appropriate behaviors are (and their rewards) and what these inappropriate behaviors are (and their punishments).

Schools go through all this effort to create and communicate discipline policies because they believe firmly that all students and all teachers have a right to be treated with respect and to spend their day in an environment that is free from disruption, violence, intimidation, bullying, victimization, harassment, and discrimination. Schools acknowledge that these inappropriate behaviors exist in any society and, because of this, they want to offer their school community a clear framework (the discipline policy) to guide everyone toward appropriate behavior and competent functioning.

THE TEACHER'S WORRIES AND CONCERNS, HOPES AND ASPIRATIONS

Like the school, the teacher wants to create an environment in which effective teaching and learning can take place and, like the school, the teacher wants all students to experience security, acceptance, support, and multiple opportunities for wellness and achievement. Thus, teachers follow the school's lead to establish and communicate

DOI: 10.4324/9781003091738-16

TABLE 13.1 Teachers' "Big 3" Worries and Concerns

Serious Misconduct

- Students act disrespectfully and use disrespectful language.
- They act irresponsibly and ignore classroom procedures.
- They break the rules.
- They act aggressively.
- They bully classmates.

Disengagement

- Students are off-task or display only token effort.
- They come to class unprepared, and the work they do is superficial.
- They fail to participate.
- They show little initiative and, instead, just sit passively.
- They procrastinate, come to class late, or skip class altogether.

Poor Performance

- Students produce sloppy, careless work.
- They perform incompetently.
- They underperform classroom standards.
- They feel lost and overwhelmed by classroom challenges and requirements.
- They cheat; they plagiarize.

rules, norms, values, and appropriate ways of behaving (i.e., a discipline policy for the classroom).

Why do teachers do this? Table 13.1 answers this question by listing teachers' "Big 3" worries and concerns—overlaid with their hopes and aspirations. The first cluster revolves around issues of discipline and classroom management. The concern is to minimize or eradicate serious misconduct. Teachers want to minimize disrespectful behavior, irresponsible behavior, rule breaking, aggression, and bullying. The second cluster revolves around issues of engagement and learning. The concern is to convert disengagement into learning-enabling engagement. Teachers want to minimize students' being off task, coming to class unprepared, failing to participate, chronic passivity, and the many varieties of procrastination. The third cluster revolves around issues of performance and achievement. The concern is that students will under-perform both their potential and classroom standards. Teachers want to minimize sloppy work, displays of incompetence, episodes of under-performance, feelings of being lost, and instances of cheating and plagiarism.

CLASSROOM STRUCTURE

Teachers want to see their students showing responsible behavior, high engagement, and excellent performance. To accomplish these aspirations and to purge their opposites (Table 13.1), teachers can create a classroom structure. Such structure guides students toward appropriate behavior and away from inappropriate behavior. For instance, teachers can be really clear about what the classroom rules and priorities are. But classroom structure can do much more than this. It is also the instruction-based means through which the teacher helps students advance from relatively immature, poorly functioning, and maladaptive ways of behaving (e.g., antisocial behavior) to that which is instead more mature, better functioning, and adaptive (e.g., prosocial behavior). To make this transition, students need the teacher's help. For instance, a student may be fully aware that it is right and good to set goals, perform up to standards, and be prosocial, yet that same student might lack the core feelings of competence and personal control needed to motivate and enable such behavior change. In these cases, what students need is guidance and mentoring.

Structure is a teacher's interpersonal tone of guidance that provides students with the support they need to develop skill, perform well, and function adaptively (Aelterman, Vansteenkiste, Haerens, Seoenens, Fontaine, & Reeve, 2019). To do this, the teacher communicates a clear behavior change goal for students to strive toward, and then provides the help and assistance students need to make progress and feel competent enough to adjust their behavior to meet those expectations and goals. Specifically, with guidance, the teacher demonstrates what competent functioning looks like, provides step-by-step guidance for how to make progress and attain desired outcomes, scaffolds for progress, offers help and assistance, adjusts task difficulty as needed, and provides constructive feedback (Carpentier & Mageau, 2016; Cheon, Reeve, & Vansteenkiste, 2020; Grolnick & Pomerantz, 2009).

Structure features three core dimensions—namely, clarifying expectations, providing guidance, and providing feedback (Aelterman, Vansteenkiste, Haerens, Soenens, Fontaine, & Reeve, 2019). A *clarifying* teacher communicates expectations in a clear and transparent way. The teacher introduces a goal or standard for students to strive for and monitors students' progress in meeting the communicated expectation. A *guiding* teacher nurtures students' progress by providing appropriate help and assistance as needed. The teacher demonstrates and explains the steps necessary to make progress, complete the task, and attain desired outcomes. With *feedback*, the teacher provides a post-behavior or a post-performance commentary so that students can assess whether or not they have met the teacher's expectations. Feedback identifies strengths and weaknesses, and it shows the student a future pathway to more competent functioning and behavior change.

Teacher-provided structure offers two motivational benefits: A feeling of competence and a sense of personal control over desired outcomes. As introduced in Chapter 2, *competence* is the psychological need to experience effectance during environmental interactions. Competence satisfaction occurs when students take on classroom challenges (e.g., write a paper, converse in a foreign language, play a musical instrument) and, while doing so, feel and say:

- I feel competent.
- I am doing well—even at the hard things.
- I am able to complete even the difficult stuff.

Alternatively, competence frustration occurs when students take on classroom challenges and, while doing so, feel and say:

- I feel inadequate.
- I feel overwhelmed by this task.
- I keep making stupid mistakes that makes me feel incompetent.

To better support students' feelings of competence satisfaction, teachers can take three steps. First, teachers can learn how to *clarify expectations*—how to offer a clear goal or a standard of excellence for students to strive for (e.g., "Write a concise topic sentence that foreshadows the paragraph to come"). Second, teachers can learn how to *provide guidance*—how to mentor students' progress and skill building (e.g., "One way to get started is to generate a title for your paragraph and then have your topic sentence reflect that title"). Third, teachers can learn how to *provide feedback*—how to offer a post-task commentary to help students do in the future what they are not yet able to do in the present (e.g., "Let's look at the verb in your topic sentence—Is it active? Does it generate vivid imagery?").

Clarify expectations

As students begin to engage in a learning activity or undertake a behavioral request, they wonder "What represents a good performance?" and "How good is 'good enough'?" A clear goal or an explicit standard answers these questions. By providing these things, teachers help students realize what is expected of them, what needs to be done, and when it needs to be done. It becomes clear what "a job well done" means. It becomes clear what "a good performance" is (e.g., one that is at or above the goal level, while a poor performance is one that is below the goal level). Table 13.2 offers some specific examples of what teachers might say during instruction to communicate clear expectations (goals, standards) to students.

TABLE 13.2 Instructional Behaviors to Clarify Expectations

Instructional Behavior	What a Teacher Might Say
1. Offer a Goal to Strive for	"Author a topic sentence that beautifully foreshadows the paragraph to come."
2. Communicate a Standard of Excellence	"Here is an example of great writing. See if you can write sentences as good as this."
3. Clarify Expectations (Define What Competence Is)	"I don't want to see your first draft. What I want is a carefully revised topic sentence that you can feel proud to call your own."

TABLE 13.3 Instructional Behaviors to Provide Guidance

Instructional Behavior	What a Teacher Might Say
1. Provide a Model, Example	"Let's watch this videoclip of an expert."
2. Offer Tips, Strategies	"Here is a good way to get started..." "Notice how the expert..."
3. Provide Needed Resources	"This website might give you some good ideas."
4. Provide Mentoring, Coaching	"How can I help?" "Are you having any particular trouble?"
5. Add Well-Timed Hints and Suggestions	"You might recall what the video-model did at this point in the task."

Provide guidance

As students invest their effort to meet the teacher's expectations, they wonder "Will I be able to do this?," "Will this task overwhelm and frustrate me?," and "How can I improve—how can I do this better?" A teacher's progress-enabling guidance and mentoring answers these questions. By providing students with step-by-step instruction, one-on-one scaffolding, and worked-out examples, teachers help students clear away their doubts and uncertainties ("Can I do this?"). How to make progress becomes clear through the teacher's modeling, examples, tips, strategies, mentoring, coaching, help, resources, and well-timed suggestions. If progress dips below the goal level, the student need not panic because the teacher is there to provide the guidance needed to turn things around. Table 13.3 offers some specific examples of what teachers might say during instruction to offer such guidance.

Provide feedback

As students' display their skill and generate products, they wonder "Is this any good?," "What should I work on next?," and "How can I advance from good to great?" The teacher's post-performance commentary answers all of these questions. By offering students a post-performance analysis, students come to understand what they need to change to put themselves on a path to future progress. Without such a post-task commentary, students typically find it difficult to judge their performances and products (e.g., "Was my presentation good?"). In a post-task commentary, the teacher comments on the quality of the students' work, identifies strengths and weaknesses, and provides improvement-enabling information, strategies, suggestions, and resources (i.e., the "secrets to success"). Table 13.4 offers some specific examples of what teachers might say to provide students with a post-task commentary.

The problem with structure

There is a potential problem with teacher-provided structure. By itself, teacher-provided structure may or may not enrich students' motivation, engagement,

TABLE 13.4 Instructional Behaviors to Provide Feedback

Instructional Behavior	What a Teacher Might Say
1. Facilitate Personal Reflection	"How well do you think you did?"
2. Provide Information	"I videotaped your performance. Take a look and notice how..."
3. Communicate Strengths	"Your topic sentences are much improved over your first draft."
4. Identify Weaknesses	"Your conclusion sentences do not yet explain the point being made in the paragraph."
5. Offer a Path Forward to Future Progress	"Let's compare your performance to the model's performance. If you could strengthen your conclusion sentences up to the model's level that would be a sure-fire way to improve your writing."

performance, effective functioning, and well-being (Grolnick & Pomerantz, 2009). This is because teachers can provide structure in either an autonomy-supportive or a controlling way. That is, the teacher can communicate their expectations, guidance, and feedback with perspective-taking, choice, and a supportive tone of voice (i.e., structure provided in an autonomy-supportive way), or the teacher can introduce the same expectations, guidance, and feedback with pressure, demands, and a harsh tone of voice (i.e., structure provided in a controlling way).

Here is the problem. When teachers impose a rule in a controlling way, that rule will actually undermine (rather than promote) students' motivation and performance (Koestner, Ryan, Bernieri, & Holt, 1984). The same is true when teachers set expectations in a controlling way (Trouilloud, Sarrazin, Bressoux, & Bois, 2006), state directions in a controlling way (Eckes, Großmann, & Wilde, 2018), recommend goals in a controlling way (Vansteenkiste, Simons, Lens, Sheldon, & Deci, 2004), communicate in a controlling way (Curran, Hill, & Niemiec, 2013), provide feedback in a controlling way (Mouratidis, Lens, & Vansteenkiste, 2010), make behavior change requests in a controlling way (Vansteenkiste et al., 2018), and assess students' work in a controlling way (Haerens et al., 2018). In all these cases, a teacher's controlling structure puts students' motivation and behavior change at risk.

The conclusion from all this research is that controlling structure actually undermines motivation and generates few, if any, benefits. If structure does not support students' competence need satisfaction, it will leave the problems of serious misconduct, disengagement, and underperformance (recall Table 13.1) hanging around the classroom. It may even exacerbate these problems and make things worse than they were before. Fortunately, when teachers are able to provide all these elements of classroom structure in an autonomy-supportive way, then the acts of instruction listed in Tables 13.2–13.4 can be expected to enhance students' motivation, generate numerous benefits, and clear away the problems of misconduct, disengagement, and underperformance.

IDEAL INSTRUCTION: PROVIDE STRUCTURE IN AN AUTONOMY-SUPPORTIVE WAY

For structure to support and empower students' motivation (need satisfaction), effective functioning, and well-being, it needs to be provided in an autonomy-supportive way (Cheon et al., 2020; Cheon, Reeve, & Song, 2019). Figure 13.1 illustrates how teachers typically learn how to do this.

First, teachers learn how to support students' autonomy, and they do this by learning how to take their students' perspective (Chapter 6), invite students to pursue their personal interests (Chapter 7), present learning activities in need-satisfying ways (Chapter 8), provide explanatory rationales (Chapter 9), acknowledge negative feelings (Chapter 10), rely on invitational language (Chapter 11), and display patience (Chapter 12). Second, teachers learn how to provide classroom structure, and they

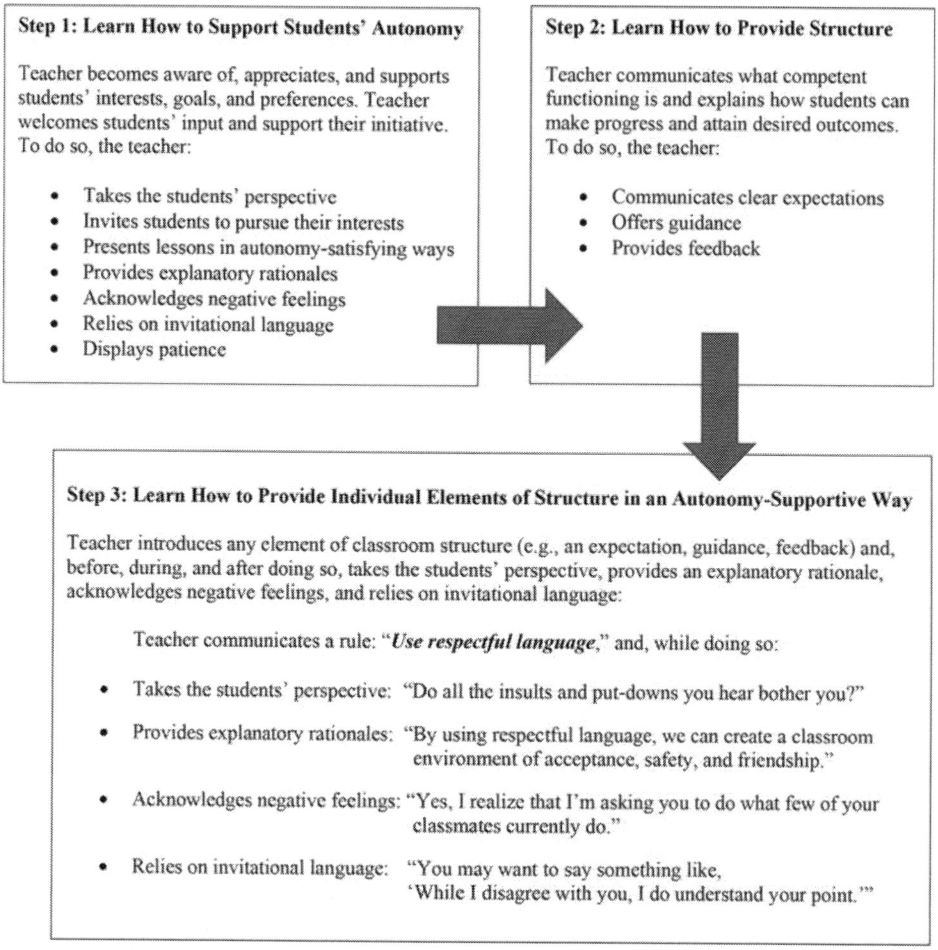

Step 1: Learn How to Support Students' Autonomy

Teacher becomes aware of, appreciates, and supports students' interests, goals, and preferences. Teacher welcomes students' input and support their initiative. To do so, the teacher:

- Takes the students' perspective
- Invites students to pursue their interests
- Presents lessons in autonomy-satisfying ways
- Provides explanatory rationales
- Acknowledges negative feelings
- Relies on invitational language
- Displays patience

Step 2: Learn How to Provide Structure

Teacher communicates what competent functioning is and explains how students can make progress and attain desired outcomes. To do so, the teacher:

- Communicates clear expectations
- Offers guidance
- Provides feedback

Step 3: Learn How to Provide Individual Elements of Structure in an Autonomy-Supportive Way

Teacher introduces any element of classroom structure (e.g., an expectation, guidance, feedback) and, before, during, and after doing so, takes the students' perspective, provides an explanatory rationale, acknowledges negative feelings, and relies on invitational language:

Teacher communicates a rule: "***Use respectful language***," and, while doing so:

- Takes the students' perspective: "Do all the insults and put-downs you hear bother you?"
- Provides explanatory rationales: "By using respectful language, we can create a classroom environment of acceptance, safety, and friendship."
- Acknowledges negative feelings: "Yes, I realize that I'm asking you to do what few of your classmates currently do."
- Relies on invitational language: "You may want to say something like, 'While I disagree with you, I do understand your point.'"

FIGURE 13.1 Step-by-Step Process to Learn How to Provide Structure in an Autonomy-Supportive Way

do this by learning how to communicate clear expectations (Table 13.2), offer step-by-step guidance (Table 13.3), and provide progress-enabling feedback (Table 13.4). Finally, teachers learn how to provide these three elements of classroom structure in an autonomy-supportive way.

Using the example of introducing a classroom rule (i.e., "Use respectful language."), the lower panel of Figure 13.1 illustrates how teachers can do this. The skill is to communicate the rule clearly but to do so while fully supporting students' autonomy (i.e., by taking students' perspective, providing an explanatory rationale, acknowledging negative feelings, and using invitational language; based on Cheon et al., 2019).

To provide rules in an autonomy-supportive way, the teacher can suggest that, when playing board games, there are rules to play by (e.g., take turns) so that everyone can have fun. The teacher can ask, "So which rules and guidelines would you like to have?" With such a preface, the teacher can invite students to speak up to suggest the rules, to agree on them, to decide what happens whenever a student does not follow the rules, and so forth. If the rules emerged out of students' input and reflection, then they will likely be internalized by the students as their own. The guidelines are not imposed on the students by the teacher but, rather, are seen as self-generated, logical, fair, and beneficial.

As a second example, Table 13.5 provides what a teacher might say to support students' autonomy during a challenging behavioral request. In the example, the teacher states clearly what her expectation for competent functioning is: "Complete your homework tonight." To support students' volitional internalization (i.e., autonomy), that teacher expectation needs to be communicated in an understanding and autonomy-supportive way. An excellent starting point for the teacher is to first take the students' perspective on what they are expected to do. The teacher may ask,

TABLE 13.5 How a Teacher Might Communicate an Expectation in an Autonomy-Supportive Way

The teacher **communicates an expectation**: *"Complete your homework tonight."*
To begin, the teacher **takes the student's perspective**: *"How do you feel about this homework assignment?"*
The teacher **acknowledges any negative feelings** students may have with the assignment: *"Yes, this will take a lot of time. I realize that I am asking you to work on your lesson instead of doing other things, like hanging out with your friends. You might also worry about getting confused or stuck on a problem, which is understandable, as everyone in class feels this same way, at least to some extent."*
The teacher **provides an explanatory rationale** to justify students' effort: *"The reason why I am asking you to spend an hour or two on your homework is because all this extra effort and practice will help you improve and develop greater skill."*
The teacher **relies on invitational, informational language**: *"If you get stuck on a difficult problem—and get really frustrated, what might you do about that? Let's talk about that for a moment."*

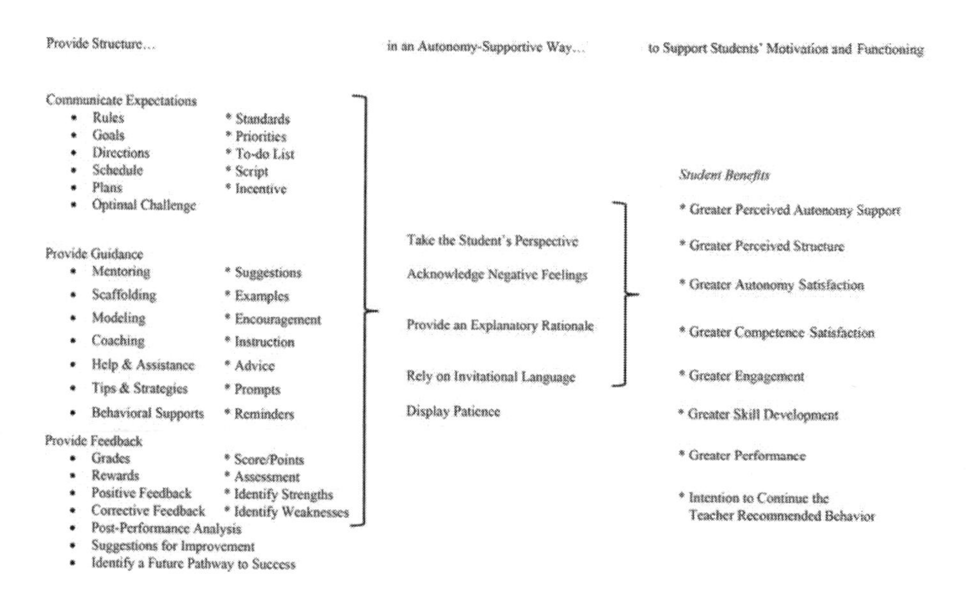

FIGURE 13.2 How to Provide Any Element of Classroom Structure in an Autonomy-Supportive Way

"How do you feel about this homework assignment? Do you feel mostly confident that you can complete it, or a bit unsure and hesitant?" To further support students' volitional engagement, the teacher may further acknowledge any negative feelings the students express upon hearing the assignment, provide a rationale to explain the homework's personal usefulness, and rely on invitational language while communicating that expectation.

Figure 13.1 and Table 13.5 provide single-case examples of how teachers can provide structure in an autonomy-supportive way. But teachers can learn how to provide *any* aspect of classroom structure in an autonomy-supportive way. To show how this might be, the left-side of Figure 13.2 list many frequently-used elements of structure to clarify what the teacher expects students to do. The center portion of Figure 13.2 recommends that each of these acts of instruction be communicated to students through an autonomy-supportive motivating style. The right portion of the figure summarizes the substantial benefits students experience when their teachers learn how to do this. This list of student benefits comes from the findings from several workshop-based experimental studies specifically designed to test the merits of providing different elements of classroom structure in an autonomy-supportive way (Cheon et al., 2020; Cheon, Reeve, & Song, 2019; Meng & Wang, 2016). Across all of these studies, results showed that the students of teachers who participated in the workshop (1) perceived their teachers as both highly autonomy supportive and well-structured, (2) reported high levels of both autonomy and competence satisfaction, (3) showed high levels of in-class engagement, skill development, and performance, and (4) reported their intentions to continue to pursue the teacher's recommended goals in the future.

CONCLUSION

Teachers want to see their students showing responsible behavior, high engagement, and excellent performance. To realize these aspirations, teachers can structure the learning environment by clarifying expectations, providing guidance, and providing progress-enabling feedback. When teachers offer such structure in an autonomy-supportive way, students tend to make progress toward more competent functioning.

Part 4

Workshop

CHAPTER 14
The workshop

A skill is an ability to do something well, and the development of an autonomy-supportive motivating style is an acquired skill. Like all skills, motivating style is learned, developed, and refined through modeling, mentoring, deep explaining, and hours of both deliberate practice and personal reflection (Ericsson, Krampe, & Tesch-Romer, 1993). For many years, we have visited classrooms and schools all around the globe to provide teachers with such a professional development opportunity.

WHAT HAPPENS DURING THE WORKSHOP?

To provide a well-structured opportunity to develop greater motivating style skill, we developed the *Autonomy-Supportive Teaching Workshop*. The workshop begins with personal reflection and information on what autonomy-supportive teaching is, but it is mostly a hands-on learning experience. Its contents are derived from self-determination theory (SDT), and its recommendations arise out of evidence-based empirical studies published in scholarly journals. In essence, what we have done is to translate SDT and empirical findings into a professional learning experience to help any interested teacher work through the process of upgrading the quality of his or her motivating style. Overall, the published research studies document three core findings that made the workshop both possible and useful (Reeve & Cheon, 2021):

1. Teachers can learn how to become more autonomy supportive.
2. When teachers are able to do this, students benefit in educationally important ways.
3. Like their students, teachers themselves benefit in numerous ways.

The workshop's step-by-step procedure appears in Figure 14.2. As shown on the left side of the figure, we first invite a group of 50 or so certified teachers from the local area or an interested school to participate in a formal research study. This occurs prior to the beginning of the academic year (or semester). Once teachers (or the whole school) agree to participate, half are randomly assigned into the experimental condition ($n = 25$) to participate in the Workshop while the other half are randomly assigned into the control condition ($n = 25$). The teachers in the control group are typically placed on a wait list to receive the workshop experience after the data collection phase of the research study. During the conduct of the research study, teachers in the control group do not participate in the workshop. Instead, they teach using

DOI: 10.4324/9781003091738-18

FIGURE 14.1 Reeve and Cheon Offering the Workshop to Korean Paralympic Coaches

their preexisting and naturally occurring motivating style, which informs us what represents "standard practice" and "typical instruction" for these teachers and their students. For teachers in the experimental group, they begin their participation in the 3-part workshop one week before the school year begins.

The 3-part workshop

We deliver the workshop in 3 parts. As shown on the left side of Figure 14.2, Parts 1 and 2 typically take place on the same day. Part 1 is a 3-hour morning workshop. Teachers first complete a couple of reflective activities to help them think about their existing classroom motivating style. We then introduce autonomy-supportive

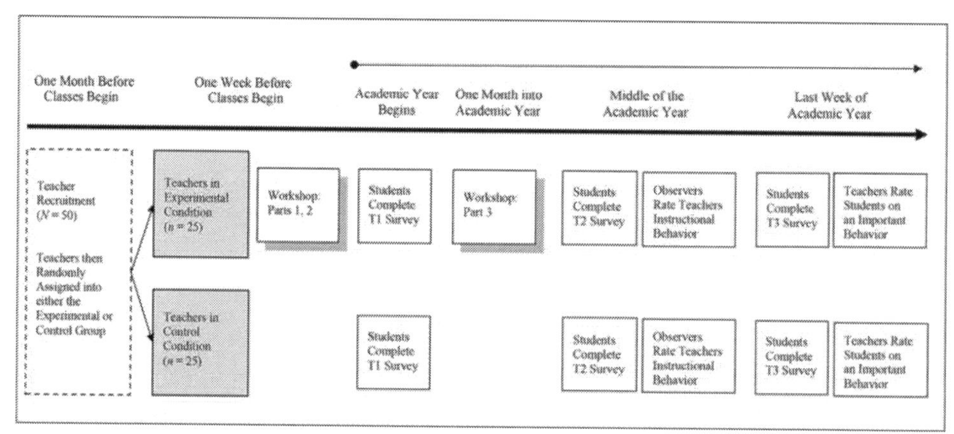

FIGURE 14.2 Procedural Timeline for the 3-Part Autonomy-Supportive Teaching Workshop Experience and the Three Waves of Data Collection

teaching, contrast it against teacher control, provide empirical evidence on the benefits of autonomy support and the costs of interpersonal control, and introduce and model each of the seven recommended autonomy-supportive instructional behaviors featured in Chapters 6–12. Part 2 is a 3-hour afternoon workshop. It is a skill-based ("how to") workshop. It is during these 3 hours that we offer teachers the modeling, mentoring, training, and practice, they need to develop greater motivating style skill. Part 3 takes place one month into the school year—after teachers have had the opportunity to try out autonomy-supportive teaching in their own classrooms with their own students. It is a 2-hour teacher-led group discussion in which teachers share their experiences, report how their students reacted to autonomy-supportive teaching, discuss the obstacles they encountered, and learn from their fellow teachers new and perhaps better ways to provide autonomy-supportive teaching.

Research design

The research design is both experimental and longitudinal. It is important for scientific purposes that we use an experimental research design, which essentially means that we use random assignment to condition. By randomly assigning teacher-participants into either the experimental (workshop) or control (no workshop) condition at the start of the study, we can be confident that the two groups of teacher-participants begin the study with similar scores on all dependent measures. This is the benefit of random assignment. Then, by the end of the study, if the two groups of teacher-participants differ on the dependent measures, we can then confidently infer that it was the condition effect that caused that difference (because participation in the workshop was the only difference between the two conditions). In the language of experimental research, teacher participation (or not) in the workshop represents the independent variable (i.e., the cause), while students' motivation and functioning represent the dependent measures (i.e., the effects).

It is also important for scientific purposes that we use longitudinal data collection. A longitudinal data collection means that we measure the study's dependent measures (e.g., students' need satisfaction) multiple times throughout the academic year (e.g., at the beginning, middle, and end of the year). By doing so, we can determine whether teacher participation in the workshop caused a gain or a decline in the dependent measures (relative to their beginning-of-year starting points, or baseline levels).

Data collection

To evaluate how workshop-enabled changes in teachers' motivating styles affect changes in students' motivation and classroom functioning, we collect many dependent measures. Generally speaking, data are collected from three sources (or informants). First, students complete questionnaires at the beginning, middle, and end of the academic year to report their perceptions of their teachers' motivating style, their own classroom motivations (e.g., need satisfaction, need frustration), and various indices of their classroom functioning (e.g., engagement, learning, prosocial behavior). Students of teachers in both the experimental and control groups complete the Time 1 (T1, week 1) questionnaire to establish baseline scores for each dependent measure. These T1 baseline scores reveal the motivation and functioning that students bring with them into the classroom at the beginning of the year. Students complete the Time 2 (T2, week 10) questionnaire to reveal how their motivation and functioning have increased or decreased compared to the beginning of the year (or semester). Finally, students complete the Time 3 (T3, week 17) questionnaire to reveal their year-end motivation and functioning due to being in that particular class with that particular teacher.

Second, trained raters observe teachers' actual classroom instruction to score the frequency and intensity of teachers' usage of autonomy-supportive (and controlling) instructional behaviors. Raters visit the classroom of each teacher-participant in the middle of the academic year (or semester), and their ratings provide an objective perspective on what teachers in the experimental and control groups say and do as they deliver their instruction and relate to their students.

Third, teachers complete a questionnaire to make an objective rating of some aspect of their students' classroom functioning that is especially important to that specific research study (e.g., classroom engagement, prosocial behavior). These teacher ratings are important to make sure that any changes in classroom functioning their students report are not just taking place in their students' heads. That is, teachers' objective ratings confirm or validate students' subjective ratings of how engaged or how prosocial they were during the year. In many investigations, teachers themselves complete a questionnaire to self-report their own motivation and functioning (e.g., teaching efficacy, job satisfaction).

Finally, at the end of the study, teachers in the experimental group complete a brief questionnaire assessing the fidelity (or "social validity") of the workshop. These questions ask the teacher-participant if he or she found the workshop experience to be understandable, important, useful, and satisfying.

PART 1

The workshop begins with two or three reflective activities to help teachers think about and get ready to work on their classroom motivating style:

- Motivating and Demotivating Teachers
- Is My Subject Matter Interesting? Valuable?
- My Current Motivating Style

We typically begin the workshop with the interactive activity that introduced Chapter 3, which was the *Motivating and Demotivating Teachers* activity. This is followed by the reflective activity that was introduced in Box 4.1, which was the *Is My Subject Matter Interesting? Valuable?* activity. Together, these two activities help teachers

FIGURE 14.3 Matos Offering the Workshop to Peruvian Teachers

think about and ready themselves to work on their motivating style. If time allows and if teachers express an interest in the activity, we offer the *My Current Motivating Style* activity as a third warm-up activity. This activity asks the teacher to complete (and score) a self-report questionnaire, which is either the Situations in School questionnaire (Table 5.1) or the Teaching Scenarios Questionnaire (Table 5.2).

If only a small number of teachers are present during the Part 1 session, then all teachers participate in these activities together as a small group. If many teachers are present during the Part 1 session (e.g., the full faculty of a school), we break the teachers into smaller groups, typically based on subject matter taught. The value of the small group format is that teachers will have greater opportunity to be agentic, to voice their concerns, and to benefit from the reactions and perceptions of their fellow teachers (rather than simply receive Part 1 as an audience).

In our minds, the workshop is not ready to begin until teachers think to themselves, "I want this—I want to learn how to upgrade the quality of my classroom motivating style." Of course, some teachers will remain skeptical, but we offer the three warm-up activities mentioned above to encourage participating teachers to begin to think, "I want to be a best teacher," "I want to know how to communicate my subject matter interest and value to my students," and "I want to know how to become more autonomy-supportive than I currently am."

To the extent that participating teachers express such readiness, the workshop transitions to an information-based PowerPoint presentation in which a member of the research team briefly provides a SDT-based overview of the nature of student motivation, which is that all students possess naturally endowed and engagement-generating inner motivational resources (e.g., intrinsic motivation, psychological needs; Chapter 2). The basic idea is that all students possess motivation of their own (the teacher does not have to create or manufacture it for students), and that motivation can be supported (via autonomy support), though it can also be neglected (via indifference) and thwarted (via teacher control). Teachers then learn what autonomy-supportive and controlling teaching are. We then introduce each of the seven recommended instructional behaviors presented earlier in Chapters 6–12. To do this, the research team introduces each autonomy-supportive instructional behavior one-by-one, defines it, offers a brief sample script of what a teacher might say to enact that instructional behavior. To provide a guiding model for each recommended act of instruction, teachers view a series of professionally created video clips showing teachers-in-action as they put each recommended instructional behavior into classroom practice (e.g., 5–10 videoclips lasting about 20 seconds each). We next present empirical evidence to show the educational benefits of autonomy-supportive teaching. For instance, we often show PowerPoint slides of figures taken from published research studies, such as those presented throughout Chapter 15 (see Figures 15.1–15.4). The final minutes of the morning workshop feature a group-based Q&A (Question and Answer) exchange.

PART 2

Part 2 is a 3-hour skill-based ("how to") workshop that builds on the earlier-modeled autonomy-supportive instructional behaviors with coaching, explaining, and practicing. To begin Part 2, teachers are placed into small groups, typically based on some shared characteristic, such as their grade level or subject matter taught. The primary activity is to conduct a series of simulations in which a teaching situation of interest to teachers is introduced so that teachers can practice enacting autonomy-supportive instructional behaviors to address that teaching situation. Some of these teaching situations are suggested by the research team, and some of the teaching situations are nominated from the participating teachers themselves (e.g., "Students come to class unprepared," "Establishing a class rule," "Students are unresponsive to the teacher's questions," "Introduce a learning activity in a way that students respond with enthusiastic engagement," and "Students perform poorly on a test."). Typically, one participating teacher takes the lead to role-play through an autonomy-supportive approach to instruction in that particular situation. For instance, for the teaching situation "Students come to class unprepared," the teacher first tries to understand why (i.e., takes the student's perspective) and, once done, then explains why coming to class prepared is important (i.e., provides an explanatory rationale). While the first teacher performs, the other teachers benefit by seeing how a peer teacher interprets and applies autonomy-supportive teaching to that situation. The performing teacher also benefits from the group's encouragements, tips, and possible revisions to make his or her approach to the teaching situation potentially more effective and easier to implement. By watching their fellow teachers in action, teachers often pick up new

FIGURE 14.4 Part 2 of the Workshop in Australia

ideas to try (e.g., "Hey, that's a good idea, maybe I'll try to do it that way too."; following Ozer & Bandura, 1990). Then, a second teacher takes the lead to role play through a second teaching situation. This procedure repeats until teachers begin to get the sense that they are ready to take the recommended autonomy-supportive teaching practices to try out in their own classroom with their own students.

To help teachers bridge the theory-to-practice gulf, we sometimes invite one or more guest teachers to join the research team as co-presenters. These guest teachers have all participated in an earlier workshop, so they know what it is like for the teachers who are currently going through the workshop. Participating teachers relate especially well to the guest teachers because of their shared perspectives, concerns, and experiences. For example, one guest teacher might be a grade-level specialist (e.g., a late elementary-grade teacher) while another might be a subject matter specialist (e.g., a math or physical education teacher).

As teachers practice enacting autonomy-supportive teaching, their approach often blends together both autonomy-supportive and controlling teaching. So, we build in additional skill-building practice opportunities for teachers to learn how to replace any existing controlling instructional behavior with an alternative (substitute) autonomy-supportive instructional behavior. For instance, we make the following recommendations shown in Table 14.1.

Teachers are asked to develop one final skill—namely, how to combine and integrate the individual acts of autonomy-supportive instruction into an overall, coherent autonomy-supportive motivating style. In particular, teachers practice integrating three acts of instruction into the larger purpose of "support intrinsic motivation": Take the students' perspective; invite students to pursue their personal interests; and present learning activities in need-satisfying ways. Similarly, teachers

TABLE 14.1 Recommendations That Teachers Replace an Existing Controlling Act of Instruction with an Alternative (Replacement) Autonomy-Supportive Behavior

Instead of Teaching in This Way	Consider This Alternative Way of Teaching
Take only the teacher's perspective	Take the students' perspective
Introduce extrinsic incentives	Invite students to pursue their interests
Assign all students the same task	Offer choice
Directives without explanations	Provide explanatory rationales
Change/Fix students' negative feelings	Acknowledge negative feelings
Use pressuring language	Use invitational language
Push students to produce an immediate desired behavior or a right answer	Display patience

practice integrating five acts of instruction into the larger purpose of "support internalization": Take the students' perspective; provide an explanatory rationale; acknowledge negative feelings; use invitational language; and display patience. The final 15 minutes of Part 2 feature a whole group discussion and Q&A exchange. As teachers practice the recommended instructional behaviors, many questions emerge. An occasional question is of a theoretical nature and a member of the research team can answer these questions. The majority of questions, however, are of a practical nature (e.g., "What about cellphones?") and the participating teachers themselves and invited guest speakers answer and discuss these questions.

PART 3

Part 3 is a 2-hour teacher-led, peer-to-peer group discussion. Part 3 takes place approximately one month into the school year. This schedule allows the group discussion to occur after teachers have had some actual classroom experience in trying to be autonomy supportive. We realize that trying to learn how to become more autonomy supportive in a single day can be overwhelming, and that teachers need a month of experimentation, trial-and-error, innovation, discussions with one's colleagues, personal reflection, etc. to refine their initial understanding of autonomy-supportive teaching into something that eventually becomes a coherent, confident autonomy-supportive motivating style. The group discussion is an opportunity for teachers to refine, integrate, and advance their maturing autonomy-supportive motivating style. In the group discussion, teachers share their experiences, discuss what they have been able to do effectively (and ineffectively), report how their students reacted to autonomy-supportive teaching, discuss the obstacles and setbacks they encountered, exchange tips and strategies for how to better handle particular teaching situations, and ask each other questions about what they might do in their future classes (see Figure 14.5).

FIGURE 14.5 Three Teacher-Led Learning Communities in Israel (Faces Blurred Intentionally)

Years ago, when we were conducting our first workshops, we would bring in a list of prepared questions and skill-checks to stimulate the group discussion. For instance, some of these questions were:

- How did your students react to your autonomy-supportive teaching?
- How did your peer teachers react to your autonomy-supportive teaching?
- Have you found autonomy-supportive teaching to be effective?
- Compared to last semester, what are you doing differently?
- Do you feel that autonomy-supportive teaching is any better than what you used before?
- Are there particular classroom situations you would like to talk about?

Similarly, some of the skill-checks were:

- Can you present learning activities in an interesting (need-satisfying) way?
- Can you promote students' valuing (internalization) during an engagement request?
- Is there one particular instructional behavior you are having trouble with?

Fairly quickly, however, we realized that teachers did not need us to provide them with such discussion prompts. We found that teachers always came to Part 3 with plenty of questions and stories to tell. The group discussion actually works best when we just give teachers an opportunity to talk among themselves about the issues that are most pressing to them. The biggest problem we have in conducting Part 3 is calling time after 2 hours, because teachers find these conversations to be important and helpful.

The fruits of the group discussion are many, but three seem paramount: (1) conceptual change, (2) skill refinement, and (3) shared experiences. By talking things through with their fellow teachers, participating teachers clarify their understanding and sense of purpose behind autonomy-supportive teaching. Teachers begin to move away from the idea that autonomy-supportive teaching is a classroom luxury to understand that it is more of a classroom necessity. That is, autonomy-supportive teaching is not something that just a few special teachers do, but it is an approach to instruction that seems fundamental to good teaching more generally. Teachers further advance their thinking about autonomy-supportive teaching from a provisional "this sort of works" assessment to one that is more definitive in a "this definitely works" way that reflects greater skill refinement. One of the key take-aways from the group discussion is that teachers discover new-and-better ways to solve particular classroom situations (e.g., how to increase student engagement on a particular learning activity). The group discussion further fuels teacher-to-teacher collaborations. It is very helpful for teachers to hear how other teachers have understood, addressed, and solved the same classroom problems that most concern them, especially when those other teachers offer new insights and strategies. Plus, there is something special and relatedness need-satisfying for teachers who go through this shared experience, especially when all the teachers feel that they are making progress toward becoming a better teacher.

On those occasions that we work with several teachers at the same school, or perhaps the entire faculty (e.g., Reeve, Jang, & Jang, 2018), the schools themselves sometimes set up a support system that takes place between Parts 2 and 3. The typical structure is for a head (or master) teacher (or a member of the research team; Cheon, Reeve, Lee, & Lee, 2015) to serve as a group leader who helps teachers work through the professional development process of becoming more autonomy supportive. These are on-going teacher-led learning communities (that often include a mentor) who work together throughout the semester or academic year. Together, the learning community listens and understands each other, asks and answers questions, visits and observes each other's classrooms, suggests new things to try, scaffolds each other's progress, and basically acts as a support system.

CONCLUSION

Autonomy-supportive teaching is an acquired skill. Recognizing this, we developed a 3-part professional development learning opportunity to help interested teachers develop the knowledge and skill needed to advance from a self-belief of "I am an okay teacher who can sort of motivate and engage my students" to one of "I am a confident, skilled teacher who can definitely motivate and engage my students."

CHAPTER 15

Does the workshop work?

To evaluate whether a particular workshop worked or not—such as the one depicted in Figure 15.1, researchers apply a series of statistical tests to determine whether teachers who participated in the workshop (experimental condition) became significantly more autonomy supportive toward students than did a comparable group of teachers who did not participate in the workshop (control condition). When these statistical tests show positive results, researchers judge the workshop a success. These results are often reported in scientific journals.

In a classic psychology experiment, one variable is manipulated to test whether its presence vs. its absence has a causal effect on another variable. The manipulated variable is referred to as an independent variable (the cause), while the second variable is referred to as the dependent measure (the effect). In an autonomy-supportive teaching workshop experiment, the manipulated independent variable is always the same—namely, teacher participation in the workshop. The dependent measure is some measure of autonomy supportive teaching. In our studies, we have included three such dependent measures: (1) students' perceptions of how autonomy-supportive their teachers are; (2) trained raters' objective scoring of teachers' in-class usage of autonomy-supportive teaching behaviors; and (3) teachers' self-reports of their own autonomy-supportive teaching. Across all three measures, the prediction is always the same—namely that, post-workshop, teachers who participate in the workshop will provide instruction in a more autonomy-supportive way than will teachers who do not participate in the workshop.

DEPENDENT MEASURE #1: ASK THE STUDENTS

In every study, we ask students to report their perceptions of their teachers' autonomy-supportive and controlling teaching at the beginning, middle, and end of the semester (or academic year). Typically, students complete the Learning Climate Questionnaire to assess perceived autonomy-supportive teaching (see Table 5.4). Students also routinely complete the Controlling Teaching Questionnaire to assess perceived controlling teaching (see Table 5.5). With these scores in hand, researchers plot students' scores on perceived autonomy-supportive teaching and perceived controlling teaching over time, as illustrated in Figure 15.2 (data from Cheon, Reeve, & Ntoumanis, 2018). At Time 1 (T1, beginning of the academic year), scores for students of teachers in the experimental and control groups do not differ significantly,

DOI: 10.4324/9781003091738-19

FIGURE 15.1 Matos Begins the Workshop in Peru

because teachers have been randomly assigned into condition and because it is still the first week of classes (i.e., teacher-student interactions have not yet taken place).

As shown in the upper panel in Figure 15.2, the consistent finding is that students of teachers in the no-workshop control condition (the dashed line) show unchanged scores on the measure of perceived autonomy-supportive teaching. That is, teachers in the control condition begin the school year with some level of an autonomy-supportive motivating style and they generally maintain that same style month after month (*M* scores at T1, T2, and T3 = 4.80, 4.89, and 4.83, using a 1–7 scale). In contrast, students of teachers in the experimental condition perceive a rising level of autonomy support from their teachers throughout the school year, as can be seen in the solid line. That is, like the teachers in the control group, these teachers begin the school year with some level of an autonomy-supportive motivating style, but their participation in the workshop leads them to be perceived by their students as significantly more autonomy-supportive by the middle of the year (T2). In fact, students perceive a rather dramatic jump in perceived autonomy-supportive teaching during the first half of the year (see the upwardly sloped solid line from T1 to T2). Thereafter, students' perceived autonomy-supportive teaching continues to rise a little more by the end of the academic year (T3), presumably because teachers continue to develop a more autonomy supportive style month-after-month (*Ms* = 4.67, 5.66, and 5.82).

As shown in the lower panel in Figure 15.2, a second consistent finding is that students of teachers in the no-workshop control condition show a steady and unchanged level of perceived controlling teaching (see dashed line; *M* scores at T1, T2, and T3 = 2.91, 2.83, and 2.91, using a 1–7 scale). That is, teachers in the control

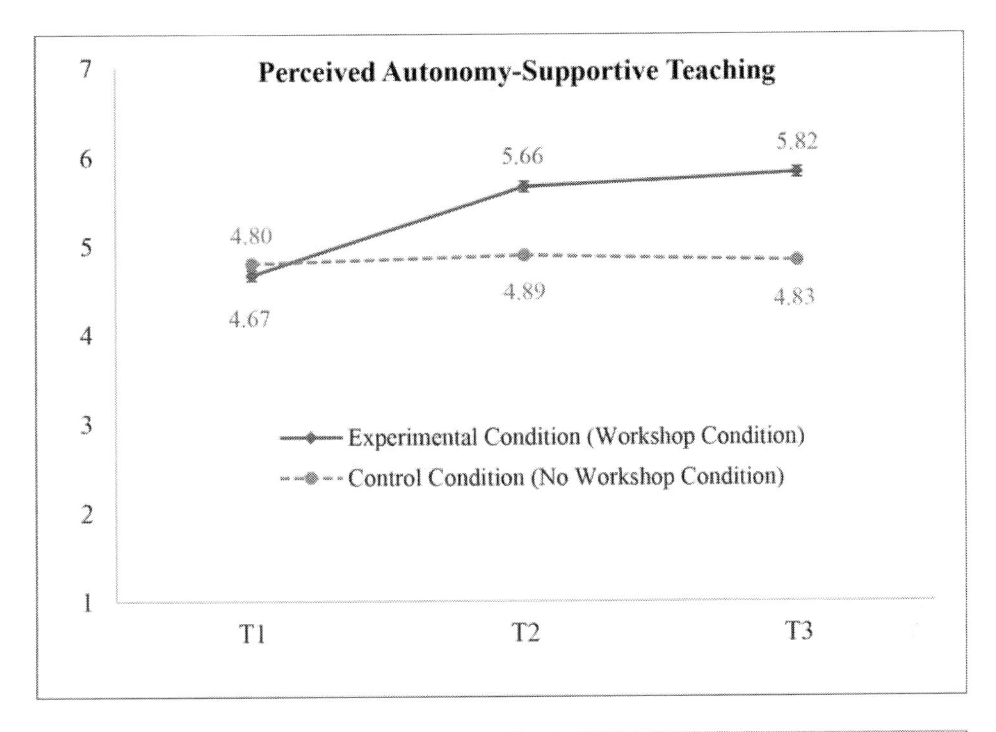

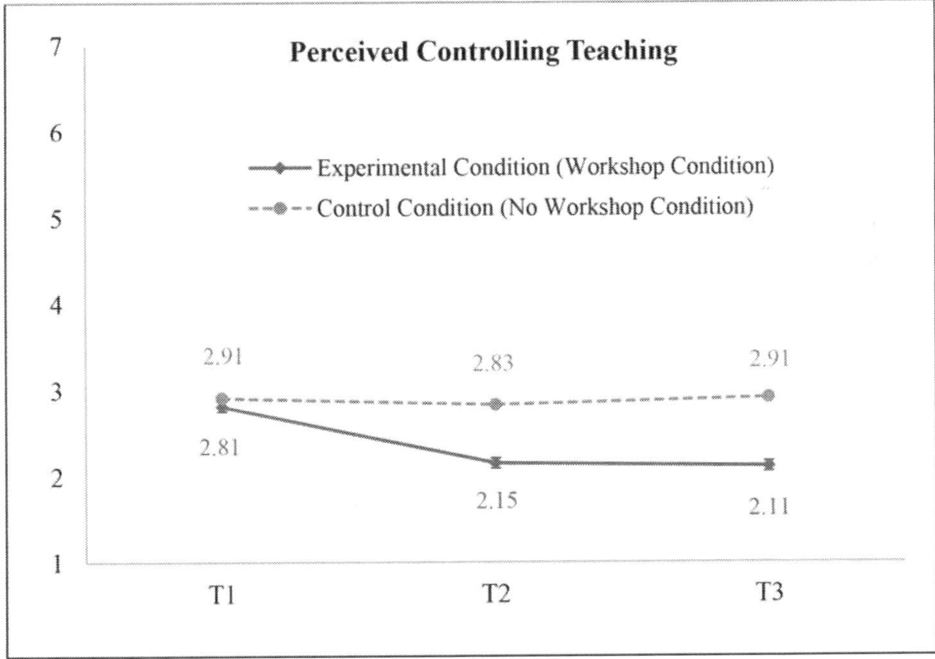

FIGURE 15.2 Students' Mean Scores for Perceived Autonomy-Supportive (Upper Panel) and Perceived Controlling (Lower Panel) Teaching Broken Down by Experimental Condition and Time of Assessment

condition begin the year with some level of a controlling style and they continue to rely on that same level of a controlling style throughout the academic year. In contrast, students of teachers in the experimental condition perceive a declining level of teacher control throughout the school year. Teachers in the experimental condition also begin the school year with some level of a controlling style, but their participation in the workshop leads them to be perceived by their students as significantly less controlling by the middle of the school year. Again, this mid-year decline in perceived controlling teaching is rather dramatic (see the downwardly sloped solid line from T1 to T2), and this decline continues throughout the rest of the school year (T3), presumably because the teachers continue to substitute autonomy-supportive behaviors for their former controlling instructional behaviors month-after-month (*M*s = 2.81, 2.15, and 2.11).

Together, the data summarized in the two panels of Figure 15.2 confirm that the workshop tends to produce its intended effect. Statistical tests show that the perceived motivating style scores of the two groups of teachers differed significantly from one another at both T2 and T3. That said, an important question is, "How big were these effects?" To answer this question, researchers use a statistic called "effect size" (Cohen, 1988). An effect size (denoted by the statistical symbol "*d*") is defined as the magnitude or "size" of the difference between the experimental vs. control groups. This statistic is interpreted as follows: $d = 0.20$ represents a small effect (i.e., a classroom phenomenon that is difficult to see with the naked eye, such as seeing that 8th graders are taller than 7th graders); $d = 0.50$ represents a medium effect (i.e., a classroom phenomenon that is visible to the naked eye of a careful observer, such as seeing that 8th graders are taller than 6th graders); and $d = 0.80$ represents a large effect (i.e., a classroom phenomenon that is big enough for anyone to see with the naked eye, such as seeing that 8th graders are taller than 5th graders).

The effect size for data summarized in the upper part of Figure 15.2 for perceived autonomy-supportive teaching was $d = 1.27$, while the effect size for the data summarized in the lower part of Figure 15.2 for perceived controlling teaching was $d = 0.71$. These effect sizes mean that anyone who walked into the classroom of a teacher who participated in the workshop would easily see that the teacher's motivating style had changed from pre-workshop to post-workshop, and substantially so. This means that teachers who participated in the workshop were able to successfully work through the professional development experience of upgrading the quality of their classroom motivating style, and that their success in doing so was obvious (i.e., a large effect size).

DEPENDENT MEASURE #2: ASK THE RATERS

In almost every study, we ask trained, expert observers to visit the classrooms of each teacher in the research study to score his or her actual usage of autonomy-supportive and controlling instructional behaviors. This visit occurs about two months into the academic year and about one month after teachers in the experimental group complete Part 3 of the workshop experience (recall Figure 14.2). Raters visit, observe, and score the in-class instructional behaviors of teachers in both the experimental and control groups, though raters do not know into which condition—experimental or control—the teacher being observed has been assigned. This is a one-time visit (unlike the students who complete their questionnaire three times). Raters find that observing a teacher in action for a single teaching session is fully sufficient to gauge instructional behaviors related to motivating style. To make their ratings, the classroom observers typically complete the Behavior Rating Sheet (see Figure 5.1) during a 55-minute classroom session.

As shown in the solid vs. dashed bars on the left side of Figure 15.3, raters consistently score that teachers in the experimental group use more autonomy-supportive instructional behaviors than do teachers in the control group (*Ms* = 5.51 vs. 4.23, using a 1–7 scale). Further, as shown in the right side of Figure 15.3, raters consistently score that teachers in the experimental group use fewer controlling instructional behaviors than do teachers in the control group (*Ms* = 2.67 vs. 3.57). These overall differences in autonomy-supportive and controlling instructional behaviors extended across all seven individual acts of autonomy-supportive teaching (e.g., take the students' perspective, acknowledge negative feelings) and across all individual acts of controlling teaching as well. Basically, what these raters observed was that, for teachers in the control group, their autonomy-supportive and controlling instructional behaviors were roughly balanced in their frequency and intensity (scores of

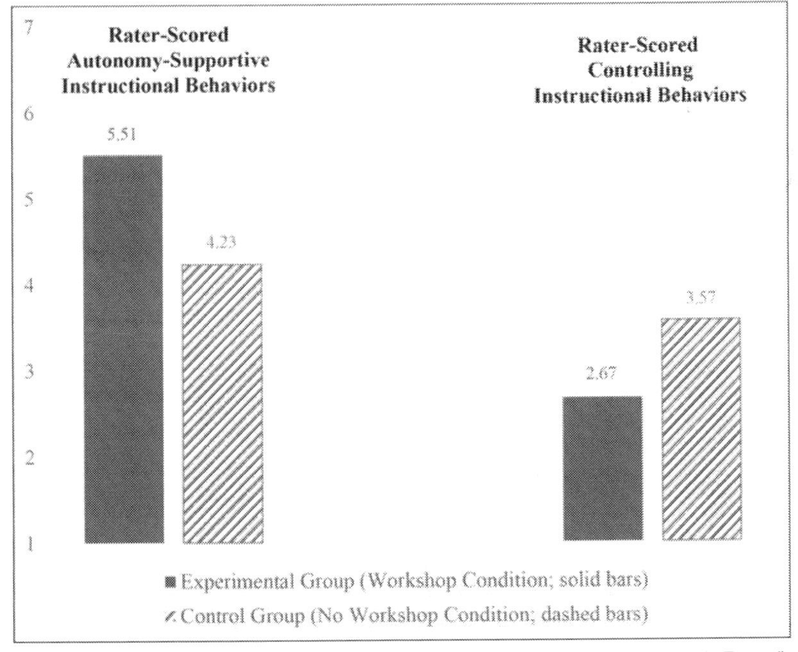

FIGURE 15.3 Mean Scores for Rater-Scored Autonomy-Supportive (Left Panel) and Controlling (Right Panel) Instructional Behaviors Broken Down by Experimental Condition and Time of Assessment

Ms, 4.23 and 3.57). Notice that the height of the two dashed bars is roughly the same. For teachers in the experimental group, however, their autonomy-supportive teaching was decidedly more pronounced than was their controlling teaching (scores of *Ms*, 5.51 and 2.67), using data from Cheon et al. (2018). Notice that the height of the left solid bar is substantially higher than the height of the right solid bar. The effect size for the rater-scored autonomy-supportive behaviors was $d = 2.26$, while the effect size for the rater-scored controlling behaviors was $d = 1.27$. These are very large effect sizes, which suggests that teachers in the experimental group taught their classes in a fundamentally different way than did teachers in the control group (i.e., much more autonomy supportive, much less controlling).

Autonomy-supportive teaching features three essential teaching tasks: take the students' perspective; support students' intrinsic motivation; and support students' internalization of external regulations (recall Figure 4.1). As shown earlier in Figure 5.1, the observers' rating sheet includes separate items to score (1) one aspect of "take the students' perspective" (takes the students' perspective), (2) two aspects of "support intrinsic motivation" (invite students to pursue their personal interests, present learning activities in need-satisfying ways), and (3) four aspects of "support internalization" (provide explanatory rationales, acknowledge negative feelings, use invitational language, and display patience). These three aggregated scores can be seen in Figure 15.4 for both teachers in the experimental (solid bars) and control (dashed bars) groups (data from Cheon & Reeve, 2015; Cheon et al., 2019). Moving from the left to the right in the figure, raters scored teachers in the

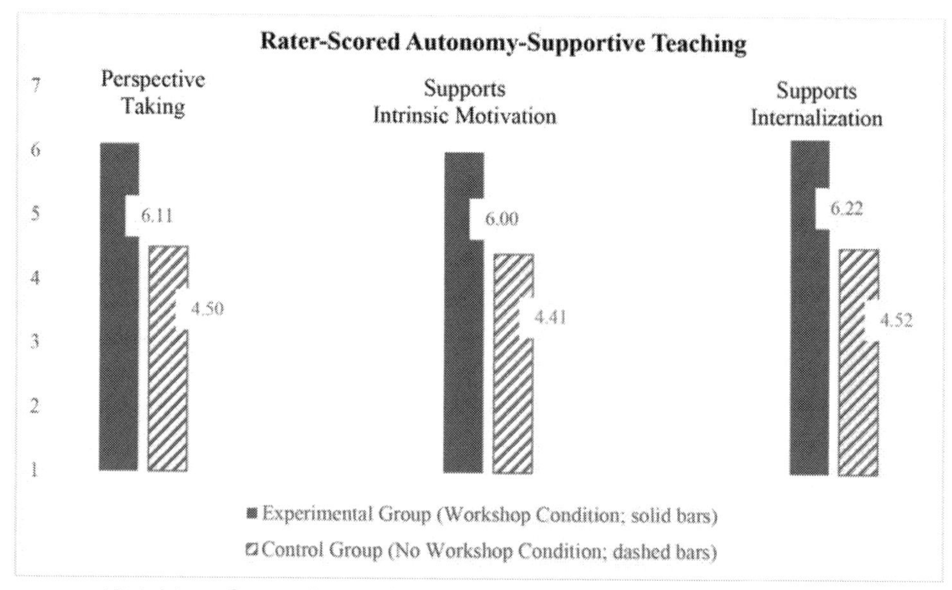

FIGURE 15.4 Mean Scores for the Three Rater-Scored Instructional Behaviors of Takes the Students' Perspective (Left Bars), Supports Intrinsic Motivation (Center Bars), and Supports Internalization (Right Bars) Broken Down by Experimental Condition and Time of Assessment

experimental group, compared to teachers in the control group, higher on takes the students' perspective (*Ms* = 6.11 vs. 4.50), supports intrinsic motivation (*Ms* = 6.00 vs. 4.41), and supports internalization (*Ms* = 6.22 vs. 4.52). Once again, the effect sizes for all three of these rater-scored aspects of autonomy-supportive teaching were quite large (*d*'s > 1).

DEPENDENT MEASURE #3: ASK THE TEACHERS

In some (but not all) studies, we ask teachers to self-report their own motivating styles. In these studies, teachers report (on a questionnaire) how autonomy supportive they perceived themselves to be both at the beginning of the semester (or academic year) and at the end of the semester (Reeve & Cheon, 2016). To do this, teachers report their self-rated autonomy-supportive teaching (e.g., "I try to understand how students see things before I suggest a new way they might do things"), personal endorsement of autonomy-supportive teaching (using the Teaching Scenarios measure, see Table 5.5; "This is an accurate and true description of what I do during my teaching"), and intentions to use autonomy-supportive teaching in their future teaching (e.g., "In the future, I intend to motivate my students this way").

As shown in Figure 15.5, teachers who participate in the workshop report greater autonomy-supportive teaching on all three measures (data from Reeve & Cheon, 2016), including greater self-reported autonomy-supportive teaching (*Ms* = 5.52 vs. 4.83; see left panel), greater personal endorsement of autonomy-supportive teaching (*Ms* = 5.21 vs. 3.75; see center panel), and stronger future intentions to use autonomy-supportive teaching (*Ms* = 5.73 vs. 4.37; see right panel). The effect size produced by the workshop effect was again quite large across all three teacher-reported measures (*ds* > 1).

DOES THE WORKSHOP EFFECT ENDURE?

Teachers receive a great deal of support from our team throughout the workshop experience. So, it would be understandable if teachers who became highly autonomy-supportive during the workshop reverted back to their naturally occurring (pre-workshop) motivating style in the absence of the workshop team's formal support. After all, everyday classroom teaching takes place within a context of daily pressures that push teachers toward a more controlling style, such as time pressures, teacher accountability for student outcomes, and the press for immediate solutions to problems such as student misconduct (Pelletier, Seguin-Levesque, & Legault, 2002; Taylor, Ntoumanis, & Standage, 2008).

Despite these near-relentless professional pressures, teacher participation in the workshop is designed to produce long-lived, enduring, and constructive effects on teachers' motivating styles. One reason to expect some endurance is because the workshop experience allows teachers to become aware—often for the first time in

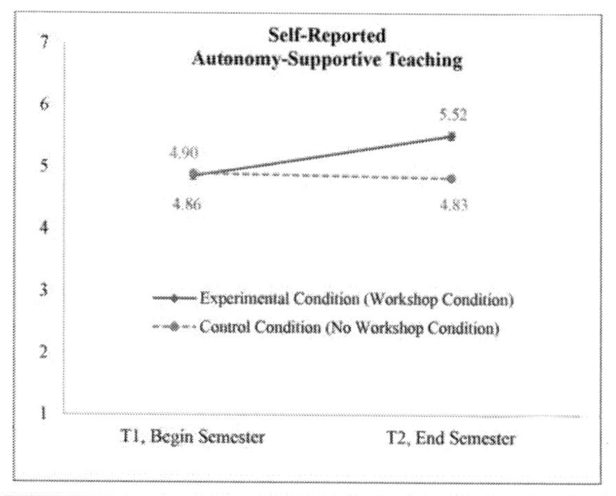

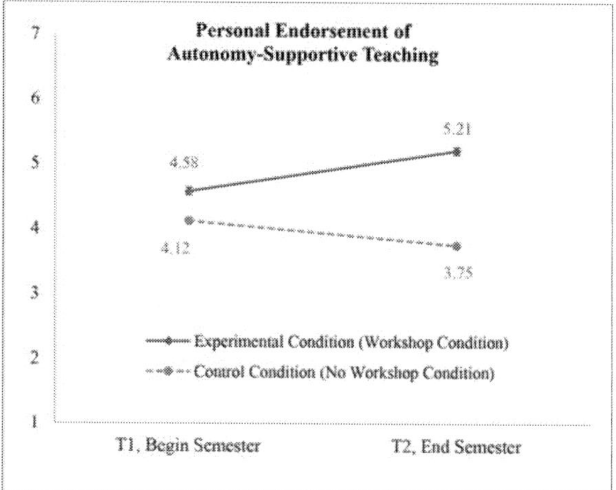

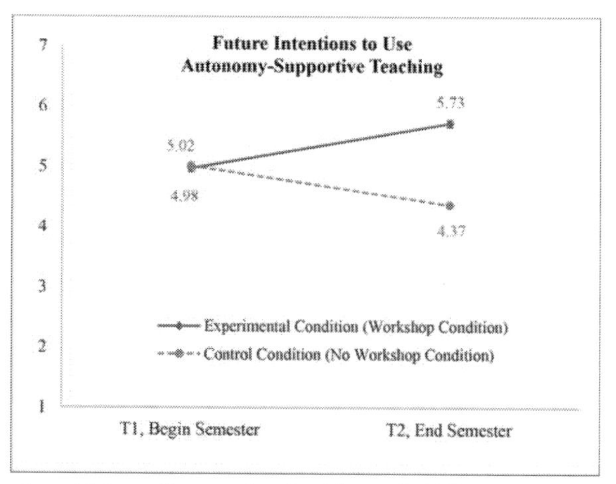

FIGURE 15.5 Teachers' Mean Scores for the Three Self-Reported Measures of Autonomy-Supportive Teaching Broken Down by Experimental Condition and Time of Assessment: Self-Reported Autonomy Supportive Teaching (Upper Panel), Personal Endorsement of Autonomy-Supportive Teaching (Center Panel), and Future Intentions to Use Autonomy-Supportive Teaching (Lower Panel)

their professional careers—of the benefits of autonomy support and the costs of teacher control. Teachers who participate in the workshop can easily see the classroom benefits from their greater autonomy-supportive teaching, a claim we make because of the large effect sizes observed in the research studies. That is, teachers can see that their students are more engaged than before (see Chapter 16). Witnessing these benefits first-hand, especially for the first time in one's career, it makes sense that these teachers would want to continue to teach in this way.

To test if the workshop effects endured, we returned one year later to the schools of the teachers who participated in a workshop a year before to reassess all the same dependent measures as described earlier in the chapter (Cheon & Reeve, 2013). (For a similar study, see Tilga, Kalajas-Tilga, Hein, Raudsepp, & Koka, 2020.) That is, in the original study, teachers in the experimental group showed greater student-reported and rater-scored autonomy-supportive teaching and lesser student-reported and rater-scored controlling teaching (compared to teachers in the control group). A year later, these same teachers were now teaching a different group of students. We asked the teachers' new students to complete the same questionnaires as completed the year before by the teachers' original students, and we again had trained raters visit each teacher's classroom to score each teacher's usage of autonomy-supportive and controlling instructional behaviors. Results from all of these measures showed that these teachers were still just as autonomy supportive and just as non-controlling as they were one year earlier. Further, across all the study's additional dependent measures (e.g., students' motivation, classroom engagement), the students of these teachers showed significantly better scores than did students of teachers in a control group. From these results, it was clear that, yes, the benefits from teacher participation in the workshop endured over time, or at least over a year's time.

In addition, we asked each teacher who had participated in the year-ago workshop the following question: "Compared to last year when you completed the informational session on how to be autonomy supportive toward your students, would you say that you were, this year, more autonomy supportive, less autonomy supportive, or about the same in terms of autonomy support?" (Cheon & Reeve, 2013, pp. 511–512). Every teacher who participated in the workshop the year before reported being significantly "more autonomy supportive."

Finally, we asked each teacher to author a brief anonymous essay to explain why his or her autonomy-supportive motivating style was more, less, or about the same as a year ago. In their essays, practically all teachers cited gains in their teaching efficacy and benefits to their students. One excerpt from a physical education teacher was as follows (Cheon & Reeve, 2013, p. 515):

> "The quality of physical education was enhanced when I supported students' autonomy. I felt happy and supported their autonomy when I found that students actually recognized what they truly valued and enjoyed. I was more confident in how to manage my students. Now, I always think before my class how to support students' autonomy."

CONCLUSION

The workshop is designed to help teachers learn how to become substantially more autonomy supportive toward their students during classroom instruction. The capacity of the workshop to produce this effect has been assessed in three ways—namely, by asking students, by asking raters, and by asking teachers themselves. In every study we have conducted, the workshop has produced its intended effects.

CHAPTER 16

Why the workshop works

About 1,300 teachers from all around the globe have used the workshop experience to improve their motivating style. How did they do it? What personal resources did they develop during the workshop that allowed them to advance from an unsure and moderately effective motivating style to one that was confident and highly effective?

TEACHERS DEVELOP FOUR PERSONAL-PROFESSIONAL RESOURCES

Most teachers capitalize on the workshop's professional development opportunity to successfully upgrade their motivating style, though this is truer for some teachers than for others. In one analysis, 90% of the workshop's teacher-participants showed a meaningful improvement in their autonomy-supportive motivating style, while 10% did not (see Figure 2.2a and b in Reeve & Cheon, 2020, p. 20). Of the teachers who did show improvement, some showed a very large improvement, some showed a large improvement, and some showed a moderate improvement. These data raise two questions: Why do some teachers improve their motivating style more than others? And, why do a few teachers show no improvement at all?

The answer to both questions is that, during the workshop, teachers more or less develop a constellation of four crucial personal-professional developmental resources that allow them to improve their motivating style. Among the teachers who do develop these personal resources, some develop them fully while others develop them only partially. Because this is so, it is helpful to examine carefully what these resources are and, once identified, understand how and why they develop. The four critical resources teachers develop, more or less, are (1) teaching skill, (2) teaching efficacy, (3) positive beliefs about autonomy-supportive teaching, and (4) adoption of intrinsic instructional goals (Cheon, Reeve, Lee, & Lee, 2018; Reeve & Cheon, 2016, 2021).

Greater teaching skill

Successfully motivating students revolves around mastering two teaching challenges. The first is to learn how to provide instruction in a way that energizes and supports students' intrinsic motivation. The essential instructional challenge is, "*How do I present this learning activity so students will find it interesting and enjoyable?*" The second is to learn how to provide instruction in a way that supports students'

DOI: 10.4324/9781003091738-20

volitional internalizations. The essential instructional challenge is, "*How do I present this learning activity so students will find it personally useful and important enough to deserve their time and effort?*"

Before teachers participate in the workshop, they already possess teaching skill related to these two teaching challenges. But the workshop experience reveals a new-and-improved repertoire of evidence-based instructional strategies that are fully capable of promoting students' intrinsic motivation (i.e., take the students' perspective, invite students to pursue their interests, and present learning activities in need-satisfying ways) and volitional internalizations (i.e., take the students' perspective, provide explanatory rationales, acknowledge negative feelings, use invitational language, and display patience). Because these are tried-and-true engagement-generating instructional behaviors, teachers who put these autonomy-supportive instructional behaviors into practice have students who show strong, robust classroom motivation and engagement.

Thus, the first reason why the workshop produces its positive effects is because it helps teachers gain the instructional skill they need to promote their students' intrinsic motivation and volitional internalizations. In many ways, this observation repeats the theme of the previous chapter (Chapter 15) in that teachers who participate in the workshop develop greater autonomy-supportive teaching skill—according to their students, according to classroom observers, and according to the teachers themselves.

Greater teaching efficacy

Teaching efficacy is the teacher's confident judgment that he or she has the capacity to cope with the teaching situation in ways that bring about desired outcomes. This confidence vs. doubt judgment revolves around whether or not the teacher expects he or she can "do what it takes" to boost students' learning, engagement, and effective behavior (Tschannen-Moran & Woolfolk Hoy, 2001). To measure high vs. low teaching efficacy, teachers often complete the Teachers' Sense of Efficacy Scale (TSES; Tschannen-Moran & Woolfolk Hoy, 2001). The 12-item TSES assesses three aspects of teaching efficacy, using a 1-9 scale: (1) teaching efficacy to implement instructional strategies that promote students' learning (e.g., "How much can you do to provide an alternative explanation when students are confused?"); (2) teaching efficacy to implement instructional strategies to promote classroom engagement (e.g., "How much can you do to motivate students who show low interest in school work?"); and (3) teaching efficacy to implement instructional strategies to successfully handle issues of classroom management (e.g., "How much can you do to calm a student who is disruptive or noisy?").

Teachers who participate in an autonomy-supportive teaching workshop report a pronounced increase in all three of these aspects of teaching efficacy, as illustrated in Figure 16.1 (data from Cheon et al., 2018). Over the course of the academic year, teachers who participate in the workshop show an ever-increasing, month-after-month rise in their (a) teaching efficacy to promote students' learning (Ms = 6.09, 6.64, 6.98, 1-9 scale; see solid line in the upper panel of Figure 16.1), (b) teaching

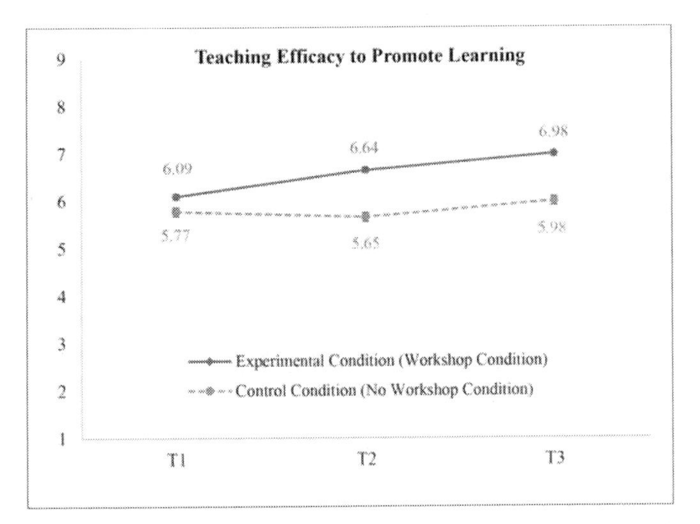

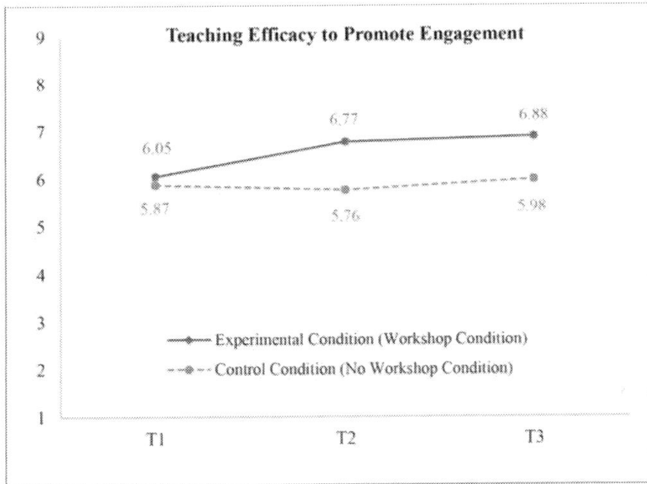

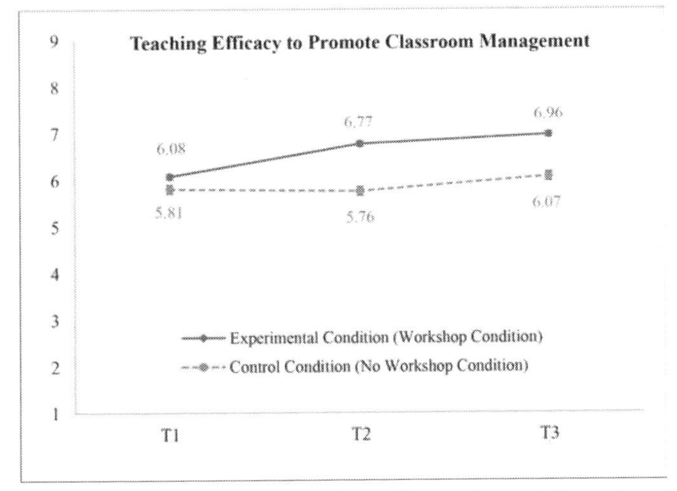

FIGURE 16.1 Teachers' Mean Scores on Three Dimensions of Their Teaching Efficacy Broken Down by Experimental Condition and Time of Assessment

efficacy to promote students' engagement (*Ms* = 6.05, 6.77, 6.88; see solid line in the middle panel of Figure 16.1), and (c) teaching efficacy to manage students' behavior (*Ms* = 6.08, 6.77, 6.96; see solid line in the lower panel of Figure 16.1). In contrast, teachers who do not participate in the workshop show a moderate level of teaching efficacy that stays fairly stable throughout the academic year (see dashed lines).

After the workshop, the findings summarized in Figure 16.1 show that teachers gained confidence from T1 to T2 that they could increase their students' learning, engagement, and effective behavior. As the academic year progresses, these teachers saw tangible evidence of their students' greater learning, engagement, and effective behavior from T2 to T3, which further boosted their confidence (their teaching efficacy). By the end of the academic year, the teachers who participated in the workshop possessed a significantly greater amount of the personal-professional resource of teaching efficacy than did non-participating teachers.

These gains in teaching efficacy occur for two reasons. First, teachers were able to expand their existing repertoire of instructional behaviors to incorporate new-and-improved, evidence-based ways to enhance their students' learning, engagement, and behavior. During the workshop, teachers (1) observe effective role models, (2) receive encouragement and support as they learn how to enact these new autonomy-supportive instructional behaviors, (3) receive hands-on practice rich in guidance, scaffolding, and coaching, and (4) receive progress-enabling positive feedback. All four of these experiences (i.e., modeling, encouragement, guidance, and positive feedback) are well-known antecedent conditions to build strong and resilient teaching efficacy beliefs (Tschannen-Moran & Woolfolk Hoy, 2007).

Second, once teachers who participate in the workshop put the recommended autonomy-supportive instructional behaviors into practice, they saw with their own eyes how effective these newly learned instructional behaviors really are. Students respond to autonomy-supportive teaching with gains in learning, engagement, and effective behavior. As teachers see the connection between the changes in their instruction and the corresponding changes in their students' learning, engagement, and behavior, they realize that, through their teaching, they have some personal control over gains in their students' positive outcomes.

Gaining teaching skill and gaining teaching efficacy are complementary resources. Learning the new autonomy-supportive instructional behaviors gives teachers the "skill" they needed to become more autonomy supportive, while building a greater sense of efficacy gives teachers the confidence and "will" they need to become more autonomy supportive.

Positive beliefs about autonomy-supportive teaching

Many teachers harbor a not-so-positive view of autonomy-supportive teaching (see Turner, 2010; Turner, Warzon, & Christensen, 2011). Some teachers see autonomy-supportive teaching as "foreign" (Skinner & Belmont, 1993), while other teachers fear that autonomy-supportive teaching will leave them vulnerable to permissiveness (Aelterman, Vansteenkiste, Haerens, Soenens, Fontaine, & Reeve, 2019). Others see autonomy-supportive teaching as "naïve" (Boggiano, Barrett, Weiher, McClelland, & Lusk, 1987). Still other teachers worry that autonomy-supportive teaching fails to prepare students for "real life." This skepticism generalizes across three different beliefs about autonomy-supportive teaching:

1. Is autonomy-supportive teaching *effective*?

   Does it work?
   Does it produce good and desirable results?
   Is it an effective and reliable approach to motivating and engaging students?

2. Is autonomy-supportive teaching *easy to do*?

   Is it simple (vs. difficult and complicated) to do?
   Is it effortless and manageable (rather than too demanding and impractical)?
   Can most teachers teach this way, or is it simply asking too much from teachers?

3. Is autonomy-supportive teaching *normative*?

   Do most teachers teach this way?
   Is this way of teaching the norm in my school (or my country)?
   Does this approach to teaching represent "standard practice"?

The third belief—the normative belief—is a matter of culture. As such, teacher participation in the workshop does not affect a change in this belief. The exception, however, would occur if all the teachers in the same school or community participated together in the workshop to become more autonomy supportive. If an entire school faculty learned how to become more autonomy supportive and observed together the benefits of autonomy-supportive teaching, then a cultural change toward seeing autonomy-supportive teaching as normative would likely occur. But improving the motivating style of an entire faculty, community, or nation would be the exception, rather than the rule. The remaining two beliefs—the effectiveness and the easy-to-do beliefs, however, are open to positive change during the workshop.

Irrespective of what teachers' baseline "pro vs. con" beliefs are concerning autonomy-supportive teaching, teachers who participate in the workshop do come to believe that autonomy-supportive teaching is both highly effective and easy to do. These more positive beliefs can be seen in Figure 16.2. The upper panel shows that, after the workshop, teachers believed that autonomy-supportive teaching was both (a) more effective (*Ms*, 4.33 increased to 5.35; see solid line) and (b) easier to do (*Ms*, 5.04 increased to 5.91; see solid line) than they first thought, while teachers who did not participate in the workshop showed no such constructive change in these two beliefs (see dashed lines). These new ways of thinking were important, because the more teachers came to endorse these two beliefs, the more autonomy-supportive toward students they became in the classroom (Reeve & Cheon, 2016). That is, increases in these beliefs led to (and explained) increases in autonomy-supportive teaching.

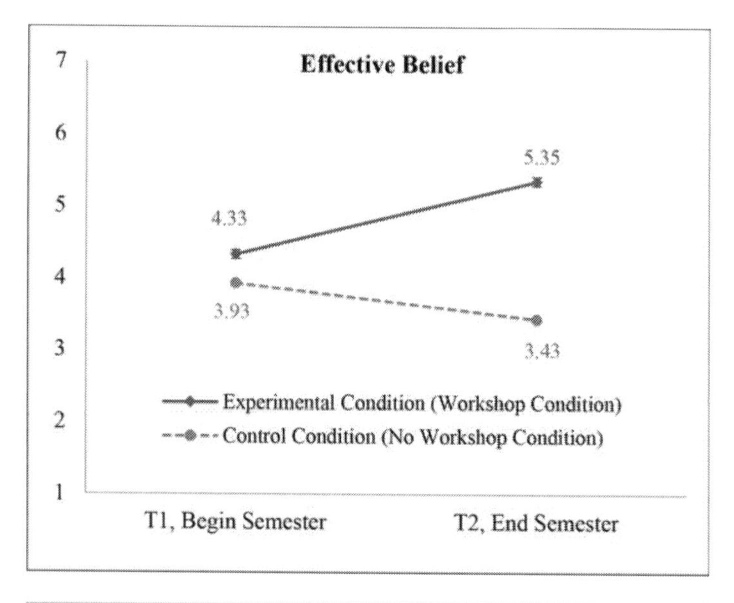

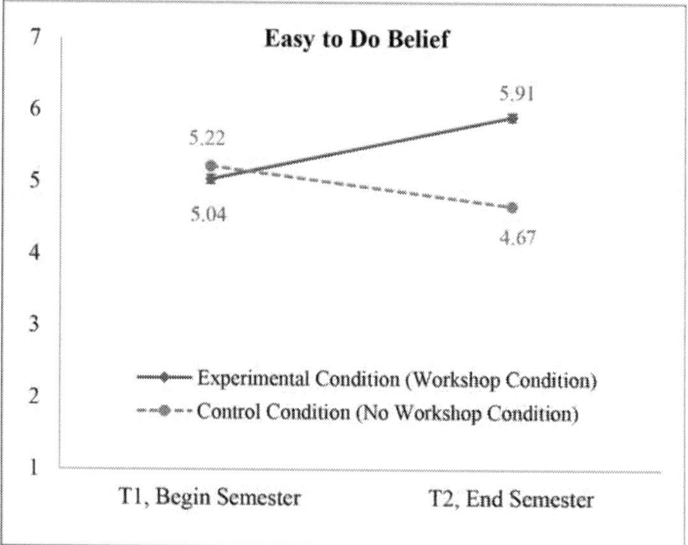

FIGURE 16.2 Teachers' Mean Scores on Two of Their Positive Beliefs about Autonomy-Supportive Teaching Broken Down by Experimental Condition and Time of Assessment

Before they participate in the workshop, teachers show wide individual differences in how effective and how easy-to-implement they believe autonomy-supportive teaching to be. As they begin the workshop experience, some teacher-participants already believe autonomy-supportive teaching is effective and easy, though many teacher-participants believe that autonomy-supportive teaching is ineffective and too difficult. What participation in the workshop does is stir up the process of conceptual change. Conceptual change is the cognitive process of changing a belief. Those who study conceptual change find that changing a belief is a very difficult thing to do (Richardson, 1990; Turner et al., 2011; Weinstein, Madison, & Kuklinski, 1995). This is because successful conceptual change for teachers hinges on the presence of all of the following: support for professional development; opportunities for ongoing dialogue; the sharing of new ideas and new sources of evidence; opportunities to refine one's classroom practice; and opportunities for personal reflection.

To help teachers work through this conceptual change process, Part 1 of Workshop focuses on promoting the effectiveness belief, Part 2 focuses on promoting the easy-to-do belief, and Part 3 focuses on providing teachers with the opportunities for dialogue and reflection that make conceptual change possible. After that, teachers' own post-workshop classroom experiences give them first-hand practical experience that speaks to the credibility of these two beliefs.

When teachers first hear about autonomy-supportive teaching, they often take a cautious, provisional "Hmm. I'm not sure. Maybe. Let's see how this goes" approach. This shows an openness to consider one's beliefs about autonomy-supportive teaching, but it is not conceptual change. As teachers experiment with autonomy-supportive strategies, however, they typically have validating classroom experiences. They see with their own eyes their students' improved motivation and engagement. After a couple of months, teachers tend to advance from a provisional "Let's see if this works" open-mindedness through a conceptual change process that produces something approaching a professional commitment to teaching in an autonomy-supportive way.

Workshop-enabled changes in these two beliefs do explain post-intervention changes in teachers' motivating style (Reeve & Cheon, 2016). Just as gains in teaching skill and teaching efficacy are complementary resources, gains in teaching efficacy and changes in beliefs about motivating style are also complementary. Gains in teaching efficacy are an important part of the conceptual change process because efficacy gains fuel changes in one's beliefs (Gregoire, 2003). As teachers gain confidence that they "have what it takes" to support students' intrinsic motivation and volitional internalizations, teachers become increasingly likely to endorse autonomy-supportive teaching as (1) highly effective (e.g., "It works!") and (2) easy to practice (e.g., "It is easy to do—once you know how.").

Adopting intrinsic instructional goals

Instructional goals are the priorities or sought-after outcomes teachers build into their lesson plans (Jang, 2019). Instructional goals tend to be intrinsic or extrinsic in nature (Kasser & Ryan, 1996). An intrinsic instructional goal is an intention to promote students' personal or relationship growth, while an extrinsic instructional goal is an intention to produce socially valued indicators of educational success, such as right answers and high test scores. To assess intrinsic and extrinsic instructional goals, teachers often completed the 16-item Teacher Goals Questionnaire (TGQ; Jang, 2019). An example of an instructional goal to promote personal growth is, "My goal in this class is to help my students become the person they want to become,"

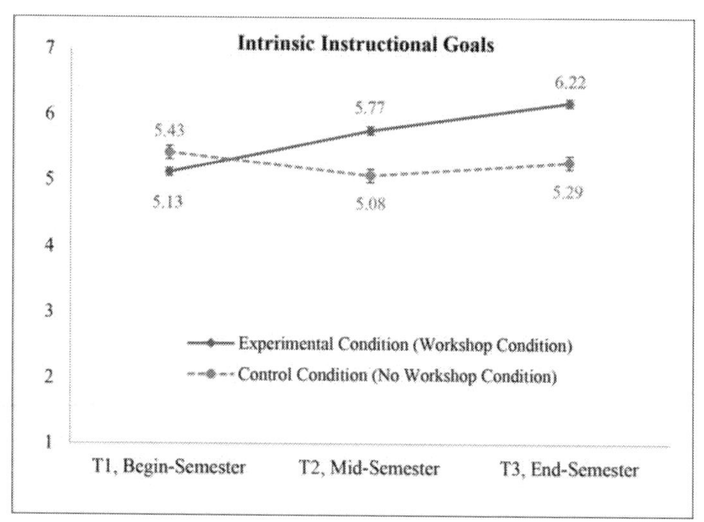

FIGURE 16.3 Teachers' Mean Scores for Their Adoption of Intrinsic Instructional Goals Broken Down by Experimental Condition and Time of Assessment

while an example of a goal to promote relationship growth is, "My goal in this class is to encourage close bonds between classmates."

Teachers who participate in an autonomy-supportive teaching workshop adopt more intrinsic instructional goals. These positive effects of the workshop on teachers' greater reliance on intrinsic instructional goals appear in Figure 16.3 (data from Cheon, Reeve, Yu, & Jang, 2014). Over the course of the academic year, teachers who participate in the workshop showed a month-after-month rise in their incorporation of intrinsic instructional goals into their lesson plans and daily teaching (*Ms* = 5.13, 5.77, 6.22, 1–7 scale; see solid line in Figure 16.3), compared to teachers who did not participate in the workshop (Ms = 5.43, 5.08, 5.29; see dashed line in Figure 16.3).

Adopting intrinsic goals catalyze autonomy-supportive teaching because autonomy support is literally the means by which teachers pursue and attain their intrinsic instructional goals [i.e., "To accomplish my intrinsic instructional goal (e.g., promote students' personal growth), I will need to teach in an autonomy-supportive way."]. That is, as shown in Figure 16.4, the link between adopting an intrinsic instructional goal and teaching in an autonomy-supportive way is a two-step process. What the adoption of an intrinsic instructional goal does is to orient the teacher toward a student focus and an understanding tone (process 1 in Figure 16.4). Once adopted, a student focus and an understanding tone together enable, foreshadow, and empower the teacher's forthcoming autonomy-supportive instructional behaviors (process 2 in Figure 16.4), because a student focus and an understanding tone are the roots of autonomy-supportive teaching (Reeve & Cheon, 2021).

Given the close relation between intrinsic instructional goals and autonomy-supportive teaching practices (Jang & Reeve, 2021), researchers have tested the

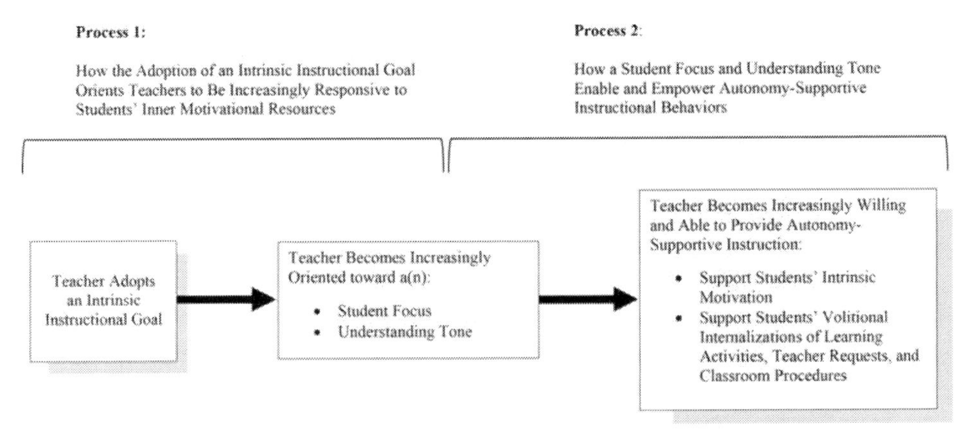

FIGURE 16.4 Two-Step Process to Explain How the Adoption of an Intrinsic Instructional Goal Orients Teachers toward Autonomy-Supportive Teaching

possibilities that (1) teacher participation in an autonomy-supportive teaching workshop increases that teacher's reliance on intrinsic instructional goals and that (2) building intrinsic instructional goals into one's daily lesson plans increases that teacher's reliance on autonomy-supportive teaching. That is, stated a bit too simply, autonomy-supportive teaching causes intrinsic instructional goal adoption just as intrinsic goal adoption causes autonomy-supportive teaching. Both hypotheses have been confirmed by empirical research (Cheon et al., 2018). Hence, the fourth reason why the workshop helps teachers develop a more autonomy-supportive motivating style is because it encourages teachers to adopt intrinsic instructional goals.

THE BIG PICTURE

Figure 16.5 shows the big picture to explain why the workshop works. Participation in the workshop helps teachers develop greater teaching skill, teaching efficacy, positive beliefs about the effectiveness and practicality of autonomy-supportive teaching, and the adoption of intrinsic instructional goals (see the four downwardly slopped lines in the upper left of Figure 16.5). Importantly, gains in all four of these personal-professional developmental resources, once developed, explain why teachers become, over time, significantly more autonomy supportive toward their students (see the four downwardly slopped lines in the lower right of Figure 16.5).

CONCLUSION

During the Workshop, teachers develop—more or less—four personal-professional resources, all of which are catalysts to greater autonomy-supportive teaching. By knowing what these critical agents of change are, the interested reader has a

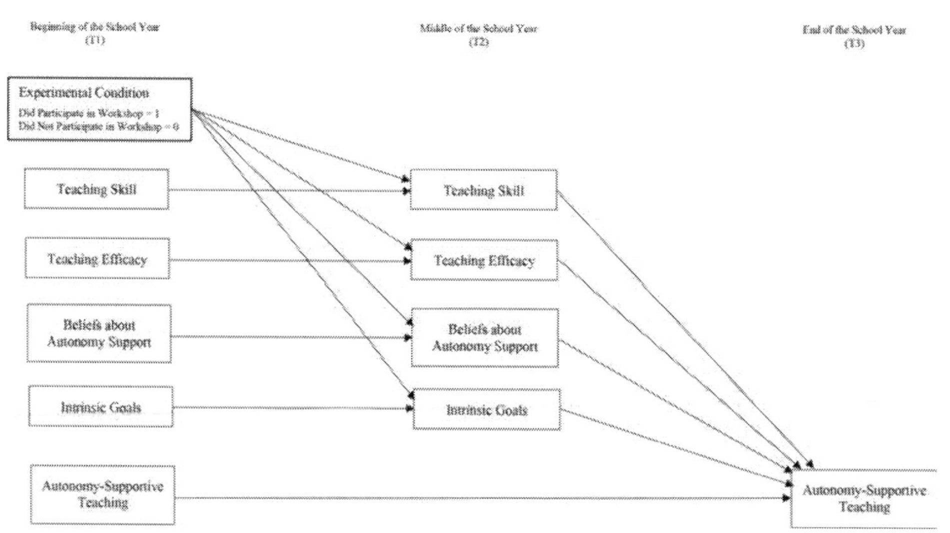

FIGURE 16.5 Mediation Model to Show How Four Workshop-Enabled Personal Resources Explain Why Teachers Become More Autonomy Supportive

"scorecard" to provide the feedback needed to know if he or she is (or is not) making progress toward greater autonomy-supportive teaching:

- Do I have the skill to enact each of the seven autonomy-supportive instructional behaviors?
- Am I confident that I have what it takes to promote students' learning, engagement, and desirable behavior?
- Do I believe that autonomy-supportive teaching is highly effective? Easy to do?
- Do the objectives built into my lesson plans encourage students to pursue intrinsic instructional goals?

If the teacher is gaining teaching skill, raising teaching efficacy, endorsing positive beliefs about autonomy-supportive teaching, and prioritizing intrinsic instructional goals, then it is very likely that greater autonomy-supportive teaching will be forthcoming.

Part 5

Benefits

CHAPTER 17

Student benefits

Student benefits are at the heart of every autonomy-supportive teaching workshop. Autonomy-supportive teaching is need-satisfying teaching—it provides students with opportunities to experience greater need satisfaction and lesser need frustration (Cheon, Reeve, & Ntoumanis, 2018, 2019; Cheon, Reeve, & Song, 2016, 2019). It also increases students' intrinsic motivation and internalization of social regulations (Cheon & Reeve, 2013; Cheon, Reeve, & Moon, 2012). Once motivationally empowered with high need satisfaction, low need frustration, high intrinsic motivation, and high internalizations, students then experience and display a wide range of educationally important benefits, such as greater engagement, skill development, and academic achievement (Cheon & Reeve, 2013; Cheon et al., 2012; Cheon, Reeve, & Vansteenkiste, 2020).

MOTIVATIONAL BENEFITS

To evaluate whether or not participation in the workshop allows teachers to provide more need-satisfying and less need-frustrating instruction, students complete questionnaires such as the Basic Psychological Need Satisfaction and Need Frustration scale (BPNSNF; Chen et al., 2015). By having students complete the BPNSNF scale, students report on six classroom experiences—autonomy, competence, and relatedness satisfaction along with autonomy, competence, and relatedness frustration.

Greater need satisfaction

As shown in Figure 17.1, students of teachers who participate in the workshop report significantly greater overall need satisfaction after a few weeks of instruction (T2, Mid-Semester) and they continue to report significantly greater need satisfaction throughout the rest of the course (T3, End-Semester), compared to students of teachers who do not participate in the workshop. Students of teachers in the control group generally report an unchanged level of need satisfaction (*M*s = 4.56, 4.75, 4.67; see dashed line). This mostly unchanged level of need satisfaction is understandable because their teachers rely on an unchanged level of autonomy-supportive teaching (recall the upper panel in Figure 15.1). In contrast, students of the teachers in the experimental condition consistently show a rising level of need satisfaction, as can be seen in the solid line (*M*s = 4.51, 5.12, 5.22). This consistently rising level of need

DOI: 10.4324/9781003091738-22

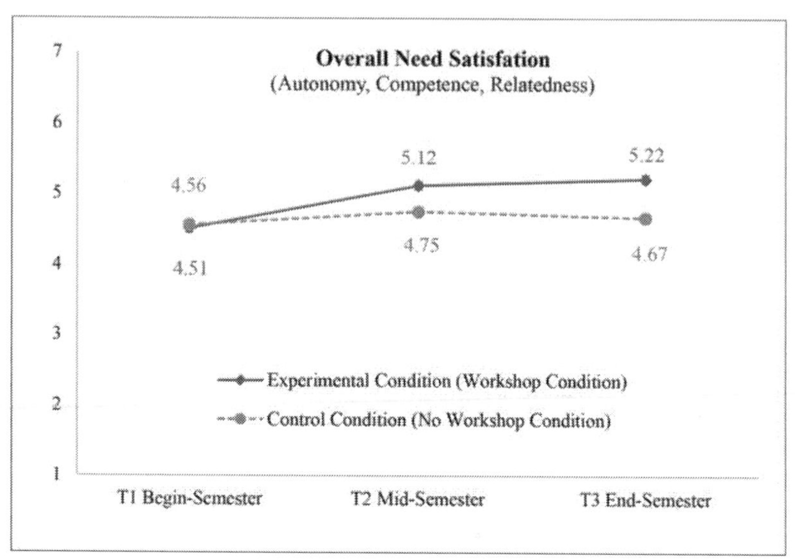

FIGURE 17.1 Students' Overall Need Satisfaction Broken Down by Experimental Condition and Time of Assessment
Source: Data are from Cheon et al. (2016).

satisfaction is also understandable because their teachers rely on a rising level of autonomy-supportive teaching (recall the upper panel of Figure 15.2). Most of this rise in need satisfaction occurs during the first half of the year (see the upwardly-sloped solid line from T1 to T2), as this was the time that their teachers were in the middle of becoming more autonomy supportive.

As shown in the three panels in Figure 17.2, this need satisfaction benefit applies across all three psychological needs—autonomy, competence, and relatedness (Cheon, Reeve, & Ntoumanis, 2018, 2019; Cheon, Reeve, & Song, 2016, 2019; Cheon, Reeve, Yu, & Jang, 2014; Cheon & Reeve, 2013, 2015). The effect sizes for the autonomy (upper panel), competence (center panel), and relatedness (lower panel) need-satisfaction effects graphed in Figure 17.2 were $d = 0.98$, 0.90, and 0.72, respectively. These are large, obvious student benefits.

Lesser need frustration

As shown in Figure 17.3, students of teachers who participate in the workshop report significantly lesser overall need frustration after a few weeks of instruction (T2, Mid-Semester) and they continue to report significantly lesser need frustration throughout the rest of the course (T3, End-Semester), compared to students of teachers who do not participate in the workshop. Students of teachers in the control group generally report an unchanged level of need frustration, though they do often show a rise in need frustration in the later part of the semester (*Ms* = 2.50, 2.51, 2.66; see dashed line). This mostly unchanged level of need frustration is understandable because

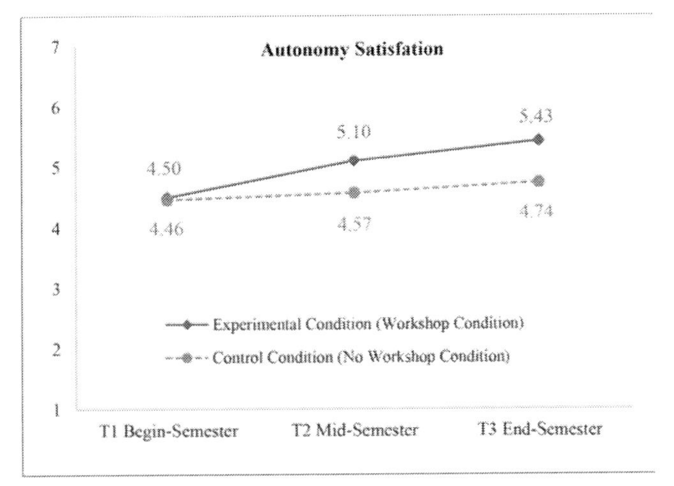

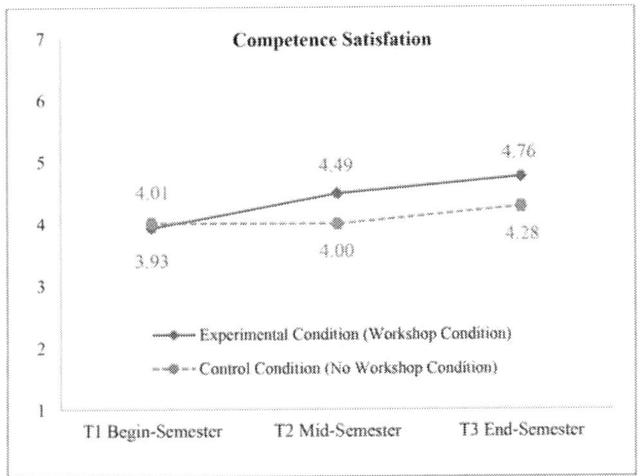

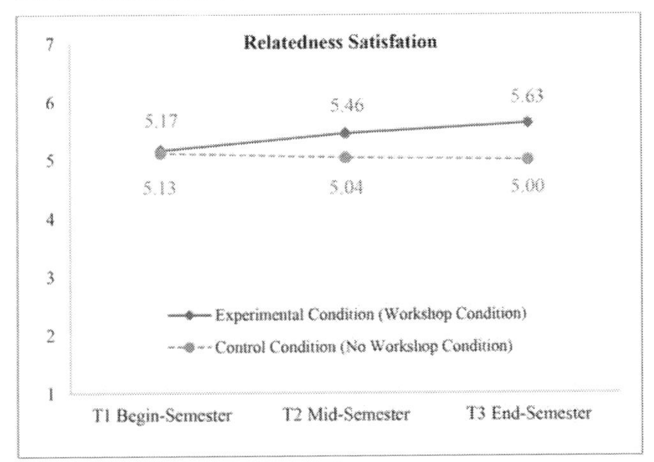

FIGURE 17.2 Students' Autonomy (Upper Panel), Competence (Center Panel), and Relatedness (Lower Panel) Satisfaction Broken Down by Experimental Condition and Time of Assessment.

Source: Data are from Cheon and Reeve (2013).

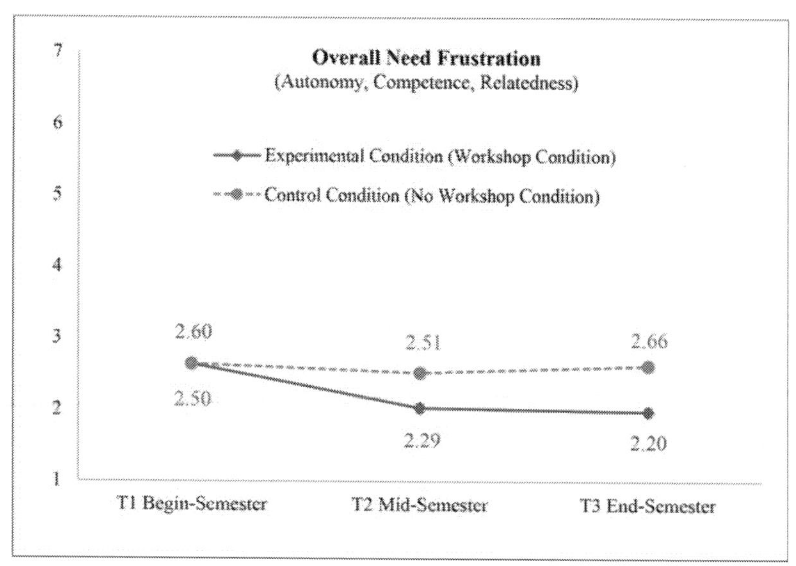

FIGURE 17.3 Students' Overall Need Frustration Broken Down by Experimental Condition and Time of Assessment
Source: Data are from Cheon et al. (2018).

their teachers showed an unchanged level of perceived controlling teaching (recall the lower panel in Figure 15.2). In contrast, students of teachers in the experimental condition consistently show falling need frustration, as can be seen in the solid line (*M*s = 2.60, 2.29, 2.20), because their teachers rely on a declining level of controlling teaching (recall the lower panel in Figure 15.2). As with the case with students' rising need satisfaction, most of the decline in need frustration occurs during the first half of the year (see the downwardly-sloped solid lines from T1 to T2), as this was the time that their teachers were in the middle of learning how to replace their existing controlling instructional behaviors with alternative autonomy-supportive acts of instruction.

As shown in Figure 17.4, this benefit of lesser need frustration applies across all three psychological needs—autonomy, competence, and relatedness (Cheon, Reeve, & Ntoumanis, 2018, 2019; Cheon, Reeve, & Song, 2016, 2019; Cheon, Reeve, Yu, & Jang, 2014). The effect sizes for the autonomy, competence, and relatedness frustration effects depicted in Figure 17.4 were also large: $d = 0.68$, 0.65, and 0.74, respectively.

Greater intrinsic motivation and internalization

Autonomy-supportive teaching generates experiences of need satisfaction, but it further supports and enables students' experiences of intrinsic motivation and internalization of social regulations. As shown in the upper panel in Figure 17.5, students of teachers who participate in the workshop report significantly greater intrinsic

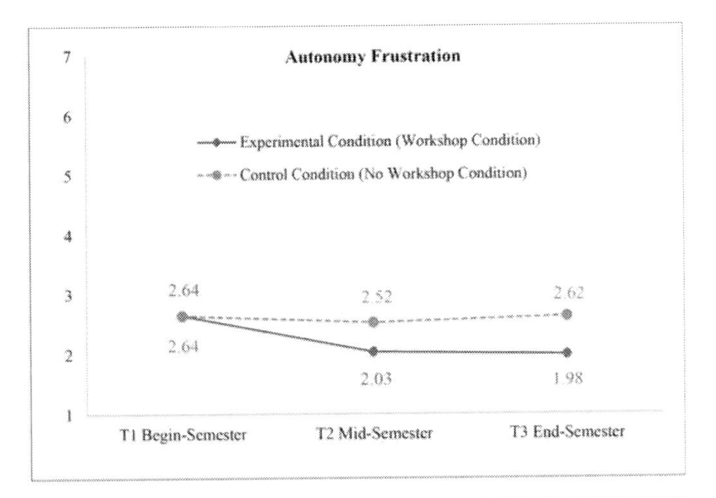

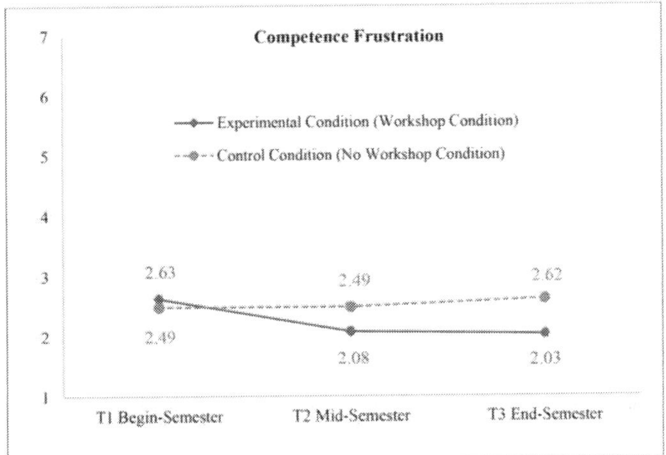

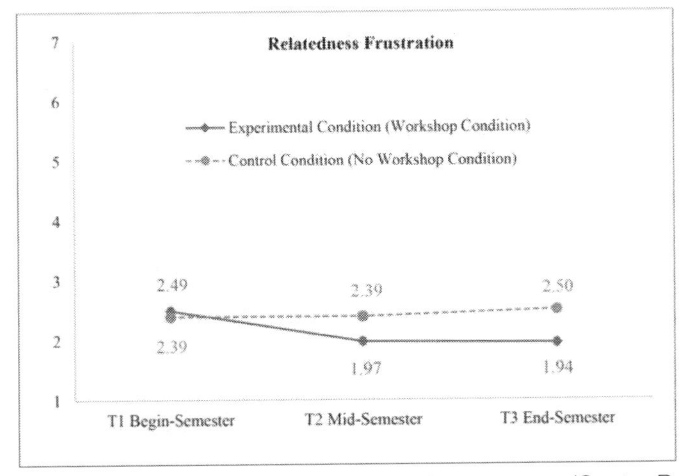

FIGURE 17.4 Students' Autonomy (Upper Panel), Competence (Center Panel), and Relatedness (Lower Panel) Frustration Broken Down by Experimental Condition and Time of Assessment

Source: Data are from Cheon et al. (2019).

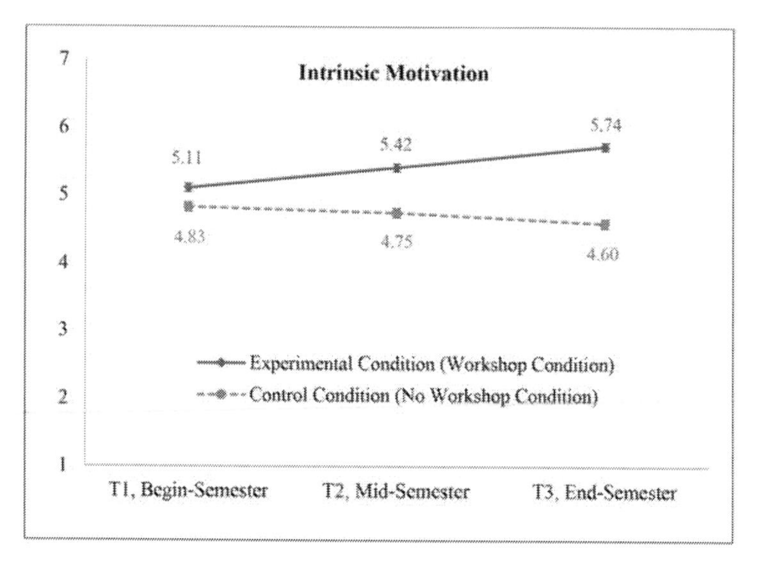

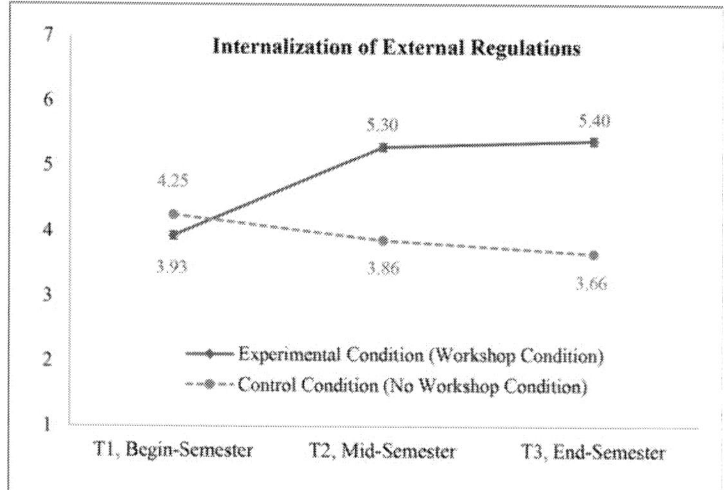

FIGURE 17.5 Students' Self-Reports of Intrinsic Motivation (Upper Panel) and Internalization of External Regulations (Lower Panel) Broken Down by Experimental Condition and Time of Assessment

Source: Data for the Upper Panel from Cheon et al. (2012); Data for the Lower Panel from Cheon & Reeve (2013).

motivation throughout the course (T2, T3), compared to students of teachers who do not participate in the workshop (Cheon & Reeve, 2013; Cheon, Reeve, & Moon, 2012). For these students, their intrinsic motivation steadily rises throughout the semester (*Ms*, 5.11, 5.42, 5.74; see solid line); while intrinsic motivation actually declines throughout the semester for students of teachers in the control group (*Ms*, 4.83, 4.75, 4.60; see dashed line).

As shown in the lower panel in Figure 17.5, students of teachers who participate in the workshop report significantly greater internalizations of external regulations throughout the course (T2, T3), compared to students of teachers who do not participate in the workshop (Cheon & Reeve, 2013; Cheon, Reeve, & Moon, 2012). For these students, their internalized motivation rises throughout the semester and shows a rather dramatic increase during the first half of the semester (*Ms*, 3.93, 5.30, 5.40; see solid line); while internalized motivation declines throughout the semester for students of teachers in the control group (*Ms*, 4.25, 3.86, 3.66; see dashed line).

Lesser amotivation

Amotivation literally means "without motivation." It is a state of motivational apathy in which students harbor little or no reason (motive) to invest the energy and effort necessary to learn or to accomplish something (Legault, Green-Demers, & Pelletier, 2006). Students with amotivation are typically passive, lethargic, and, when they do participate, mostly "just go through the motions" to act like they are engaged in the classwork. As shown in Figure 17.6, students of teachers who participate in the workshop report significantly lesser amotivation throughout the course (T2, T3) than do students of teachers who do not participate in the workshop (Cheon & Reeve, 2013, 2015; Cheon et al., 2016; Cheon et al., 2012). As shown in the rising dashed line, students of teachers in the control group show a gradual and disturbing increase in course-related amotivation (*Ms*, 2.37, 2.57, 2.65). Teachers who participate in the workshop, however, are able to support their students' motivation such that

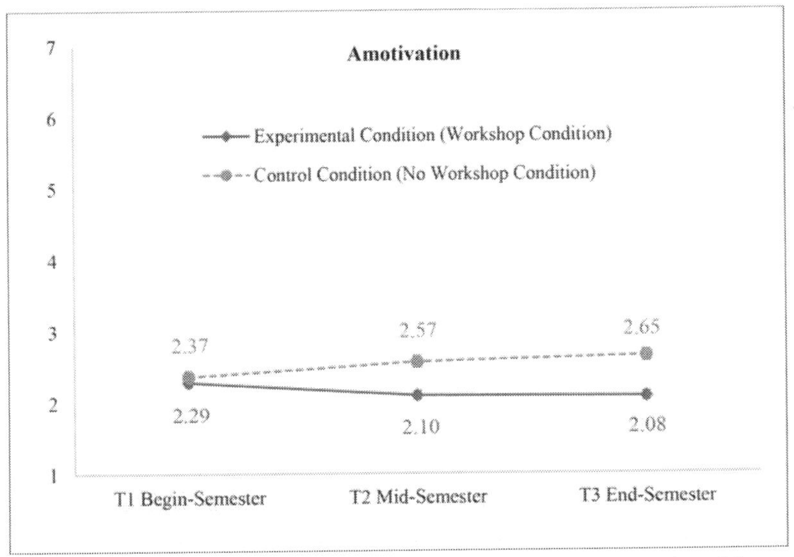

FIGURE 17.6 Students' Amotivation Broken Down by Experimental Condition and Time of Assessment

Source: Data are from Cheon, Reeve, and Song (2016).

amotivation not only does not rise but actually declines significantly as the weeks go by (*Ms*, 2.29, 2.10, 2.08; see solid line).

EDUCATIONAL BENEFITS

The data summarized in Figures 17.1–17.6 show that students of teachers who participate in the workshop experience a boost in many aspects of their classroom motivation. These motivational boosts, once experienced, produce favorable effects on a wide range of educationally-important benefits.

Gains in positive outcomes

The list of gains in students' positive outcomes enabled by autonomy-supportive teaching is a long one. Compared to students of teachers who do not participate in the workshop, students of teachers who do participate in the workshop show gains in all of the following: *classroom engagement* (Cheon & Reeve, 2013, 2015; Cheon et al., 2019; Cheon et al., 2016; Cheon et al., 2020; Cheon et al., 2012; Reeve, Jang, Carrell, Jeon, & Barch, 2004), *agency and initiative* (Reeve, Cheon, & Yu, 2020), *self-regulated learning* (Flunger, Mayer, & Umbach, 2019), *course-specific skill development* (Cheon, Reeve, & Ntoumanis, 2019; Cheon & Reeve, 2013; Cheon et al., 2012; Cheon, Reeve, & Vansteenkiste, 2020), *general life skills development* (Cheon, Reeve, & Song, 2021), *academic achievement* (Cheon, Reeve, & Ntoumanis, 2019; Cheon & Reeve, 2013; Cheon et al., 2012; Cheon, Reeve, & Vansteenkiste, 2020), *course grade* (Cheon et al., 2019), *positive emotions* (Kaplan & Assor, 2012), and a positive domain-specific *self-concept* (Cheon et al., 2019). For illustrative purposes, Figure 17.7 shows workshop-enabled gains in three of these educational benefits: classroom engagement (upper panel; data from Cheon et al., 2019), skill development (middle panel; data from Cheon & Reeve, 2013), and self-concept (lower panel; data from Cheon et al., 2019).

Declines in negative outcomes

The list of declines in students' maladaptive functioning enabled by autonomy-supportive teaching is also a long one. Compared to students of teachers who do not participate in the workshop, students of teachers who do participate in the workshop show declines in all of the following: *classroom disengagement* (Cheon et al., 2019), *passivity* (Reeve, Cheon, & Yu, 2020), *problematic relationships* (Cheon et al., 2019), *acceptance of cheating* (Cheon et al., 2018), *negative feelings* (Kaplan & Assor, 2012), and *biological/physical upset* (e.g., lesser cortisol reactivity; Reeve & Tseng, 2011a). For illustrative purposes, Figure 17.8 shows workshop-enabled declines in three of these educational vulnerabilities: classroom disengagement (upper panel; data from Cheon et al., 2019), problematic peer relationships (middle panel; data from Cheon et al., 2019), and acceptance of cheating as okay (lower panel; data from Cheon et al., 2018).

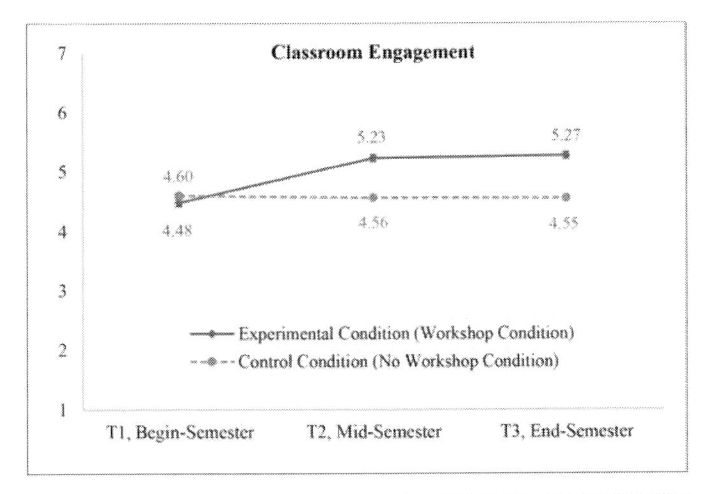

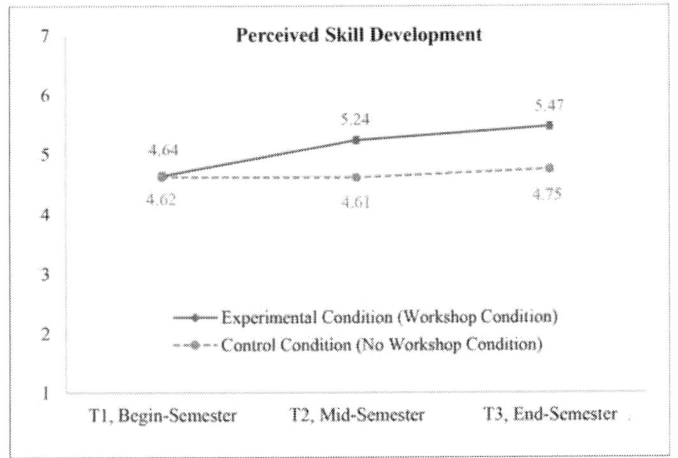

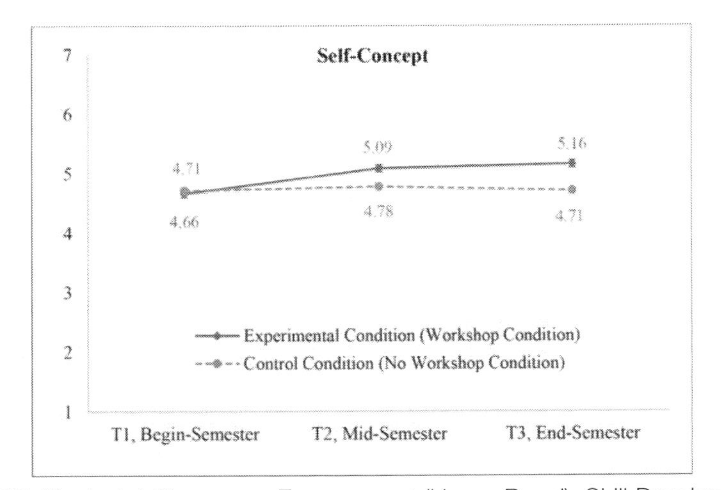

FIGURE 17.7 Students' Classroom Engagement (Upper Panel), Skill Development (Middle Panel), and Self-Concept (Lower Panel) Broken Down by Experimental Condition and Time of Assessment

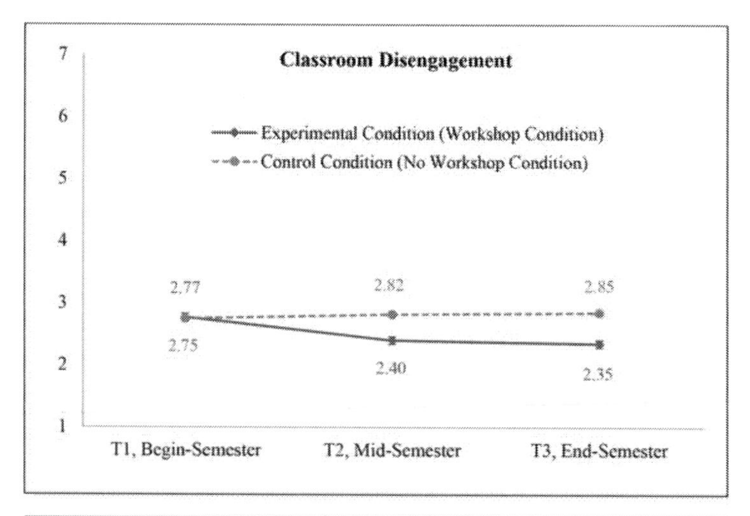

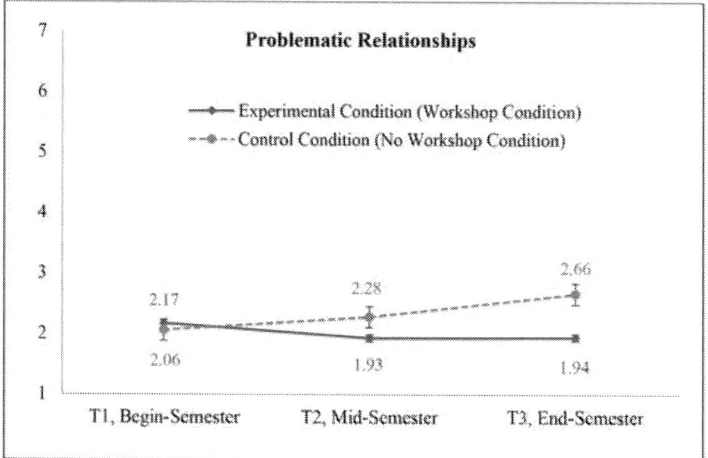

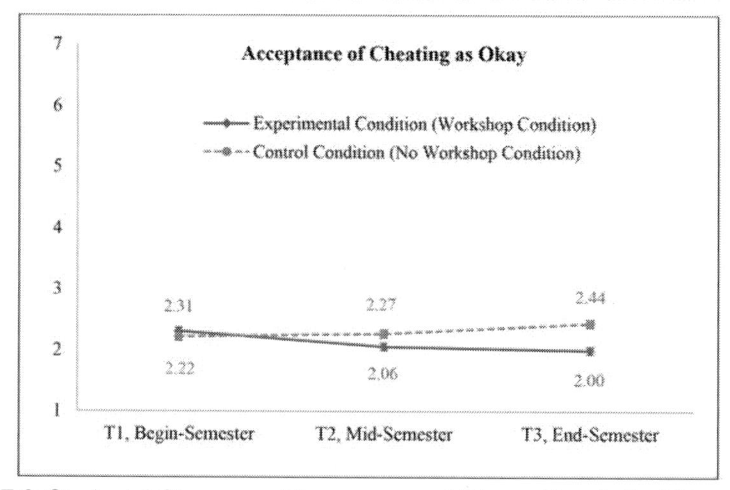

FIGURE 17.8 Students' Classroom Disengagement (Upper Panel), Problematic Peer Relationships (Middle Panel), and Acceptance of Cheating (Lower Panel) Broken Down by Experimental Condition and Time of Assessment

WHY THESE EDUCATIONAL BENEFITS OCCUR

Greater autonomy-supportive teaching catalyzes students' motivational assets (e.g., need satisfaction, intrinsic motivation, internalizations), while lesser controlling teaching soothes away students' motivational vulnerabilities (e.g., need frustration, amotivation). To show how gains in motivation boost effective functioning and lessen maladaptive functioning, self-determination theory (SDT) proposes its dual-process model (Bartholomew, Ntoumanis, Ryan, Bosch, & Thøgersen-Ntoumani, 2011). As shown in Figure 17.9, teacher-provided autonomy support enables motivational assets (e.g., need satisfaction) which then energizes a multitude of educational benefits, while teacher control galvanizes motivational liabilities (e.g., need frustration) which then energizes a multitude of educational vulnerabilities.

The dual-process model highlights two parallel (i.e., "dual") explanatory processes through which (1) a teacher's autonomy-supportive style vitalizes and supports the "brighter" side of students' motivation and functioning (though it also has a mild, supplemental effect in diminishing students' need frustration and maladaptive functioning, as indicated by the dashed, downwardly-sloped "cross-over" path drawn on the right side of Figure 17.9) and (2) a teacher's interpersonal control galvanizes the "darker" side of students' motivation and functioning (though it also has a mild, supplemental effect on diminishing students' need satisfaction and adaptive functioning, as indicated by the dashed, upwardly-sloped "cross-over" path drawn on the right side of Figure 17.9) (Bartholomew et al., 2011; Bartholomew, Ntoumanis, Ryan, & Thøgersen-Ntoumanis, 2011; Cheon et al., 2016; Haerens, Aelterman, Vansteenkiste, Soenens, & Van Petegem, 2015; Vansteenkiste & Ryan, 2013).

For an example of how the dual-process model depicted in Figure 17.9 can explain how teacher participation in the workshop both empowers students' effective functioning and diminishes maladaptive functioning, Figure 17.10 shows the results from one study to illustrate how these teaching, motivational, and educational processes affect one another over the course of an academic semester (data from Cheon et al., 2019). In this investigation, 37 Korean secondary-grade teachers and their 2,669 students were first randomly assigned to participate (or not) in the

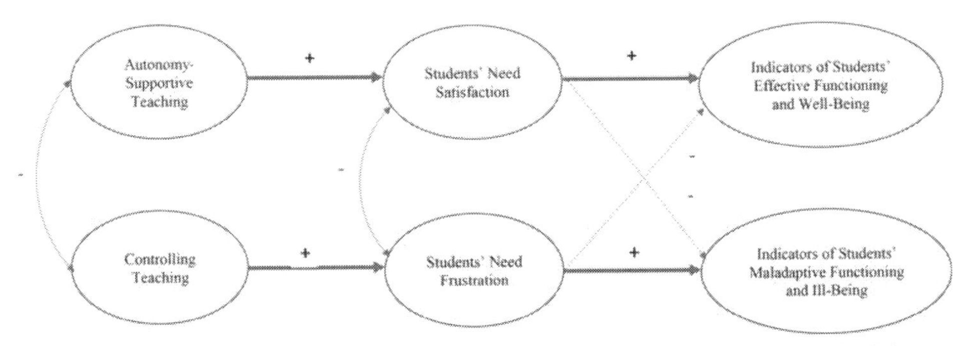

FIGURE 17.9 The Dual-Process Model within Self-Determination Theory to Explain Students' Effective and Maladaptive Functioning

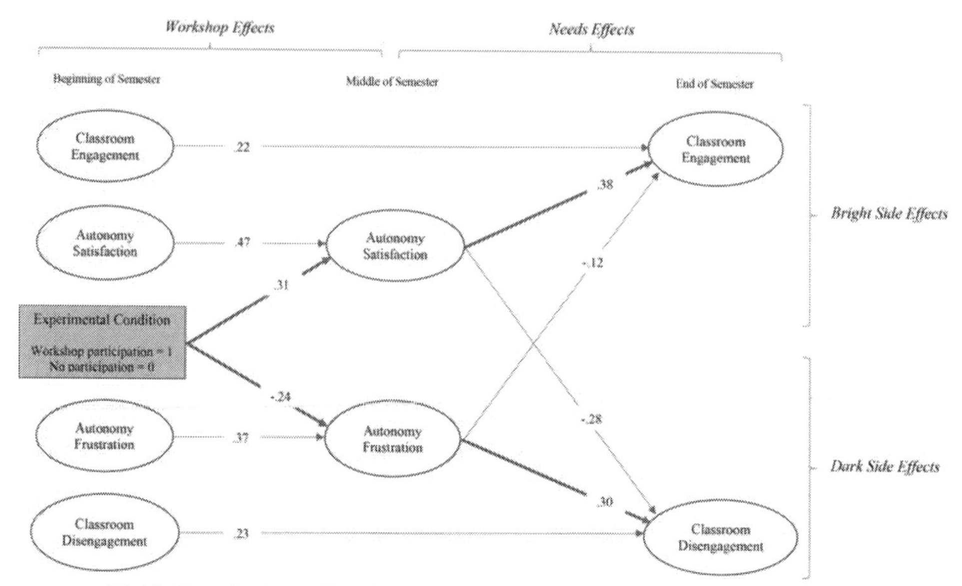

FIGURE 17.10 Results from One Workshop Investigation to Illustrate Self-Determination Theory's Dual-Process Model

Note: The numbers in the figure represent statistical *beta* weights, as explain in the text.

workshop, as depicted in the grey rectangle on the left side of the figure. Students' motivation (autonomy satisfaction, autonomy frustration) and two key indicators of students' classroom functioning (engagement, disengagement) were assessed longitudinally over the course of an 18-week semester. The numbers in the figure represent statistical beta weights to show how changes in one variable affected the subsequent changes in another variable. Beta weights ("*beta*"; possible range, 0–1) are calculated from regression analyses, and the corresponding numbers communicate the magnitude (size) of the effect of one variable on another (e.g., *beta* of .00 = no effect; *beta* of .20 = a small effect; *beta* of .40 = a medium effect; and *beta* of .60 represents a large effect, while a *beta* of 1.00 would represent a perfect effect/relation between the two variables).

The data summarized in Figure 17.10 show many of the motivational and educational effects that occur during any autonomy-supportive teaching workshop. Here, we identify four important effects that occurred in this particular study to explain how teacher participation in the workshop first supports students' high-quality motivation and these motivational gains then allow students to function more effectively and less maladaptively.

1. *Workshop effects*. As shown in the boldfaced sloped lines on the left side of the figure, teacher participation in the workshop (i.e., experimental condition) produced two effects: It increased students' mid-semester autonomy satisfaction (*beta* = .31) and decreased students' mid-semester autonomy frustration (*beta* = –.24).

2. *Needs effects.* As shown in the boldfaced sloped lines on the right side of the figure, workshop-enabled gains in students' autonomy satisfaction led to end-of-semester engagement gains (*beta* = .38), just as workshop-enabled declines in autonomy frustration led to end-of-semester disengagement declines (*beta* = .30).
3. *Dual process effects.* As shown by the labels on the far-right side of the figure, two parallel effects occurred—bright side effects in which autonomy satisfaction enhanced engagement (*beta* = .38) and dark side effects in which autonomy frustration fueled disengagement (*beta* = .30).
4. *Cross-over effects.* Students' engagement rose mostly because mid-semester gains in autonomy satisfaction, but it also rose a bit because of declines in mid-semester autonomy frustration (*betas* = .38 and –.12, respectively). Similarly, students' disengagement declined mostly because of declines in mid-semester autonomy frustration, but it also declined because of gains in mid-semester autonomy satisfaction (*betas* = .30 and –.28, respectively).

In addition to these 4 key points, the information summarized in Figure 17.10 reinforces one final point—namely, that autonomy-supportive teaching does not enhance students' effective functioning directly. Rather, what greater autonomy-supportive teaching does is support students' need satisfaction, which is the motivational factor that explains students' effective functioning. Similarly, greater autonomy-supportive teaching does not diminish students' maladaptive functioning directly. Rather, what greater autonomy-supportive teaching does is minimize students' need frustration, which is the motivational factor that explains students' lesser maladaptive functioning.

CONCLUSION

The purpose of the very first workshop was to help high-school teachers develop the teaching skill needed to enhance their students' classroom engagement (Reeve et al., 2004). Since that original investigation, two dozen similar workshop investigations have been conducted. These studies have revealed many additional educational benefits beyond enhanced engagement. Looking back, it is now clear that teacher participation in the workshop benefits students by enhancing their motivational assets and by diminishing their motivational liabilities.

CHAPTER 18
Classroom benefits

The building on the next page is the National Assembly Hall in downtown Seoul, South Korea (see Figure 18.1). Its architecture features 24 surrounding granite pillars with a blue dome on top. The 24 pillars represent the diverse opinions of the Korean people, while the blue dome represents the Assembly's consensus decisions. This design offers a visual metaphor for the present chapter. While the previous chapter on Student Benefits focused on the 24 pillars (the 24 students in a class), this chapter focuses on the dome (the classroom climate that emerges from their interactions and relationships). By doing so, the discussion transitions from a focus on individual benefits to a new focus on group-experienced benefits.

UNIT OF ANALYSIS

Reflect for a moment to ask yourself why an individual student in your class might be engaged or disengaged during the learning activity of the day. One obvious explanation is the student's individual level of interest (i.e., motivation). But there is a second, not-so-obvious reason—namely, how engaged in the learning activity all the other students in the class are (i.e., students' collective engagement). If everyone in the class is showing strong effort and initiative, then it becomes more likely that the individual student will do the same. This classroom effect also works the other way—if disengagement and passivity are the class norm, then it becomes more likely that the individual student will do the same.

When educators conduct sophisticated statistical analyses of their research data, they can divide any individual student's motivation, engagement, or prosocial behavior into two separate components. Figure 18.2 uses the example of antisocial behavior to illustrate what several research studies have shown—namely, that approximately 80% of the reason why any one individual student pushes, insults, or socially excludes is because of his or her individual factors (e.g., gender, anger, and motivational frustration) but about 20% of the reason for these acts of aggression is because of the social and classroom factors that surround the student (e.g., the prevailing classroom climate). Incidentally, the same group effect holds just as true for prosocial behavior as it does for antisocial behavior. In the figure, the oval's white section represents the individual or personal reasons that explain why a student hits, teases, and intimidates, while the oval's shaded section represents the social and classroom-wide reasons. For instance, anger and relatedness frustration represent individual student factors, while a conflictual classroom climate represents

DOI: 10.4324/9781003091738-23

FIGURE 18.1 National Assembly Hall in Seoul, Korea
Source: Wikimedia Commons. File: Korea-Seoul-Yeouido-National Assembly Building-06.jpg – Wikimedia Commons

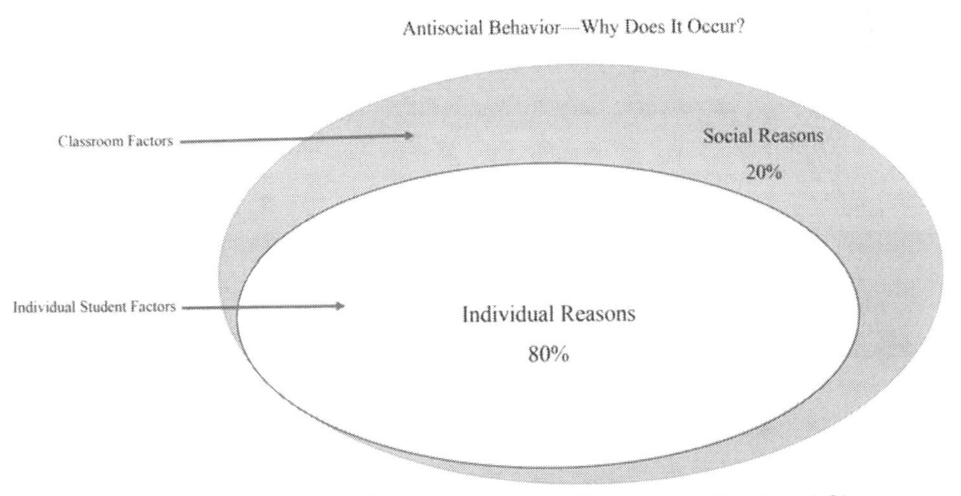

FIGURE 18.2 The Individual and Classroom Factors that Explain Students' Classroom Behavior

a classroom factor. Whereas the previous chapter focused on the motivational processes inside the white oval, the focus of this chapter is on understanding and explaining the social forces inside the shaded oval.

Figure 18.2 introduces the idea of the *unit of analysis*. The unit of analysis is the level of interpretation or explanation for why a behavior occurs. The unit of analysis can be at the individual student level, or it can be at the classroom level. Actually, the unit (or level) of analysis can be extended further to include not only the individual and classroom effects but those that occur at the school and nation levels as well. For instance, students argue and fight because of personal and classroom factors, but students also argue and fight because of the particular school they attend, because antisocial behavior is more prevalent at some schools than it is at other schools. Similarly, students also argue and fight because they live in a particular nation, because antisocial behavior is more prevalent in some nations than it is in other nations. Because of this, the reader might imagine four ovals in Figure 18.2—one for individual factors, one for classroom factors, one for school factors, and a fourth for national factors.

To keep things manageable and to maintain our focus on the classroom teacher, this chapter focuses only on classroom factors (the shaded oval)—for two reasons. First, teachers have influence over the classroom dynamics that emerge and take root in their classrooms. Second, as will be shown, if teachers can change in the prevailing classroom climate—if teachers can transition students' interactions and relationships away from a "me-against-you" culture and toward a "we" (mutually supportive and caring) culture, then this upgrade in the classroom climate will yield important benefits.

CLASSROOM CLIMATE

The classroom climate represents the norms, expectations, roles, priorities, group dynamics, and patterns of communication that prevail in a given classroom to guide peer-to-peer (student-to-student) interactions and relationships (Hodge & Gucciardi, 2015). As students begin to interact with each other, they create a classroom climate, as early classroom conduct begins to take on a normative nature and becomes contagious (as through modeling and shared expectations). What emerges over the course of a semester are peer relationships that are generally supportive, generally conflictual, or something in between.

A supportive classroom climate is one that is characterized by interpersonal acceptance (Hodge & Gucciardi, 2015). In these classes, relationships tend to be egalitarian. The climate orients students toward interpersonal inclusion, cooperation, rich interpersonal ties, encouraging each other, focusing on task mastery, and working together (Ntoumanis & Vazou, 2005). Once established, a relationship-supportive classroom climate functions as a social-contextual resource to promote students' prosocial functioning. For instance, when students find themselves surrounded by peers who support, care for, and show respect for each other, their prosocial behavior tends to follow this supportive climate to be high (Solomon, Watson, Delucchi, Schaps, & Battistich, 1988).

A conflictual classroom climate is one that is characterized by interpersonal competition. In these classes, relationships tend to be hierarchical. The climate orients students to focus on social status and proving their worth or status to their peers (e.g., ego-involvement) and, further, to emphasize social comparison, social dominance, interpersonal conflict, normative ability hierarchies, and interpersonal competition (Ntoumanis & Vazou, 2005). Once established, a status-centric conflictual classroom climate functions as a social-contextual liability that puts students' adaptive functioning at risk to, instead, promote antisocial functioning. For instance, when students find themselves surrounded by peers who are competitive and seek social dominance, their antisocial behavior tends to follow this conflictual climate to be high (Lansford, Malone, Dodge, Pettit, & Bates, 2010; Mikami, Lerner, & Lun, 2010).

Autonomy-supportive teaching improves the classroom climate

Student-to-student relationships, group processes, and a classroom culture will form in any classroom, irrespective of the teacher's motivating style. What greater autonomy-supportive teaching does, however, is bend or skew the developing trajectory of students' in-class interactions toward egalitarian relationships and interpersonal support and away from social hierarchy and interpersonal conflict (Assor, Feinberg, Kanat-Maymon, & Kaplan, 2018; Cheon, Reeve, & Ntoumanis, 2019). The teacher's motivating style is an important contributing factor to the direction the classroom climate takes.

One way autonomy-supportive teachers contribute to a supportive climate is through teacher-to-whole-class dialogues (Assor et al., 2018; Kaplan & Assor, 2012). In these discussions, autonomy-supportive teachers model and communicate caring, empathy, and perspective taking. They ask the class, "How would you feel if a classmate spread a nasty rumor about you?" They recommend prosocial solutions to resolve conflict situations, such as "What a victim needs most is a classmate who will stand at their side and say 'no' to the bully." These teachers identify the very real benefits that come from positive peer relationships and prosocial behavior (e.g., friendship, positive feelings). These dialogues focus somewhat on students' individual motivations, but they mostly focus on establishing class-wide rules, expectations, norms, and values. Research shows that when teachers model, encourage, and value interpersonal support, a prosocial classroom climate tends to emerge (Hendrickx, Mainhard, Boor-Klip, Cillessen, & Brekelmans, 2016; Joesaar, Hein, & Hagger, 2012).

Just as teachers can learn how to support the autonomy of an individual student, teachers can learn how to support the autonomy of the whole class. When teachers are able to do this, they model what interpersonal support looks like (e.g., greater perspective taking and empathy), establish prosocial norms, enrich the interpersonal ties among students, lessen the status hierarchy among students (more egalitarian), and initiate teacher-to-whole-class social dialogues. How they do this specifically is through the aforementioned seven autonomy-supportive instructional behaviors (e.g., take the students' perspective, acknowledge negative feelings, use invitational language). Once teachers learn how to support the autonomy of their individual students, they find it rather easy to extend these one-on-one skills to the whole class level. For instance, once a teacher learns how to take the perspective of an individual student, teachers who participate in the workshop find it relatively easy to further take the perspective of the whole class. Similarly, once a teacher learns how to provide explanatory rationales and acknowledge the negative feelings of an individual student, teachers who participate in the workshop find it relatively easy to further apply these skills collectively to the whole class (Cheon, Reeve, & Marsh, 2021a, 2021b; Kaplan & Assor, 2012).

Figure 18.3 presents the effects of one workshop study on (a) a supportive classroom climate and (b) students' prosocial behavior (Cheon et al., 2021a). The two panels in Figure 18.3 show that, in the absence of teacher participation in the workshop

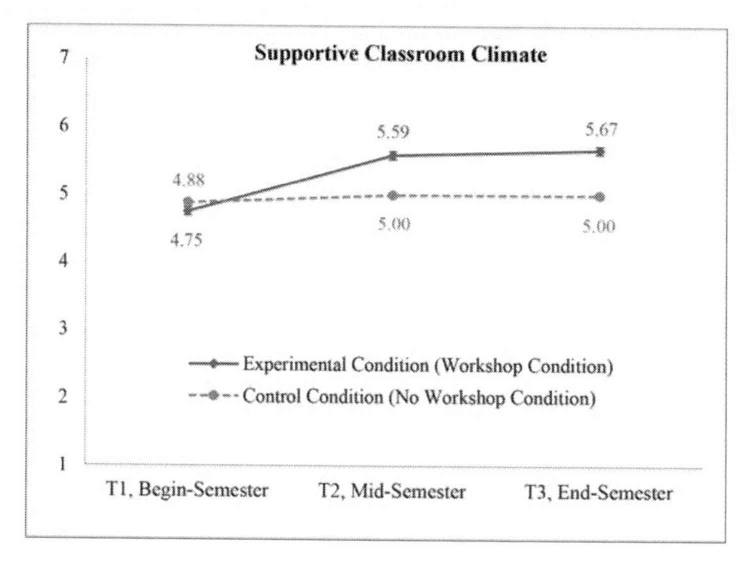

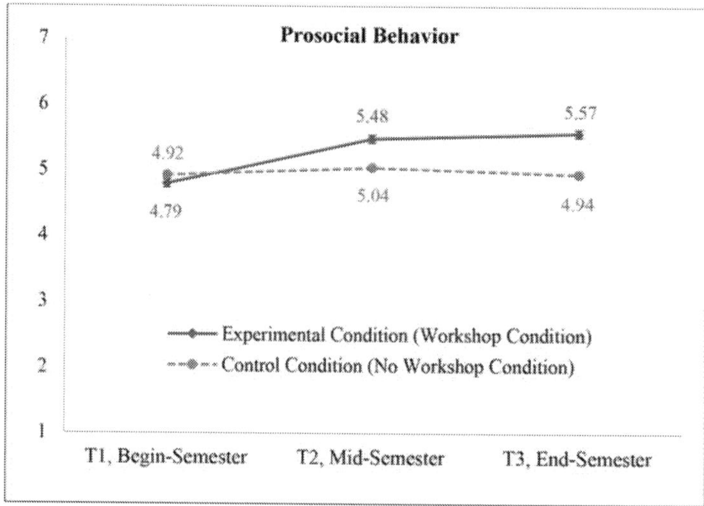

FIGURE 18.3 Autonomy-Supportive Teaching Increases both a Supportive Classroom Climate and Prosocial Behavior

(i.e., "practice as usual"; see the dashed lines of the control group participants), the supportive classroom climate and prosocial behavior start at moderately high levels (*Ms* = 4.88 for supportive climate, 4.92 for prosocial behavior, on a 1–7 scale) and maintain that moderately high level over the course of the semester. When teachers participate in the workshop, however, the supportive classroom climate and prosocial behavior start at the same moderately high levels but quickly rise to higher levels by mid-semester (*Ms*, 4.75, 5.59, and 5.67 for supportive classroom climate; *Ms* = 4.79, 5.48, and 5.57 for prosocial behavior). The reason why autonomy-supportive teachers are able to generate this upward spike in class-wide prosocial behavior (the lower panel) is because they first are able to generate an upward spike in the supportive peer-to-peer classroom climate (the upper panel) (Cheon et al., 2021a, 2021b).

Figure 18.4 presents the effects of a workshop study on (a) a conflictual classroom climate and (b) students' antisocial behavior (Cheon et al., 2021a). The two

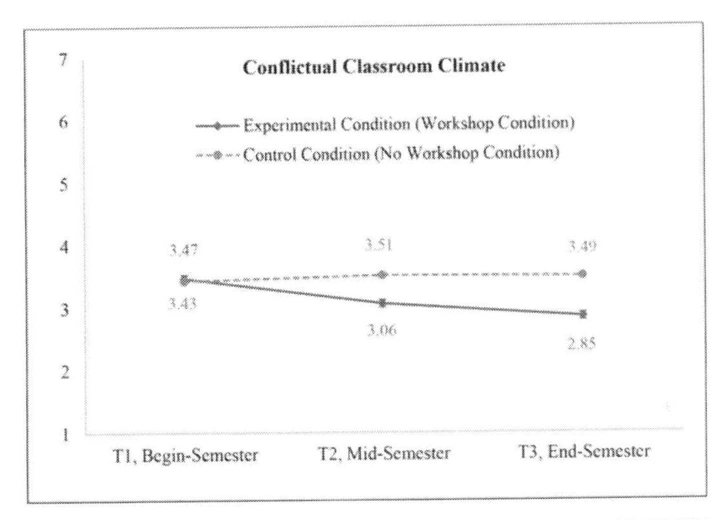

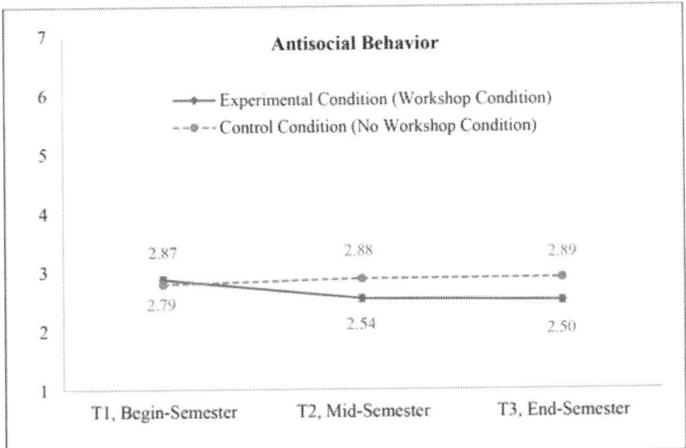

FIGURE 18.4 Autonomy-Supportive Teaching Decreases both a Conflictual Classroom Climate and Antisocial Behavior

panels in Figure 18.4 show that, in the absence of teacher participation in the workshop (i.e., "practice as usual"; see the dashed lines of the control group participants), the conflictual classroom climate and antisocial behavior start at moderate to moderately low levels (*Ms* = 3.43 for conflictual climate, 2.79 for antisocial behavior, on a 1–7 scale) and maintain that moderate level over the course of the academic semester. When teachers participate in the workshop, however, the conflictual classroom climate and antisocial behavior start at the same moderate to moderately low levels but quickly drop by mid-semester (*Ms*, 3.47, 3.06, and 2.85 for conflictual classroom climate; *Ms* = 2.87, 2.54, and 2.50 for antisocial behavior). The reason why autonomy-supportive teachers are able to generate such a downward plunge in class-wide antisocial behavior (the lower panel) is because they first are able to generate a downward plunge in the conflictual peer-to-peer classroom climate (the upper panel) (Cheon et al., 2021a, 2021b).

Implications

In thinking about the findings summarized in Figures 18.3 and 18.4, what is most notable is the strong interdependency or covariation among autonomy support, a supportive climate, and prosocial behavior on the one hand as well as the strong interdependency among teacher control, a conflictual climate, and antisocial behavior on the other hand. The twofold take-home message from these empirical studies is that, as teachers begin to provide instruction in autonomy-supportive ways, (1) the prevailing classroom climate becomes significantly more supportive and, because of this, the prevalence and intensity of students' prosocial behavior increases and (2) the prevailing classroom climate becomes significantly less conflictual and, because of this, the prevalence and intensity of students' antisocial behavior decreases.

THE SPECIAL CASE OF BULLYING

Like antisocial behavior, bullying involves intentionally harming a victim (Smith, 2016). But bullying is different in important ways. While antisocial behavior typically involves a single episode of aggression, bullying involves sustained and repeated acts of aggression and intimidation. Flair ups of antisocial behavior are often episodic events (e.g., a sudden spike in anger or need frustration), but the persistence of bullying over time and across situations suggests more enduring factors. When it occurs, bullying takes one of three forms—physical (e.g., pushing, hitting, kicking, and assaulting), verbal (e.g., name calling, teasing, insulting, and put-downs), or relational (e.g., socially excluding, spreading rumors) (Marsh et al., 2011).

Greater autonomy-supportive teaching decreases bullying (Cheon et al., 2021b). That said, bullying is different from all the other maladaptive educational outcomes emphasized in this book, because it is such a social, group-based phenomenon. Bullying is more than just a dyadic confrontation between a perpetrator and a victim, as bullying occurs in a social context in which peer observers contribute into the initiation, maintenance, promotion, deterrence, and suppression of bullying (Rodkin & Hodges, 2003; Salmivalli, 2010). Peers are present in 85-88% of school-based bully attacks, as occur in public settings such as the classroom, playground, cafeteria, and athletic field (Atlas & Pepler, 1998). Bullying escalates when peers reinforce, support, and encourage the bully, while bullying plummets when peers support and defend the victim (Hawkins, Pepler, & Craig, 2001). That is, bullies often get reinforcement and support (or criticism and opposition) from their classmates. What this means is that one of the most effective bullying prevention programs is to improve the quality of the classroom climate in which bullying typically occurs. Bystanders are crucial participants in any bullying-victimization relationship. If peers did not reinforce bullying—and if peers would in fact discourage bullying, then bullying would decline—and perhaps disappear altogether. Fortunately, this is what autonomy-supportive teachers are able to do so well (Cheon et al., 2021b). When autonomy-supportive teachers bend the prevailing climate toward interpersonal support (a classroom-level group-based process), they lessen bullying.

Figure 18.5 shows the results from one study to illustrate how greater autonomy-supportive teaching enables a more supportive and less conflictual classroom climate

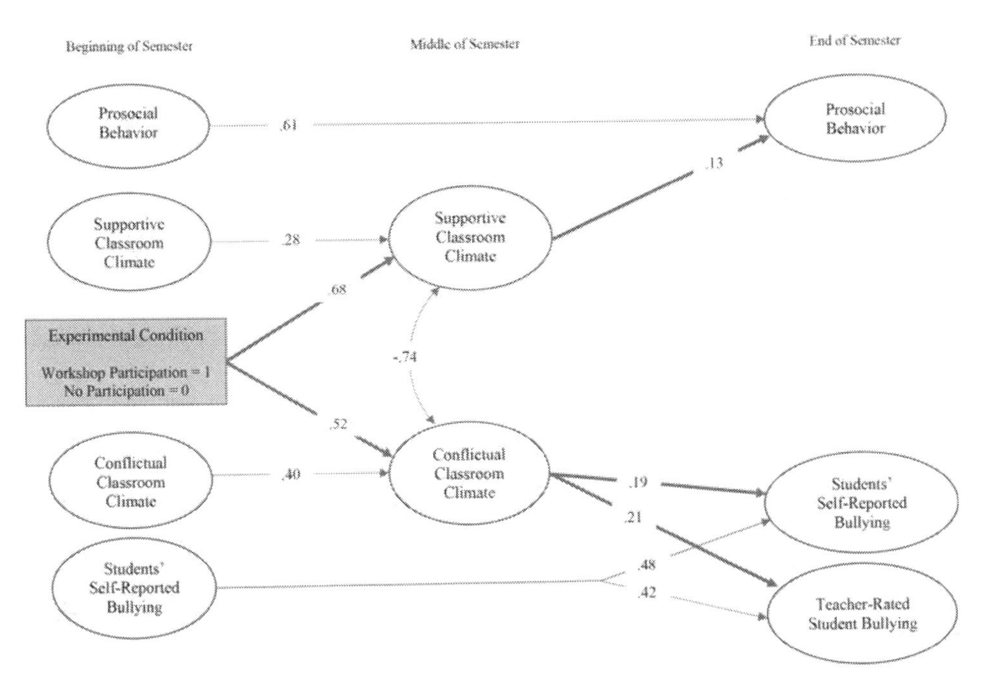

FIGURE 18.5 Teacher Participation in the Workshop Improves the Quality of the Prevailing Classroom Climate, which Increases Prosocial Behavior and Decreases Bullying

Note: The numbers in the figure represent statistical beta weights.

Source: Data are from Cheon, Reeve, and Marsh (2021b).

and, hence, greater prosocial behavior and lesser bullying (data from Cheon et al., 2021b). In this investigation, two parallel measures of bullying were recorded—students' self-reported bullying and teachers' objective-rating of each student in the class. As indicated on the left side of the figure, teachers who participated in the workshop were able to foster significantly more supportive and less conflictual classroom climates. As shown on the right side of the figure, that more supportive climate increased prosocial behavior (*beta* = .13) while the less conflictual climate decreased both indicators of classroom bullying (*betas* = .19 and .21).

The findings from this bullying study (Figure 18.5) are intentionally presented in the same format as the earlier findings from the engagement-disengagement study (Figure 17.10). The parallel presentation shows that just as workshop-enabled gains in autonomy-supportive teaching help teachers increase students' need satisfaction and decrease students' need frustration (as per Figure 17.10), workshop-enabled gains in autonomy-supportive teaching equally help teachers increase a supportive classroom climate and decrease a conflictual climate (as per Figure 18.5). Further, just as gains in need satisfaction and declines in need frustration enable students' more adaptive academic functioning (i.e., greater engagement, lesser disengagement), gains in a supportive climate and declines in a conflictual climate enable students' more adaptive social functioning (i.e., greater prosocial behavior, lesser bullying).

EXPANDING THE EXPLANATORY POWER OF AUTONOMY-SUPPORTIVE TEACHING

Autonomy-supportive teaching workshops were initially designed and implemented to boost students' individual motivational states (greater need satisfaction, lesser need frustration). What the studies introduced in the present chapter showed—for the first time—was that autonomy-supportive teaching also boosted classroom-wide social processes. This is important for two reasons.

First, because autonomy-supportive teaching improves both individual student motivation and class-wide social interactions, it is able to explain educational outcomes more completely or comprehensively. That is, part of the reason why students show high engagement or high disengagement is because their psychological needs are satisfied or frustrated, yet another part of the reason is because the other students in the class are engaged and participating actively or are disengaged and passive. As exemplified earlier in Figure 18.2, these student and classroom factors combine to explain students' engagement-disengagement better than does either a student factor alone or a classroom factor alone.

Second, because autonomy-supportive teaching improves both individual student motivation and class-wide social interactions, the range of explained educational outcomes expands. Because autonomy-supportive teaching improves students' motivational states, it supports gains in students' personal and academic functioning

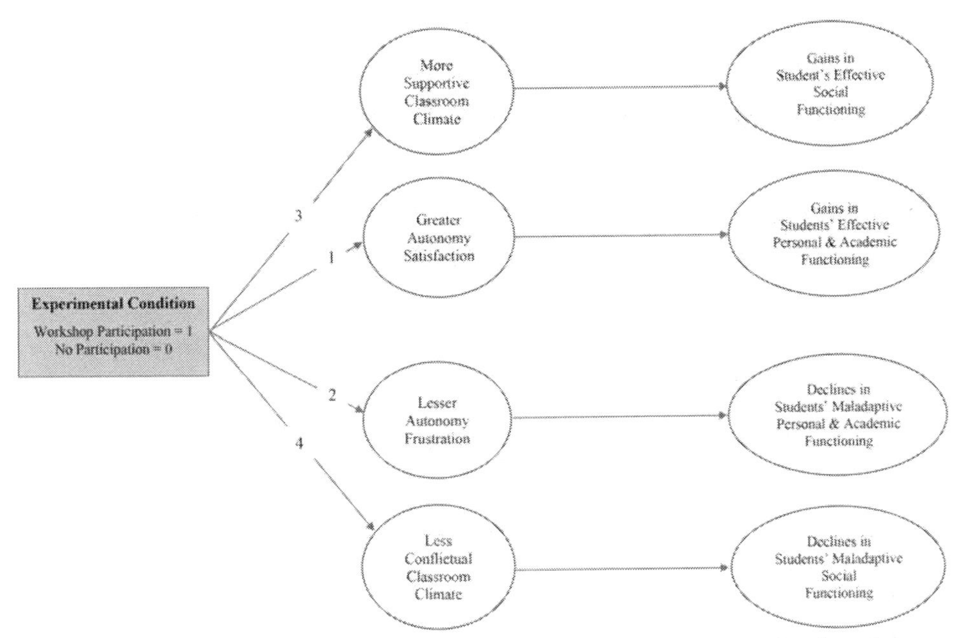

FIGURE 18.6 Teacher Participation in the Workshop Enables Gains in Students' Effective Personal, Academic, and Social Functioning and Declines in Students' Personal, Academic, and Social Maladaptive Functioning

(e.g., engagement, learning, self-concept, well-being; as per Figure 17.7). Similarly, because autonomy-supportive teaching improves the classroom climate, it supports gains in students' social functioning (e.g., gains in prosocial behavior and declines in antisocial behavior and bullying, as per Figure 18.5).

Figure 18.6 puts all this together into a single image. The figure provides a visual depiction of how autonomy-supportive teaching expands the range of important educational outcomes. Chapter 17 overviewed the empirical studies that support the conclusion that autonomy-supportive teaching increases need satisfaction and decreases need frustration and, in doing so, increases students' effective personal and academic functioning and decreases students' maladaptive personal and academic functioning. These studies are represented in Figure 18.6 by lines 1 and 2. But Figure 18.6 also presents the new line 3 to show that autonomy-supportive teaching encourages a more supportive classroom climate, which increases students' social functioning, and it also presents the new line 4 to show that autonomy-supportive teaching encourages a less conflictual classroom climate, which decreases students' social functioning. Together, students' effective personal, academic, and social functioning covers just about every positive educational outcome educators wish they could increase, just as students' maladaptive personal, academic, and social functioning covers just about every negative educational outcomes educators wish they could decrease.

CONCLUSION

Teachers worry that an episode of antisocial behavior might flare-up in their classroom. They worry that students might hit, insult, or socially exclude their classmates. When teachers are autonomy-supportive, however, they create a more supportive and a less conflictual climate—because understanding the students' perspective and acknowledging their collective negative feelings really helps. When such a climate takes root, it becomes an antidote to students' maladaptive social functioning (i.e., aggression, bullying).

CHAPTER 19

Teacher benefits

When the research was just beginning, one of the authors visited a high school to request volunteers to participate in a workshop study. Speaking at an all-hands faculty meeting, the author explained what the workshop was, what teachers would be asked to do, and how their students would likely benefit. Following the presentation, one teacher stood to protest, "It all sounds fine and good. But it sounds like students get all the benefits. What's in it for us—as teachers?" Good question. At the time, we focused only on student benefits, but the teacher's question piqued our interest to find the answer.

As we were deliberating on possible teacher benefits, an enlightening research study was published (Deci, La Guardia, Moller, Scheiner, & Ryan, 2006). In a study of friendships, the authors first showed that, as expected, receiving autonomy support from a friend was both need satisfying and personally beneficial. But the study also showed, for the first time, that *giving* autonomy support was also both need satisfying and personally beneficial. This finding opened up the new possibility that teachers might benefit in terms of their own well-being from giving autonomy support, perhaps as much as their students might benefit from receiving it!

TEACHERS BENEFIT TOO

Why students benefit from receiving autonomy support is clear—they experience greater need satisfaction and lesser need frustration. They become more engaged, and they experience both personal growth and interpersonal connection. Anybody feeling this way is going to thrive psychologically. Teachers similarly benefit from being autonomy supportive, but for different reasons. Giving autonomy support is need-satisfying (Cheon, Reeve, Yu, & Jang, 2014; Taylor, Ntoumanis, & Standage, 2008), it feels like something that is connecting (satisfying relatedness), effective (satisfying competence), and easy to endorse as one's own (satisfying autonomy).

But there is more to the story. As discussed in Chapter 16, teachers also develop the following professional developmental resources during their workshop experience:

- Refining of teaching skills
- Gaining teaching efficacy
- Strengthening positive beliefs about autonomy-supportive teaching
- Adopting intrinsic instructional goals

DOI: 10.4324/9781003091738-24

This is true professional development—a process of growing skills, gaining confidence, strengthening beliefs, and adopting goals. Developing these resources feels deeply beneficial.

But there is still more. Post-workshop, the classroom dynamics are better. The more teachers become autonomy supportive, the more motivation, engagement, learning, and achievement their students show. Being in a classroom where students show improved motivation, engagement, and learning makes the daily experience of being a teacher more professionally satisfying. Along with this, teacher-student relationships improve. The more teachers become autonomy supportive, the more prosocial and the less antisocial their students become (Kaplan & Assor, 2012). This is true for individual students, and this is true for the prevailing classroom climate. Teacher-student conflict gives way to cooperation, interpersonal support, and being "in sync" with each other (Reeve, 2015). Spending one's day with students who you feel closer to and more connected with makes the daily experience of being a teacher more emotionally satisfying.

Then there is yet another reason, which was the original phenomenon Deci et al. (2006) uncovered. There is an old adage that "It is better to give than to receive." That adage rings true because engaging in prosocial behavior is actually a highly emotionally satisfying thing to do (Martela & Ryan, 2016; Weinstein & Ryan, 2010). Prosocial behavior gives rise to benevolence, which is the pleasure one feels upon being able to give to others (Martela & Ryan, 2016). Benevolence comes in many forms (e.g., acts of kindness, volunteering one's time) but, in the teaching profession, benevolence mostly arises from giving interpersonal support (Figure 19.1).

FIGURE 19.1 Community of Satisfied Teachers in Israel

When the classroom dynamics improve, when teacher-student relationships improve, and when teachers make a positive difference in their students' lives, teacher benefits emerge. These benefits include an improved motivation to teach, job satisfaction, passion for teaching, agency, and relationship satisfaction with one's students.

Motivation to teach

Figure 19.2 displays two indicators of high-quality teaching motivation. It compares the quality of motivation for teachers who participated in the workshop (experimental condition) vs. teachers who did not participate in the workshop (control condition) on (1) need satisfaction during teaching (e.g., "I feel free to decide for

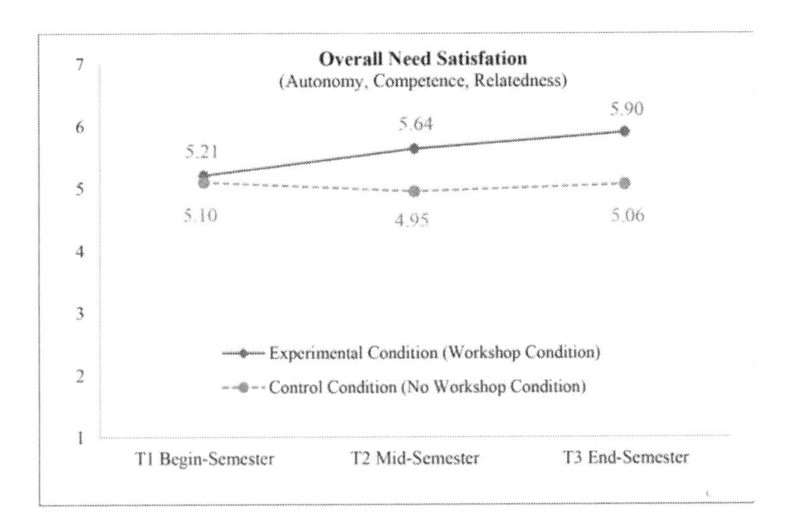

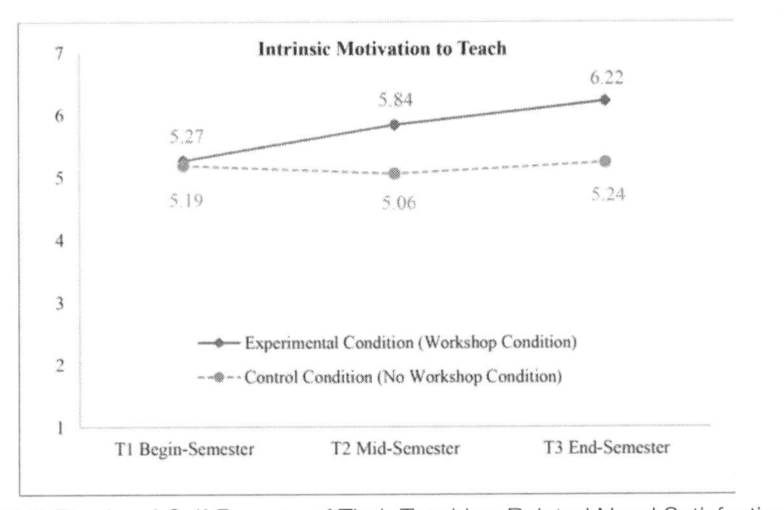

FIGURE 19.2 Teachers' Self-Reports of Their Teaching-Related Need Satisfaction (Upper Panel) and Intrinsic Motivation (Lower Panel) Broken Down by Experimental Condition and Time of Assessment

myself how to teach my class.") and (2) intrinsic motivation to teach (e.g., "The reason I teach my students is because I enjoy it."), using data from Cheon et al. (2014). As shown in the upper panel of Figure 19.2, while teachers who provide instruction via "standard practice" show a moderate and unchanging level of need satisfaction during their teaching (see dashed line), teachers who participate in the workshop show a semester-long rise in their teaching-related need satisfaction (see solid line) (Cheon et al., 2014; Cheon, Reeve, Lee, & Lee, 2018). As shown in the lower panel of Figure 19.2, teachers who participate in the workshop also show a steady rise in their intrinsic motivation to teach (solid line), while teachers in the control group do not show this same rise in intrinsic motivation (dashed line) (Cheon et al., 2014).

Well-being

Psychological well-being is about life going well—one feels good and functions effectively. In the teaching profession, well-being means that one feels good and functions well in the classroom—before, during, and after one's teaching. One gold standard of such wellness is job satisfaction, which is typically measured by asking teachers how much they agree with the statement, "In general, I am satisfied with my job" (Caprara, Barbaranelli, Borgogni, & Steca, 2003). Teacher participation in the workshop increases teachers' job satisfaction (Cheon et al., 2014; Cheon, Reeve, & Vansteenkiste, 2020). As show in the upper panel of Figure 19.3, teachers who do not participate in the workshop tend to show a moderately high and steady level of job satisfaction (*Ms* on a 1–7 scale = 4.94, 4.76, 5.03; see dashed line), while teachers who do participate in the workshop show a semester-long rise in their job satisfaction (*Ms* = 4.74, 5.60, 5.70; see solid line).

Job satisfaction asks teachers to take a step back from the everyday and make an overall rating of how things are going, all things considered. Another way of assessing well-being is in-the-moment. Some days teachers feel energetic and full of enthusiasm (i.e., vitality), while other days leave teachers feeling only exhausted, drained, and tired (i.e., emotional exhaustion). Teachers who participate in the workshop experience greater vitality and lesser emotional exhaustion (Cheon et al., 2014, 2020).

Vitality is the excess psychological energy one feels (Ryan & Fredrick, 1997). When possessing excess energy, one feels alive, energetic, and vital. The bell rings at the end of class, and vitalized teachers want to keep going, because they have more to say and more to give. As shown in the middle panel of Figure 19.3, teachers who participate in the workshop show a steady rise in their vitality while teaching (*Ms* = 4.51, 5.21, 5.99; see solid line). On the other hand, emotional exhaustion is feeling drained, overwhelmed, and fatigued. Emotional exhaustion reflects burnout. The bell rings, and emotionally exhausted teachers are glad to see its end, as the idea of taking a break and holding a calming cup of coffee sounds good. As shown in the lower panel of Figure 19.3, teachers who participate in the workshop show a steady decline in emotional exhaustion (*Ms* = 3.64, 2.31, 1.88; see solid line).

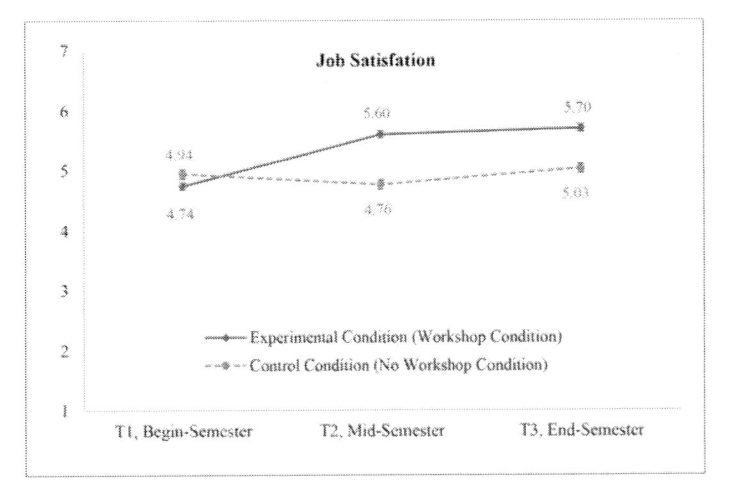

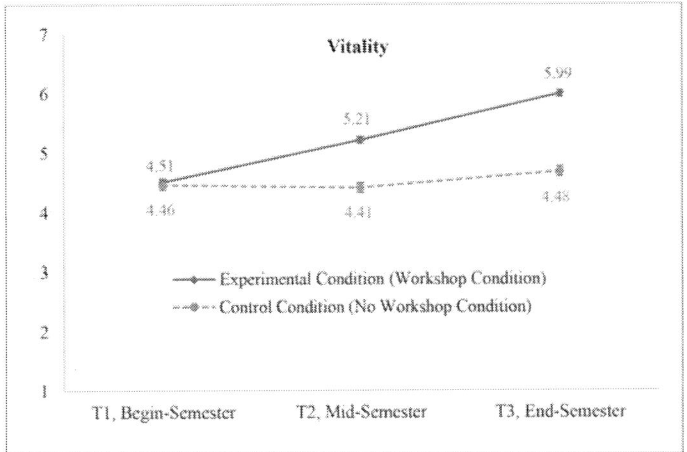

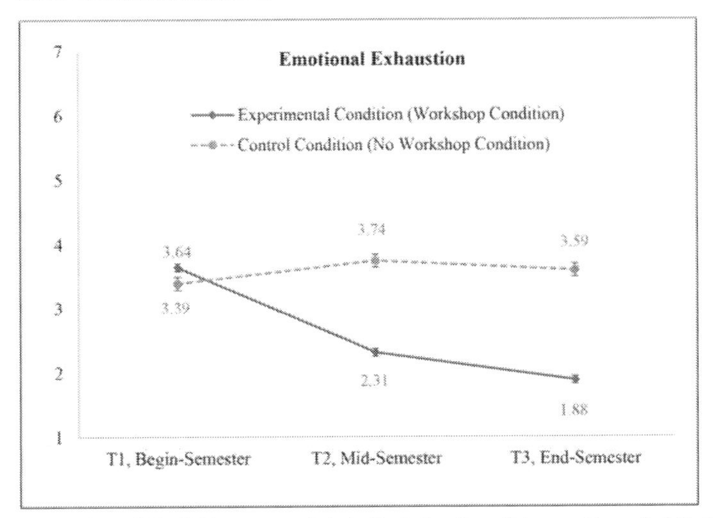

FIGURE 19.3 Teachers' Self-Reports of Job Satisfaction (Upper Panel), Vitality while Teaching (Middle Panel), and Emotional Exhaustion/Burnout from Teaching (Lower Panel) Broken Down by Experimental Condition and Time of Assessment

It is interesting to compare the end-of-semester well-being profiles of the two groups of teachers. By the end of the semester, teachers who participate in the workshop show a terrific well-being profile with high job satisfaction ($M = 5.79$), high vitality ($M = 5.99$) and low emotional exhaustion ($M = 1.88$), while those who teach using "standard practice" show only a blasé profile of moderate job satisfaction ($M = 5.03$) moderate vitality ($M = 4.48$), and moderate burnout (i.e., emotional exhaustion, $M = 3.59$).

Passion for teaching

Passion is a deep involvement in an activity that a person likes (even loves), finds important, values, invests time and energy, and integrates into one's personal identify and self-definition (Vallerand, 2010, 2015). A passionate teacher does not just value and enjoy teaching; he or she embraces "teacher" within the identity (specifically "harmonious passion"; Vallerand, 2015). Teacher participation in the workshop increases the passion for teaching (Cheon et al., 2020; Cheon, Reeve, Jang, & Yu, 2021). As shown in Figure 19.4, teachers who do not participate in the workshop tend to show a fairly high passion for teaching, though it does tend to slip a bit as the semester takes its toll ($Ms = 5.49, 5.42, 5.23$; see dashed line). Teachers who participate in the workshop tend to show the opposite pattern, as they experience a mid-semester upward spike in their passion for teaching ($Ms = 5.22, 6.11, 6.29$; see solid line). It is worth noting how high those end-of-semester passion scores are for teachers who participate in the workshop (i.e., $M = 6.29$ on a 1–7 scale).

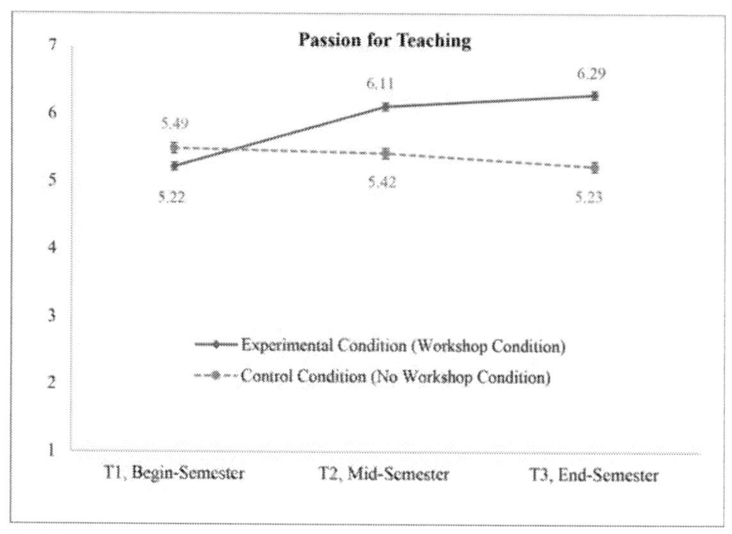

FIGURE 19.4 Teachers' Self-Reports of Passion for Teaching (i.e., Harmonious Passion) Broken Down by Experimental Condition and Time of Assessment
Source: Data are from Cheon et al. (2020).

Relationship satisfaction with one's students

Teachers who learn how to support their students' autonomy report having more positive, satisfying (i.e., high-quality) interpersonal relationships with their students. Relationship satisfaction is a multidimensional construct, as it includes working well together, being happy and content while together, attachment security, an emotional reliance on the other (e.g., "I can turn to this person in a time of need"), inclusion of the other in one's own sense of self, high positive emotionality, and low negative emotionality (Deci et al., 2006). For teachers, relationship satisfaction with one's students is typically expressed rather simply as, "I have a good and satisfying relationship with my students." As shown in Figure 19.5, teachers who participate in the workshop show a steady and meaningful rise throughout the semester in their relationship satisfaction with their students (*Ms* = 5.39, 5.94, 6.28; see solid line; data from Cheon et al., 2020). For teachers who do not participate in the workshop, their relationship satisfaction tends to remain largely unchanged, and it actually deteriorates a bit by mid-term (*Ms* = 5.33, 5.24, 5.24; see dashed line).

Agency

Agency is the teacher's desire, intention, and sense of purpose to find new ways, new opportunities, and new resources to improve as a teacher—to learn, develop, and perform better as a teacher (Bandura, 2006). Agency in one's teaching is rooted in the teacher's personal initiative to develop greater skill and greater capacity. It often takes the form of talking to and learning about teaching with one's colleagues and head teacher, especially those who the teacher considers to be experts. But it mostly

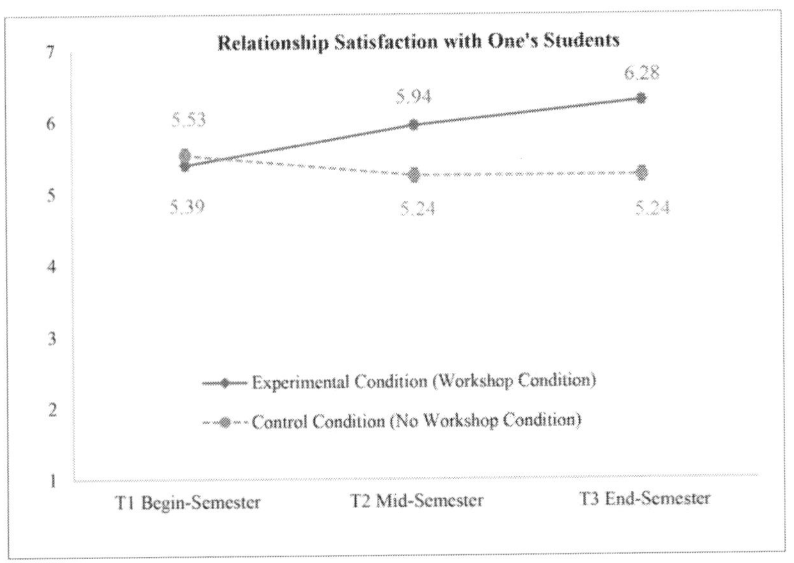

FIGURE 19.5 Teachers' Self-Reports of Their Relationship Satisfaction with Their Students Broken Down by Experimental Condition and Time of Assessment

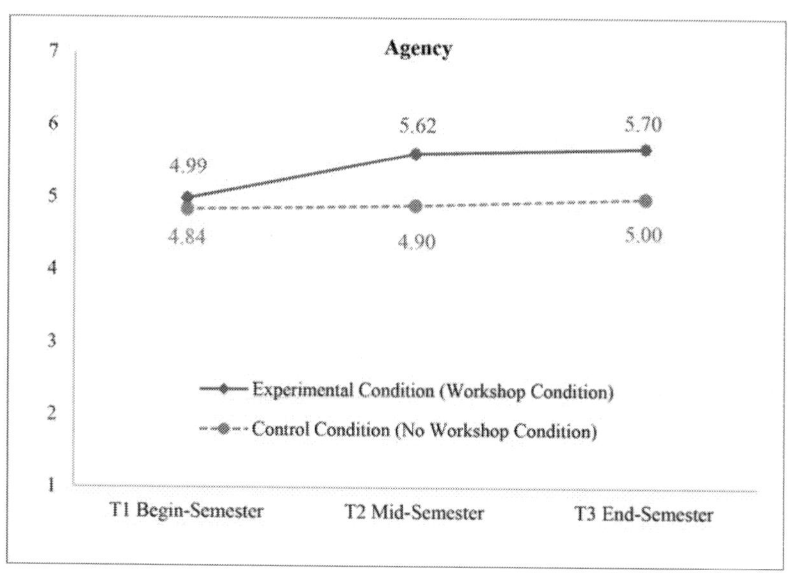

FIGURE 19.6 Teachers' Self-Reports of Teaching Agency Broken Down by Experimental Condition and Time of Assessment

involves a curiosity to find, discover, and invent new and better ways to teach. Such desire opens up a teacher's willingness to generate new opportunities to be autonomy supportive with one's students, to collect formative assessment data from one's students, and to pursue formal and informal professional development opportunities. As shown in Figure 19.6, teachers who participate in the workshop tend to show a steady rise in their sense of agency and initiative to grow professionally as a teacher (*Ms* = 4.99, 5.62, 5.70; see solid line; data from Cheon et al., 2021). For teachers who do not participate in the workshop, their sense of agency tends to remain largely unchanged week-after-week (*Ms* = 4.84, 4.90, 5.00; see dashed line).

ADDITIONAL POSSIBLE TEACHER BENEFITS

The take-away message from the research on teacher benefits is that giving autonomy support is beneficial for teachers, just as receiving it is beneficial for students. Many important teacher benefits have been discovered, but it is possible to imagine some additional teacher benefit candidates that may accrue from greater autonomy-supportive teaching.

Teaching evaluations

It is common practice to have students complete an end-of-course evaluation of the teaching they received, at least in post-secondary classrooms (Marsh, Dicke, & Pfeiffer, 2019). These teaching evaluations typically ask students to rate teachers on their enthusiasm, classroom management, use of technology, organizational clarity, capacity to promote learning, and whether or not the student would recommend the teacher to a classmate. Autonomy-supportive teaching does lead to higher end-of-course teaching evaluations (Filak & Sheldon, 2003), but this pioneering study was only a correlational study. While this study showed that autonomy-supportive teachers receive better student evaluations than do non-autonomy-supportive teachers, it would be interesting to see if teacher participation in the workshop would show a cause-and-effect relation. It is also worth noting that teacher effectiveness can be measured in multiple ways beyond student evaluations, including principal evaluations, head of department ratings, tenure and promotion decisions, and teaching awards.

Teaching self-concept

Self-concept is the person's self-perceptions of how he or she defines and evaluates the self in a particular domain (e.g., "I am good at teaching"). While self-concept is a complex multidimensional construct, teaching self-concept more narrowly concerns self-perceptions of one's ability in the specific domain of teaching. These self-perceptions are formed through personal classroom experiences and through one's interpretation of these experiences (Marsh & Martin, 2011). When teachers form strong self-perceptions about their abilities as a teacher, these positive self-beliefs become building blocks for a positive teaching self-concept. Once formed, a positive teaching self-concept then predicts that teacher's positive future classroom functioning, such as high teaching performance and a continuation in the profession (i.e., greater retention, lesser attrition). Because receiving autonomy-supportive teaching boosts students' self-concepts as learners (Cheon, Reeve, & Song, 2019), it is reasonable to expect giving autonomy-supportive teaching might similarly boost teachers' self-concepts as teachers.

Anxiety

Teaching is a stressful profession, and this is particularly true for beginning teachers (Newberry & Allsop, 2017). When teaching does not go well, teachers tend to experience emotional exhaustion and burnout. As these experiences accumulate, teachers may begin to build up an anxiety that things will not go well for them in the future. With anxiety, the teacher worries about the unknown, and this emotional unease acts like a flashing warning signal that bad and uncontrollable things might happen. Fortunately, the workshop provides the modeling, guidance, scaffolding, and feedback teachers need to skillfully and successfully address and solve difficult classroom problems, which boosts one's teaching efficacy. Such teaching efficacy, once gained, then quiets, calms, and eventually displaces teaching anxiety (Bandura, 1983). Because participation in the workshop has been shown to increase teaching efficacy, it seems likely that participation in the workshop would similarly decrease teaching anxiety.

CONCLUSION

Giving autonomy support is a beneficence-enriching experience that boosts teachers' personal motivation, well-being, passion, agency, and relationship satisfaction. Given these findings, the vocal high school teacher from all those years ago might rest comfortably because, yes, teachers benefit too.

Part 6

Getting started

Can all teachers become autonomy supportive?

In each workshop—like the one we conducted in the school featured in Figure 20.1, our intention is always the same—namely, to help all teacher-participants work through the developmental process of upgrading the quality of their classroom motivating style. That is, we try to support this professional growth experience in 100% of teachers. After the semester or academic year is over and after we have looked at all the data collected during the experiment, the consistent finding is that almost all teacher-participants do indeed become more autonomy supportive, as per Chapter 15. But a few do not. Some teachers do not capitalize on the professional development opportunity we offer. They do not bring an autonomy-supportive motivating style with them into the workshop, and they do not leave the workshop with an autonomy-supportive motivating style. So, we ask ourselves, "Why not?" We wonder, "Can *all* teachers learn how to become more autonomy supportive?" or, "Can only some teachers learn how to become more autonomy supportive?"

We also notice a second phenomenon. Even before the workshop begins, teachers show wide individual differences in their classroom motivating styles. Some teachers are naturally autonomy supportive. That is, pre-workshop, these teachers are already highly supportive of their students' classroom autonomy, and this is true before they ever meet our workshop team. Other teachers are sometimes autonomy supportive, but other times not-so autonomy supportive (recall Figure 4.3). Their motivating style seems to fluctuate back and forth. Still, another group of teachers are practically never autonomy supportive. Autonomy support is just not their thing. We wonder, "Why are some teachers more naturally autonomy supportive than are others?"

In our search for answers, we ask teachers these same questions. For instance, we ask, "When you introduce a learning activity to your students, do you do anything special to support their motivation and engagement? Could you tell us what you say and do during instruction to motivate students? Why do you use that particular approach?" Most teachers do make a special effort to support their students' motivation, and most of these teaching practices reflect an underlying theory of teaching that has grown out of years of teaching experience. At some point in the conversation, however, most teachers will pause the conversation to ask why we are ignoring "the elephant in the room." Teachers will widen their eyes and make a special effort to get us to understand what they find to be so obvious—namely, that their approach to motivating students reflects how motivated (or unmotivated) their students are in

DOI: 10.4324/9781003091738-26

FIGURE 20.1 School in Ventanilla Callao, Peru (north of Lima)

the first place. They say that it is difficult to motivate an unmotivated student: "How can you motivate a student who just doesn't want to be there in the first place?"

This is an excellent question. Teachers clearly react to and are affected by students' motivation, but it is equally true that students react to and are affected by teachers' motivating styles. Recognizing this, Chapter 21 focuses on student tendencies toward low motivation and an unwillingness to take either personal initiative or personal responsibility for their own learning. This chapter, however, focuses on teachers themselves.

A teacher needs two critical ingredients to be able to advance his or her classroom motivating style up to the status of a "best teacher" or a "motivating teacher" (Chapter 2). The first is information, "how to" models, guidance, mentoring, feedback, and reflection on what skills are needed to become a highly supportive teacher. This is what the workshop provides. The second is the motivation to develop that teaching skill. To become highly skilled, the teacher needs to go into the workshop saying, "I want this; I want to learn how to support my students' motivation—better, more fully, and more authentically." This is what the teacher provides.

Every teacher wants their students to be more motivated. Every teacher wants their students to engage in and benefit from the learning activities the teacher provides. Given this, the two key questions are Where does this student motivation come from? and How might a teacher best create or support that motivation? We have found that three characteristics lead teachers to answer these two questions differently (and to have different reactions to the workshop experience). The first teacher characteristic is the teacher's personality, as some personality characteristics lead teachers to favor an autonomy-supportive style, whereas other personality characteristics lead teachers away from an autonomy-supportive style. The second is the teacher's culture, as some cultures (or schools or communities or nations) lead teachers to favor an autonomy-supportive style while other cultures lead teachers away from autonomy-supportive teaching practices. The third is the teacher's desire for professional development, as some teachers are passionate about discovering new ways to upgrade their classroom effectiveness while others are less motivated to embrace these same opportunities.

PERSONALITY

Personality refers to individual differences in patterns of thinking, feeling and behaving. Like everybody else, teachers differ in their characteristic thoughts, emotions, and behaviors. For instance, the "Big Five" personality characteristics of extraversion, neuroticism, openness to experience, agreeableness, and conscientiousness exemplify such teacher-to-teacher differences.

Agreeableness, openness to experience, an autonomy causality orientation, and the personal growth striving are four personality characteristics that predict which teachers are most likely to (1) harbor a naturally occurring autonomy-supportive motivating style and (2) respond favorably to the autonomy-supportive message built into the workshop experience (Reeve, Jang, & Jang, 2018). Authoritarianism, a control causality orientation, and closed-mindedness, on the other hand, are three personality characteristics that predict which teachers are most likely to (1) harbor a skeptical view of autonomy-supportive teaching and (2) respond unfavorably (with resistance and counter-arguments) to the workshop's message (Reeve, 1998; Reeve et al., 2018; Van den Berghe, Tellir, Cardon, Aelterman, & Haerens, 2015; Van den Berghe et al., 2013).

Personality characteristics that orient toward autonomy-supportive teaching

Agreeableness is a general concern for social harmony and for getting along well with others (e.g., being considerate, trusting, and willing to compromise). High agreeableness tends teachers toward autonomy support because it helps teachers cope with students' problems (e.g., disengagement, misconduct, and poor performance) by listening, understanding, being patient, and accepting expressions of negative affect as okay.

Openness to experience is a general appreciation to embrace a variety of experiences and to be intellectually curious, creative, and unconventional. High openness to experience tends teachers toward autonomy support because it attracts teachers to new and non-traditional ways of motivating students (i.e., try to support students' motivation, rather than control their behavior).

The *autonomy causality orientation* is a belief that what causes and what best regulates people's behavior are their inner guides (e.g., needs, interests, and personal goals). An autonomy orientation tends teachers toward autonomy support because the teacher believes that internal causalities are the most reliable and effective sources of motivation and hence to favor instructional practices such as supporting students' intrinsic motivation and internalizations.

A *personal growth striving* is a desire to reach one's potential and a willingness to change oneself (i.e., "grow") to gain greater self-knowledge and personal effectiveness. A personal growth initiative opens teachers up to be responsive to opportunities for self-improvement and to new opportunities for professional growth (e.g., the workshop).

While all four of these personality characteristics predict teachers' natural tendency to favor autonomy-supportive teaching, an autonomy causality orientation and the personal growth striving seem to be the key factors behind teachers' favorable reaction to the workshop's professional development opportunity (Reeve, Jang, & Jang, 2018). The workshop's two-fold message is that, first, students possess inner guides (i.e., psychological needs, intrinsic motivation, and desire for healthy internalizations) that are fully capable of motivating their behavior and, second, what they need most from their teachers is support for these inner guides. Teachers with an autonomy causality orientation and teachers with a strong personal growth striving are mostly likely to cognitively assimilate this message, respond favorably to the recommended instructional behaviors, and take the action necessary (e.g., deliberate practice) to become more autonomy supportive toward their students.

Personality characteristics that orient away from autonomy-supportive teaching

Authoritarianism is the belief that subordinates should submit to and obey authority figures. Out of this belief, authoritarian teachers emphasize conformity to prevailing social norms, submission to legitimate authority, and the necessity of sometimes using coercion to ensure conformity (Altemeyer, 1998).

The *control causality orientation* is a belief that what causes and what best regulates people's behavior are external guides (e.g., attractive rewards, social expectations, and external controls). If a teacher embraces the use of rewards and social controls as effective motivational strategies, then a controlling style will sound more appealing and effective than will an autonomy-supportive style.

Need for closure represents an intolerance for uncertainty and an aversion to ambiguity, and it is often described by closed-mindedness. To achieve certainty, teachers with a high need for closure prefer simplified, straight-forward instructional scripts that produce high predictability, which is the opposite of open-ended autonomy-supportive strategies, such as "What would you like to do?"

For teachers high in authoritarianism, control causality orientation, and need for closure, the information and recommended teaching practices featured in an autonomy-supportive workshop tend to conflict with and be contrary to what they understand to be true about student motivation. Beliefs that students should obey authority figures (teachers), that student motivation is best regulated by social controls, and that teachers should implement simplified ("Do this") instructional scripts limit the acceptability of the workshop's autonomy-supportive message. To teach differently would be to teach in a way that was too permissive, would leave students unnecessarily soft, and would fail to prepare one's students for the real world. For these teachers, their workshop experience is often characterized more by cognitive resistance than it is by cognitive assimilation.

We have found two ways to help this subset of teachers to accept rather than to reject the workshop message. The first is for the workshop team to practice what they teach—to listen to the teacher, to understand their counter-priorities, to accept their reactions as valid, and so forth. The second has been to expand the workshop to include principles of motivation and teaching with which they would be more likely to endorse, such as competence support (i.e., teacher-provided structure). Workshops have been designed and implemented to help teachers learn both competence-support and autonomy-support together (recall Chapter 13). The teaching recommendation to "provide structure in an autonomy-supportive way" has been highly successful (Cheon, Reeve, & Song, 2019; Cheon, Reeve, & Vansteenkiste, 2020), and part of the reason for this success is because teachers who tend toward authoritarianism, a control causality orientation, and closed-mindedness can accept a message of autonomy support—so long as it recognizes the importance of and the need for high classroom structure.

CULTURE

Cultures vary in their values, priorities, ideals, and definitions of success, and cultures use these aspirations to set expectations, establish norms, prescribe attitudes toward authorities, legitimize hierarchies, and communicate what is desirable and acceptable. This view of culture applies equally well to the local school community as it does to the national ethos. Through these processes, the culture in which the teacher lives and works can affect what acts of instruction he or she believes represent "best practices." For instance, teachers in hierarchical cultures tend to prioritize (or "value") group needs and submission to authority over individual needs and personal agency. These teachers may lean toward controlling teaching practices and away from autonomy-supportive practices, as they tend to embrace authoritative control as an effective pathway to produce cultural priorities such as students' discipline, academic achievement, and entrance to prestigious schools (Ng, Pomerantz, & Deng, 2014; Yu, Chen, Levesque-Bristol, & Vansteenkiste, 2018). In contrast, teachers in more egalitarian cultures (e.g., a Montessori educational system) tend to prioritize individual needs and student agency over group needs and submission to authority. In doing so, these teachers tend toward autonomy-supportive teaching practices as an effective pathway to nurture educational priorities such as students' personal interests, agency, and self-determination (Lillard, 2019).

Cultural values that orient away from autonomy-supportive teaching

The core features of autonomy-supportive teaching are a student focus, an understanding tone, and a willingness to take the students' perspective. Some cultures (e.g., hierarchical cultures), however, do not necessarily endorse or embrace these three building blocks of autonomy-supportive teaching. In a hierarchical culture, what is valued is for authority figures (i.e., teachers) to adopt a teacher focus that pursues teacher-emphasized priorities communicated through an authoritarian tone to legitimize the teacher's authority to trump (override) the student's personal interests and need for autonomy (Chao, 1994; Stewart, Bond, Kennard, & Zaman, 2002). The idea: The teacher, as a representative of the culture, knows what is best for the student. Because autonomy-supportive instructional behaviors flow out of a student focus, understanding tone, and taking the perspective of minors, membership in a culture that disfavors such practices could serve as a limiting condition to autonomy-supportive teaching.

The pushback against culturally-endorsed controlling teaching practices is this: Students in practically any global classroom benefit from autonomy-supportive teaching (Chirkov & Ryan, 2001; Downie, Koestner, ElGeledi, & Cree, 2004; Nalipay, King, & Cai, 2020; Taylor & Lonsdale, 2010; Zhou, Ma, & Deci, 2009). This occurs because students in practically any culture benefit from the volition-rich experiences of autonomy need satisfaction that autonomy-supportive teaching affords (Chen et al., 2015; Chen, Vansteenkiste, Beyers, Soenens, & Van Petegem, 2013). If one recognizes these near universal benefits, then it makes sense to ask why teachers all around the globe do not respond more favorably to autonomy-supportive teaching. There may be many answers to this question, but one is the teacher's deeply held values.

Value or skill?

A *value* is a guiding principle about what is desirable and important in life (Rokeach, 1973). Values are typically picked up through a socialization process, as when a person identifies with important people in the culture and then "takes on" those values and characteristics that the role model deems to be desirable or important. Once a person embraces a societal value as their own, he or she then has a guide to show the way to what is good, attractive, and worth pursuing in life. A good example of how a cherished cultural value can guide a teacher's classroom motivating style can be found in the Asian concept of filial piety (i.e., reverence for one's elders—and the values they hold). The more one values certain forms of filial piety, such as valuing obedience to elders, the more sense it makes to embrace controlling teaching practices that tell students to (a) obey teachers, (b) submit to authority, and (c) fulfill their societal duties and obligations. However, filial piety can also be focused on respect and care for the elderly, in which case it is more compatible with autonomy-supportive classrooms (Pan, Gauvain, & Schwartz, 2013).

A *skill* is an ability to do something well. It is the capacity to use one's knowledge, experience, and training to perform effectively in a particular domain, such as teaching. Skills are typically picked up through a training process, as when the person is mentored in the "how to" of that particular skill. Skills are therefore deeply rooted in training and hours of deliberate practice.

One's value system provides a nice starting point to forge a motivating style. With one's values as an anchor, the teacher can decide what approach to teaching is good, attractive, and worth pursuing (i.e., what represents "best practices"). With such an anchor in place, the teacher can then be open to skill-based suggestions and tips in how to improve what they already value. If someone visited their class, understood what they valued and were trying to do, and had the experience and expertise to suggest a new-and-improved way to accomplishing their goals, then the outsider's input would be a good and welcomed event. If the outsider really knew something that the teacher did not know and if the outsider were willing and able to show them step-by-step how to teach in that skill-based way (e.g., how to use the interactive menti technology introduced in Chapter 6), they would likely be open to that. They would feel that the outside expert was not trying to change their values and motivating style but, instead, show them a new way to solve a problem that they had not been able to solve on their own.

That is essentially the role we put ourselves in each time we meet a new group of teachers. When we explain the benefits of autonomy-supportive teaching, we acknowledge the role of personal values in motivating style. We do not try to change teachers' values. But values can be honored and pursued in one of two ways. The first way is to take the students' perspective, provide an explanatory rationale for what we value, acknowledge students' negative feelings associated with fulfilling that value, rely on invitational language, and display patience as students work through the internalization process of creating personal value within that societal value. This is an autonomy-supportive approach to internalizing cultural values. But there is a second and problematic way to promote this same socialization process. This second way is to take only the teacher's (the culture's) perspective, utter directives without explanations, counter and try to change students' negative feelings and expressions of resistance against the recommended value or way of behaving, rely on pressuring language, and display impatience to push and shame students into believing and doing what they are told to believe and do. Here, the problem is not with the value, but with the motivating style used to promote the value.

DESIRE FOR PROFESSIONAL DEVELOPMENT

In conducting workshops around the globe, we have noticed that different nations vary in how strongly their teachers desire, seek out, and respond favorably to opportunities for professional development. Teachers in China, Singapore, and Korea, for instance, are generally passionate about professional development (Tan, 2013), while we have observed that teachers in some other nations take a less enthusiastic attitude toward these same opportunities. When teachers desire professional development, they are more likely to ask question, seek out resources, work with mentors, participate in learning communities, and basically go the extra mile. Similarly, teachers in the same school often vary in their desire for professional development. To assess such motivation, researchers ask teachers, "How motivated are you, personally, to participate in professional development opportunities?"

Few studies have been conducted on whether a teacher's desire for professional learning might moderate the workshop's benefits. One might expect that teachers with a strong desire for professional development would benefit more from the workshop experience than would teachers with a lesser desire for professional development. What the research shows, however, is that teachers with a strong desire for professional development come into the workshop with a big head start on how motivationally supportive they already are, compared to teachers with a lesser desire for professional development. What the desire for professional development does is to motivate the teacher to pursue a career-long trajectory of seeking out and taking advantage of opportunities to improve their motivating style. Constantly, these teachers talk to their colleagues, get advice from master teachers (or their department head), seek out role models to emulate, read books and view videotapes, collect classroom data, and so forth. As a result, these teachers tend to walk into the workshop with an already-developed supportive motivating style. They leave the workshop more autonomy-supportive than before (they advance from moderately autonomy-supportive to highly autonomy-supportive), but teachers with a lesser desire for professional development also leave the workshop more autonomy-supportive than before, though they tend to advance from not autonomy-supportive to moderately-autonomy-supportive. What this means is that both groups of teachers benefit from their participation in the workshop, though the two groups of teachers may nevertheless leave the workshop with different levels of autonomy-supportive teaching.

ADAPTING THE WORKSHOP

Over the years, we have listened carefully to teachers' suggestions as to how the workshop experience might be improved to better speak to their needs, personalities, and priorities. Teachers who harbor some personality characteristics, live in relatively authoritarian cultures, and endorse behavior modification techniques have told us about their barriers, doubts, and misgivings that work against greater autonomy-supportive teaching. This is why, for example, we now affirm in each workshop that teachers' needs, goals, and priorities are important in the same way that students' needs, goals, and priorities are important. That is, we have adapted the workshop so that it supports not only what students need and benefit from the most (i.e., high autonomy support) but also what teachers need and prioritize the most (i.e., high structure). As we have done a better job of speaking to teachers' concerns and doubts, we have found that practically all teachers benefit from the workshop experience.

CONCLUSION

Almost all teachers who participate in the workshop experience meaningful benefits. Still, a few do not. Of the three possible limiting conditions of personality, culture, and desire for professional development, only authoritarian and control-oriented personality characteristics have been shown to explain who rejects the autonomy-supportive message within the workshop. Recognizing this, we have made adaptations to the workshop over the years to accommodate to teachers' a priori preferences and values, such as spending more time on the teaching skill of "provide structure in an autonomy-supportive way."

CHAPTER 21

Must teachers do all the work?

It is difficult to support motivation when one sees little motivation to support. Skeptical teachers ask, "Why would I 'invite students to pursue their personal interests,' when students say that they are not interested in anything related to the course?" Skeptical teachers ask, "Why would I ask students, 'What would you like to do?,' when they respond with stone-silence, by twirling their pencils nervously, and by looking at the floor to avert my inquiring eyes?" In these cases, the teacher feels that their efforts to support students' motivation have run into a roadblock.

Consider a typical classroom episode. The teacher gets things started by introducing a learning activity and by making an engagement request. Students, in turn, react with perhaps a low level of enthusiasm and engagement. The more passive students are, the more unilateral the teacher's instruction tends to be. Teachers come to feel that they have to initiate and direct all the activity and thinking. It is no wonder that when this happens teachers get the sense that they must do "all the work" in the classroom. This becomes tiresome and depleting. When in contrast students speak up to express their preferences, a two-way relationship begins to emerge in which what the teacher says and does affects what students say and do, and vice versa (Patall, Kennedy, Yates, & Vallin, 2020; Reeve, 2013). Both parties feel like they matter. The more proactive students are, the more back-and-forth and collaborative instruction tends to be, which is not only more satisfying for the student but for the teacher as well. Instruction becomes a shared journey.

STUDENT PASSIVITY VS. AGENTIC ENGAGEMENT

Sometimes students are passive rather than agentic. The passive student just sits silently, avoids asking questions, offers little or no input, and essentially does what he or she is told—but little more than that (Jang, Kim, & Reeve, 2016). The passivity of students can pull teachers into a directive style, as in the cycle above, just to make things happen.

Such passivity is not defiance or rebellion; it is a motivational, rather than a behavioral, concern. For whatever reasons, students are not feeling able or empowered to voice their questions, interests, or needs.

Such passivity is a problem because it self-sabotages the student's prospects for academic progress. It gives teachers few clues, and at the end of the day it leaves

DOI: 10.4324/9781003091738-27

TABLE 21.1 The Five-Item Agentic Engagement Questionnaire (AEQ)

AEQ
Instructions. Please respond to each of the following statements by indicating the degree to which you agree or disagree with the statement as it applies to your experience in this particular class.

	Strongly Disagree			Moderately Agree			Strongly Agree
1. I let my teacher know what I need and want.	1	2	3	4	5	6	7
2. I let my teacher know what I am interested in.	1	2	3	4	5	6	7
3. During this class, I express my preferences and opinions.	1	2	3	4	5	6	7
4. During class, I ask questions to help me learn.	1	2	3	4	5	6	7
5. When I need something in this class, I'll ask the teacher for it.	1	2	3	4	5	6	7

students with a sense that they did little or nothing at school that was interesting, worthwhile, or need satisfying.

In contrast, an agent is someone who acts to improve his or her circumstances and surroundings (Bandura, 2006, 2018). Improving one's circumstances means taking the initiative to create a more favorable learning environment for oneself. For students in the classroom, such agency has been studied as *agentic engagement*. To communicate what agentic engagement is and how students express it in the classroom, Table 21.1 provides the five items on the Agentic Engagement Questionnaire (AEQ; Reeve, 2013). Like the questionnaires introduced in Chapter 5, the AEQ has been translated into several different languages.

Agentic engagement refers to students' actively contributing into the flow of instruction they receive (Patall, Pituch, Steingut, Vasquez, Yates, & Kennedy, 2019; Reeve, 2013). When students give voice to their inner motivations (e.g., interests, preferences, and needs) and when students ask questions to help them learn, they make a constructive contribution into the flow of instruction by changing how the teacher interacts with them. When students offer their input (e.g., "Teacher, could we practice this language in a real setting, and not just memorize note cards?"), then teachers become increasingly aware of what students want, need, and are interested in doing. Knowing this, teachers are in a better position to bend (adjust, transform, alter, improve, enrich, and calibrate) their lessons in a direction that is increasingly relevant to and supportive of their students' expressed interests, preferences, and goals. When students do not offer such input, the teacher goes into the lesson guessing—not knowing what students want, need, and feel. It is through their agentic engagement that students begin to enrich and personalize what they are to learn and the circumstances under which they learn it.

TABLE 21.2 Illustrative Examples of Students' Agentic Engagement

Act of Agentic Engagement	Illustrative Student Quotation
Let the teacher know what you want.	"I want to learn how to paint."
Let the teacher know what you are interested in.	"I am interested in Stonehenge."
Express a preference.	"Reading Shakespeare is nice, but I would prefer to watch the movie version. May we do that?"
Offer input.	"Could we practice this language in a real setting, and not just memorize note cards?"
Make a suggestion.	"A trip to the computer lab would be helpful; could we do that?"
Make a recommendation.	"Can we start with a demonstration?"
Ask for a say in what to do and how to do it.	"May we work with a partner?"
Generate options.	"I would like to add a drawing to my essay; may I do that?"
Ask "why?" questions.	"Why do we need to wear these safety goggles?"
Ask a question to help you learn.	"I don't get it; why is the periodic table arranged in these columns and rows?"
Ask for support and guidance.	"Could you show me how to do this?" "Could you give an example?"
Ask the teacher for needed resources.	"Could we have a little more time?"
Recommend a goal to pursue.	"I want to learn all 12 cranial nerves."
Personalized the learning experience.	"Learning about the economy is interesting. Can I do a special project on the stock market?"
Communicate likes and dislikes.	What I like most about painting is mixing the colors."

To illustrate how students contribute constructively into the classroom flow (and to elaborate on the AEQ items in Table 21.1), Table 21.2 provides 15 examples of what agentically engaged students say and do during instruction. These examples illustrate what agentic engagement looks and sounds like in the classroom. Each example is paired with an illustrative student quotation (borrowed from Reeve & Shin, 2020).

The agentic behaviors featured in Table 21.2 illustrate the means through which students begin to forge a working partnership with their teacher. In each case, the students' initiative is proactive, reciprocal, and constructive (Reeve & Shin, 2020).

Agentic engagement is *proactive* in that the student takes the initiative to "make a difference" in their own learning and learning conditions (e.g., "Teacher, as we talk about the solar system, can we also talk about life on Mars?"). When teachers encourage and respond positively to such initiative, such agency gives some life to the forthcoming learning opportunity (Pineda-Baez, Manzuoli, & Sanchez, 2019). Before the upcoming learning opportunity becomes set, students can make a suggestion, offer some input, and express a preference. In doing so, it becomes more likely that the teacher will take these suggestions to heart to bend the lesson in a direction that becomes more relevant to the student's interests and goals. Continuing the example above, when the teacher announces that the day's lesson will be on the solar system, the agentically engaged student might ask the teacher if she will address the question as to whether life on Mars is really possible. To the extent that the teacher accommodates the student's expression of interest, the odds increase that the student will find the day's lesson to be interesting and personally relevant.

Agentic engagement is *reciprocal* in that the student's input and suggestions affect and transform what the teacher says, does, and provides (Fitzpatrick, O'Grady, & O'Reilly, 2018). For instance, the agentically engaged student might voice a privately held motivational state (e.g., "I am interested in space travel!"). What the agentically engaged student seeks is a pattern of teacher-student interaction that features reciprocal causation, which means that what students do (display engagement) affects and transforms what teachers do (provide instruction) and vice versa (Sameroff, 2009). The student is trying to work collaboratively with the teacher to create for himself or herself more need-satisfying, interest-relevant, and personally valued learning conditions.

Agentic engagement is *constructive* in that its purpose is to catalyze students' academic progress, high-quality motivation, and supportive learning environment (Bandura, 2006; Reeve, 2013). If the students' input is off topic, then it is something other than agentic engagement (e.g., distraction, avoidance, defiance, or complaining). Agentic engagement is on-task, as students are trying to produce important educational benefits for themselves.

BENEFITS OF AGENTIC ENGAGEMENT

Agentic engagement is a student-initiated pathway to (1) recruit autonomy support from one's teacher; (2) create opportunities for motivational satisfaction, and (3) make academic progress (Matos, Reeve, Herrera, & Claux, 2018; Patall & Zambrano, 2021; Patall et al., 2019; Reeve, 2013; Reeve et al., 2020; Reeve, Jang, Shin, Ahn, Matos, & Gargurevich, 2021; Reeve & Tseng, 2011b).

Autonomy support

Agentic engagement is both catalyzed by and catalyzes greater teacher-provided autonomy support. When students express their interests and preferences, teachers tend to become increasingly supportive of their publicly expressed motivations (Fitzpatrick et al., 2018; Matos et al., 2018; Patall & Zambrano, 2021; Reeve, 2013). That is, as students communicate their interests and preferences, teachers become increasingly able to take their students' perspective, appreciate these interests, and support their autonomy more generally. Agentic engagement provides teachers with the information they need to be more autonomy supportive. In contrast, when students are quiet and only passive during instruction, teachers lose an important means to come to know and appreciate what their students want. The more passive students are, the less likely teachers will be able to be autonomy supportive toward them (Reeve et al., 2020). With acts of agency, however, students essentially tell teachers how they can support their autonomy (e.g., Table 21.2).

Motivational satisfactions

Through agentic engagement, students create opportunities to experience motivational satisfaction (Patall & Zambrano, 2021; Patall et al., 2019; Reeve, Cheon, & Jang, 2020; Reeve & Lee, 2014). Agentically engaged students take the action necessary to satisfy their curiosity (e.g., ask the teacher a question, type a query into a computer search), develop their interests (e.g., volunteer for the school play, explore school resources), build their sense of competence and efficacy (e.g., watch an online how-to video of a skilled performance), and attain their personal goals (e.g., seek out and try to master an optimal challenge, spend their free time pursuing that personal goal). Passivity, on the other hand, tends to create deprivation-like conditions, motivationally speaking.

Academic progress

Agentically engaged students make more academic progress than do their passive counterparts. That is, over the course of a semester, agentically engaged students take the action necessary to develop their skills, learn new things, make higher grades, and attain higher academic achievement (Patall et al., 2019; Reeve, 2013; Reeve, Cheon, & Jang, 2020). This academic progress occurs because agentically engaged students tend to have more autonomy supportive teachers and more motivationally satisfying learning experiences.

THE TEACHER-STUDENT RELATIONSHIP

Table 21.3 shows how complementary students' agentic engagement and teachers' autonomy support can be (from Matos et al., 2018). The left side of the table lists several agentic acts of engagement students might display, while the right side lists several acts of autonomy-supportive instruction a teacher might display. What is important to notice is how each act of agency brings out in teachers a corresponding act of autonomy support (and vice versa). That is, the more students let the teacher know what they want and need (Item 1), the more likely it becomes that the teacher will respond to students' wants and needs.

Of course, just because students ask for a say in what to do (Item 7), that does not mean that teachers will actually accept and act on those recommendations. Some teachers will instead argue against such student input (e.g., "No, I am the teacher;

TABLE 21.3 Illustrative Examples of How Students' Acts of Agentic Engagement Tend to Bring Out Greater Teacher-Provided Autonomy Support

What Agentically Engaged Students Say and Do During Instruction	What Autonomy-supportive Teachers Say and Do During Instruction
1. Let the teacher know what you want and need.	1. Take the student's perspective.
2. Tell the teacher what you are most interested in.	2. Invite the student to pursue their personal interests (e.g., need for autonomy, interests, preferences).
3. Express a preference; suggest a goal to pursue.	3. Offer choices and options.
4. Ask "why?" or "why not?" questions.	4. Provide explanatory rationales.
5. Communicate likes and dislikes.	5. Acknowledge and accept expressions of positive and negative affect (i.e., expressions of dislike).
6. Make a suggestion, recommendation, or contribution.	6. Use invitational language.
7. Ask for a say in what to do and how to do it.	7. Allow the time and space the student needs to work in their own way and at their own pace (i.e., display patience).
8. Ask the teacher for help and needed resources.	8. Listen and be responsive to the student's input and initiative.

just do the assignment I gave you."). So, student-initiated agentic engagement is only a potential catalyst to greater autonomy-supportive instruction. For agentic engagement to translate into increased autonomy support, the teacher needs to listen to students, welcome their suggestions, and have the skill and experience to know how to translate, where possible, that student input into productive instruction.

Teacher-student synchrony

One scorecard to diagnose the quality of any teacher-student relationship is the extent to which the two are in sync, are independent, or are in conflict (Reeve, 2015). Two key ingredients into the quality of that relationship are how autonomy-supportive the teacher is and how agentically engaged the students are. When in sync, student agency and teacher autonomy support beget each other. This synchrony takes shape as teachers provide instruction in a motivationally satisfying way that energizes students to speak up to let the teacher know what they want and need. This, in turn, allows teachers to become increasingly willing and able to take their students' perspective and provide instruction in ways that are relevant to students' interests, goals, and values (i.e., autonomy supportive; Reeve et al., 2020). That is, just as autonomy support encourages greater agency, student agency encourages and recruits greater autonomy support (Matos et al., 2018; Reeve, 2013; Reeve et al.,

2021). As interaction partners, the teacher and student come together and benefit each other. They join forces to move the student toward a higher-quality motivation and the teacher toward a higher-quality motivating style. A constructive reciprocal causation emerges. Over time, the two become motivational and environmental assets for each other.

Teacher-student conflict

In conflict, interaction partners move apart, oppose, and undermine each other. The student shows amotivation and passivity (i.e., agentic disengagement) in response to the teacher's controlling motivating style, and the teacher tries to compensate for the students' disengagement with destructive motivational tactics (e.g., commanding, shaming, intimidating, and offering conditional regard). Instead of being in sync, the teacher-student relationship deteriorates into conflict ("me vs. you"). Over time, the two become motivational and environmental liabilities to each other.

Teacher-student independence

If the teacher is indifferent to students' initiatives, students will tend to keep their motivations to themselves, experience mostly need dissatisfaction, and their engagement tends to slip into disengagement (Cheon et al., 2019). Under these conditions, little that students say and do in the classroom is able to pull greater autonomy support out of their teacher. The teacher-student relationship dissolves into two independent actors, as what students do affects little change in what teachers do and vice versa (e.g., "You do your thing, and I'll do mine.").

A MOTIVATIONAL THERMOSTAT IN THE CLASSROOM

Supporting students' agentic engagement is easier to do than supporting students' autonomy. This is because it is easier to support what you can see. That is, as a teacher observes a student engage in a learning activity, it is difficult to see that student's private experience of autonomy while it is not so difficult to see that student's public expression of agentic engagement (e.g., "Does my student speak up and ask questions?").

Even though it is difficult to observe directly, student autonomy has a very close relation to students' agentic engagement, as the latter is simply the publicly observable expression of the former (Skinner, Kindermann, & Furrer, 2009). High agentic engagement is a tell-tale sign that students' needs for autonomy are being satisfied. In this way, students' agentic engagement is like a thermostat hanging on the wall for teachers to monitor. While most thermostats tell teachers the room's temperature, the student agentic engagement thermostat tells the teacher the room's motivation. When they see high levels of student agentic engagement, that means "all is well" (i.e., autonomy is high, the student-teacher relationship is in sync, and students are making progress). When they see only student passivity, that means "all is not well."

HELPING STUDENTS MOTIVATE THEMSELVES

The way to promote students' agentic engagement is to support their autonomy (Reeve et al., 2020). Autonomy support enriches students' motivation to the point that students can fully motivate themselves. When students are able to do this, then the answer to the chapter's title ("Must Teachers Do All the Work?") is, "No." Students who have their autonomy supported tend to become proactive agents who take responsibility for their own learning. When this occurs (e.g., Tables 21.1–21.3), students become fully able to motivate themselves. They also make it easy for a teacher to be autonomy supportive. Such students are always a joy to teach. Perhaps this is one reason that explains the many teacher benefits from autonomy-supportive teaching, such as high job satisfaction and vitality while teaching (recall Chapter 19).

CONCLUSION

With support, students can become architects of their own motivation, learning conditions, and future selves. They do this by leaving behind their academic passivity to become engaged agents. Teachers can help this process along by offering autonomy-supportive teaching.

Teachers' professional development

The primary reason to be autonomy supportive is to empower one's students. Autonomy-supportive teachers do this by providing need-satisfying instruction. But what if we paused for a moment to focus our full attention on the teachers? How might we support and empower teachers, such as those in Figure 22.1?

During their career, teachers encounter a complex reality of rapid changes and uncertainty and face multiple pedagogic, technological, and societal challenges. Daily, teachers confront instructional complexity, suffer from work overload, manage conflicting goals and demands, and do all of this within an ever-present uncertainty of what might happen next. All these professional challenges mean teachers need personal resilience and social support (Vansteenkiste, Aelterman, Haerens, & Soenens, 2019). This chapter addresses opportunities for professional development as a source of social support to help teachers build that personal resilience—the capacity to bounce back from difficulties and setbacks (Skinner, Pitzer-Graham, Brule, Rickert, & Kindermann, 2020)—throughout the three career stages of (1) initial training, (2) a transitional induction stage, and (3) full responsibility for one's own classes.

DAY-TO-DAY TEACHING

What makes a job (or activity) interesting and enjoyable is an intriguing question. In a self-determination theory analysis, interest and enjoyment emerge out of an experience of need satisfaction during activity engagement (Deci, 1992; Krapp, 2002; Tsai, Kunter, Ludtke, Trautwein, & Ryan, 2008). Teaching is enjoyable, satisfying, meaningful, and fulfilling when it is able to produce experiences of autonomy, competence, and relatedness satisfaction. Unfortunately, the reverse is also true in that teaching becomes stressful, overwhelming, and depersonalized when it produces on-the-job experiences of autonomy, competence, and relatedness frustration (Kaplan, 2021).

One framework to understand how day-to-day circumstances affect teachers' need satisfactions and frustrations is to consider sources of support versus pressure (a) from above, (b) from within, and (c) from below (Eyal & Roth, 2011; Pelletier, Seguin-Levesque, & Legault, 2002; Reeve, 2009; Soenens, Sierens, Vansteenkiste, Dochy, & Goossens, 2012).

DOI: 10.4324/9781003091738-28

FIGURE 22.1 Teacher-Led Learning Community in Israel (Faces Blurred Intentionally)

From above refers to the teachers' interactions with principals and school administrators. Principals and department heads provide teachers with resources, words of encouragement, and opportunities for professional development. Principals also, however, sometimes pressure teachers with unilaterally enforced policies, require teachers to teach in a prescribed way, and hold teachers accountable to produce bottom-line results, such as students' achievement and desired behavior.

From within refers to teachers' own personal motivations, beliefs, self-talk, and personality dispositions. Teachers sometimes support or pressure themselves, as through self-encouragement, the pursuit of intrinsic goals, and strengthening their teaching efficacy or, in contrast, through self-criticism, imposing unrealistic standards for perfectionism on themselves, and doubting their capacity for effective teaching.

From below refers to teachers' day-to-day interactions with students. While enthusiastic students are a source of support, daily teaching tends to be stressful when students show little motivation and much misbehavior and interpersonal conflict (Boyle, Borg, Falzon, & Baglioni, 1995). Unmotivated, unengaged, disobedient, and antisocial students can lead teachers to think that they need to exert pressure and control over students, which is a motivating style that can lead to teacher burnout.

Whether the source of support comes from above, within, or below, the more teachers have an experience of feeling supported, the more they tend toward need satisfaction, passion and enthusiasm, teaching efficacy, job satisfaction, and an autonomy-supportive motivating style; contrariwise, whether the source of pressure comes from above, within, or below, the more teachers have an experience of feeling pressured and constrained, the more they tend toward need frustration, stress, emotional exhaustion, depersonalization, and a controlling motivating style (Bouwma-Gearhart, 2010; Roth, Assor, Kanat-Maymon, & Kaplan, 2007; Sarrazin, Tessier, Pelletier, Trouilloud, & Chanal, 2006; Soenens et al., 2012; Taylor, Ntoumanis, & Standage, 2008).

PRE-SERVICE TEACHER PROGRAMS

Young adults from all around the world enter teacher education programs situated within colleges of education or universities to become a certified, licensed teacher. Within these teacher education programs, teachers-in-training acquire the knowledge, skills, and experience they need to become effective and confident full-time teachers who accept full responsibility for their own classrooms. Beginning teachers need to learn, develop, and refine dozens of teaching skills—from creating a lesson plan through assessing students' work to addressing problems of student misconduct. In addition, teachers-in-training need to work through a process of professional identity construction, helping them understand what it means to be a teacher.

For teacher training to promote skill development and healthy identity construction, it needs to take place in a needs-supportive environment (Kaplan & Madjar, 2017), one that appreciates and actively supports teachers' own needs for autonomy, competence, and relatedness (Evelein, Korthagen, & Brekelmans, 2008). Such an environment may also encourage exploration of issues such as "Who am I as a future teacher?," enable open dialogues regarding professional beliefs and guiding values, and promote a sense of self-actualization (Kaplan, Glassner, & Adess, 2016).

Early in their careers, preservice teachers need to engage in an on-going dialogue to help them explore and clarify their beliefs concerning learning and teaching. A dialogue of this kind is likely to support pre-service teachers' exploration of their goals and values, which is essential for their identity construction and the formulation of an educational-ideological worldview (Kaplan, Glassner, & Adess, 2016; Roth, 2014). Assor (2012) terms this a "Supporting Value/Goal/Interest Examination" process.

Faculty members need to help preservice teachers become familiar with autonomy-satisfying instructional behaviors and how to apply them during instruction. That said, traditional classroom settings in which the teacher provides whole-class instruction can reduce preservice teachers' opportunities to observe and practice autonomy-supportive teaching (Rogat, Witham, & Chinn, 2014). Still, faculty members can invite and listen to preservice teachers' questions and personal goals. They can also introduce preservice teachers to alternative approaches to instruction that make autonomy-supportive teaching easier to do, such as group work, collaborative work, inquiry-based learning, personal projects, teacher-to-whole-class dialogues, and so forth. Faculty members can also introduce preservice teachers to research publications and resources such as videoclips, websites, and guest speakers.

THE INDUCTION YEAR: CROSSING THE BRIDGE FROM TRAINING TO TEACHING

The first year of teaching is one of the most difficult periods in a teacher's career. Young teachers enter the profession imbued with a sense of mission, enthusiasm, and a desire to bring about positive change. They quickly discover, however, that the "real" world of teaching differs considerably from their ideal. Instead, they encounter social, emotional, and pedagogical hardships, and they suffer from heavy teaching workloads and difficult relationships with students (but also with some parents, school administrators, and fellow teachers; De Neve & Devos, 2017; Orland-Barak & Maskit, 2011). Problems at this stage generate experiences of need frustration and may even lead to teachers to drop out of the profession, a troubling phenomenon in many countries (Sperling, 2015).

Because these challenges and stressors are so commonplace, it becomes obvious that beginning teachers need an effective and reliable support system during their first year of teaching. When beginning teachers have access to a needs-supportive context to help them cope with the challenges of the induction stage, they tend to thrive (Fernet, Trépanier, Austin, & Levesque-Côté, 2016; Kaplan et al., 2016; Zach, Sivan, Harari, Stein, & Nabel-Heller, 2015). Such effective and reliable intervention models have been developed (Howe, 2006; Ingersoll, 2012; Ingersoll, Merrill, & May, 2014).

In Israel, for example, the Division of Internship and Induction at the Ministry of Education, in collaboration with academic institutions for teachers' training, created a support framework that offers an internship workshop, in which interns participate during their internship year, and a beginning teachers' workshop, which they take the following year. These groups constitute professional learning communities that provide teachers with opportunities for reflective dialogue and collaborative problem solving. In the workshop, teachers share relevant issues and support one another. Each beginning teacher is also paired with a veteran mentor-teacher from the same school. When provided with such a support system, beginning teachers improve the quality of their teaching, forgo burnout, deal effectively with difficult issues (e.g., student discipline), work successfully through their professional identity construction, and decrease the rate at which they drop out of the profession (Baker-Doyle, 2012; Central Bureau of Statistics, 2019; Fresko & Nasser-Abu Alhija, 2015; Ingersoll, 2012; Thomas et al., 2019).

The mentor is a key source of support (Kaplan, in press). When autonomy-supportive, an accomplished mentor can catalyze a wide range of benefits for beginning teachers, such as a boost in their sense of competence and well-being, teaching enthusiasm, investment in the school, and a sense of self-actualization and perseverance in the profession (LoCasale-Crouch, Davis, Wiens, & Pianta, 2012; Richter et al., 2013; Rots, Aelterman, Vlerick, & Vermeulen, 2007).

The gold standard to support teachers' needs is an in-school learning community. Beginning teachers can come together, along with interns and mentors, to create and maintain their own in-school professional learning community. The community operates with a shared vision, and it facilitates teachers' meaning-making processes and professional identity construction through reflective dialogue.

In Israel, these communities are called Multi Players Induction Teams (MITs). The MITs operate in schools or the local area, are based on collaborative clinical approaches, and work together with policy makers. A new national and international project called Promentors (which is part of the European Union's Erasmus+ Program, 2020-2023; promentors.org) focuses on developing mentors as autonomy-supportive figures. One such model developed at the Kaye Academic College of Education is called *Autonomy Supportive Mentoring: The ABC-C Mentoring Model* (ABC-C stands for Autonomy-Belongingness-Competence-Community) (Kaplan & Israel, 2021). This model helps the beginning teacher experience (a) *relatedness* from trust in his or her mentor and a closeness with members of the learning community, (b) *competence* from the teacher's growing capacity to execute plans, accomplish objectives, and contribute to their students and the school, and (c) *autonomy* by utilizing their inner resources, intrinsic goals, and sense of meaning in their teaching.

In a parallel process, the mentor also tends to experience his or her own sense of need satisfaction from giving autonomy support, contributing to school life, and involving oneself in a meaningful relationship with the new teacher (Kaplan & Israel, 2021). As an illustration, here are the reflections from two participating mentors:

> I learned what the mentor-teacher's role is, especially fostering the mentee's self-determination, and encouraging his personal initiatives. The mentoring experience has brought us into the world of the beginning teacher, a world of loneliness and lack of support. It is very hard to imagine how a teacher who lives in this kind of world can survive without good mentoring that helps him grow and reinforces his motivation, supports his independence and competence, and promotes his worldview...
>
> While participating in the training sessions, I decided to consciously change how I do things in order to better serve the mentee's personal needs and professional development. I tried to help her find her place and give her genuine confidence in order to help her in the more distant future to believe in her skills and abilities, and thus help the teacher to believe in herself and her skills, and to enhance her original and creative thinking.

PROFESSIONAL DEVELOPMENT FOR IN-SERVICE TEACHERS

Practicing (i.e., in-service) teachers catalyze their professional development in two primary ways. First, they participate in formal workshops that last a couple of days and are facilitated by outside experts to help them develop a particular, new, advanced skill. Second, they participate in teacher-led learning communities that are long-term collaborative support groups with their fellow teachers.

Formal professional development

For 2 or 3 days a semester (or academic year), most schools offer their teachers a formal workshop experience that is essentially a short course in a prioritized aspect of teaching. (Alternatively, some schools require teachers to complete 30 hours of diverse professional development activities throughout the year.) In these workshops, the school administrators invite outside experts to provide a structured workshop to advance the full faculty's expertise in a particular area, such as how to use technology in the classroom, incorporate cooperative learning in one's teaching, implement new assessment strategies, incorporate and celebrate diversity and inclusion, prepare students for the 21st century, and improve one's motivating style (as with greater autonomy-supportive teaching!).

Sometimes these professional developmental opportunities are mandatory and externally imposed on teachers, which frustrate teachers' autonomy, especially if teachers are evaluated in some way (Patton, Parker, & Tannehill, 2015). Recognizing the costs of unilaterally imposing such activities on teachers, many schools (a) give teachers a greater say in the highlighted topic, (b) tailor professional development days to teachers' own needs, interests, and goals, and (c) provide opportunities for teachers to collaborate, support, and care for each other's' professional development (Hargreaves & Fullan, 2012; Mikulincer & Parzachevsky Amir, 2020).

Learning communities

Many schools encourage their teachers to come together to create an in-school learning community. A learning community is a teacher-led group whose purpose is to discuss pedagogical matters, consider curricula, work through professional dilemmas, enhance the teaching-learning process, and problem-solve through classroom issues, such as how to promote students' motivation and socio-emotional learning (Lefstein, Vedder-Weiss, & Segal, 2020). These learning communities are highly collaborative, and they are based on the principles of partnership and collegiality. They are support systems that provide teachers with a forum to build their skills, reinvigorate their passion, and support each other (Owen, 2016).

In these communities, teachers within a particular school come together, often based on the grade level or subject matter they teach (see Figure 22.2). The role of the school administration in this kind of community is to support teachers' needs, promote collaboration, give teachers a greater voice and sense of agency, and convey faith in teachers' capacity for leadership and school vision. When productive, a teacher-led learning community generally focuses on the following (Lefstein et al., 2020):

- Solving practical problems, such as specific and pressing concerns that arise in the classrooms of the community's teachers.
- Reliance on reasoning, such as the use of evidence and deep explanations to analyze and interpret what is happening in the classroom and what course of action might be taken.

FIGURE 22.2 Teacher-Led Learning Community in Peru

- A rich representation of what happens in the classroom, such as video recordings of classroom practice or samples of students' work.
- Multi-voiced input, such that different perspectives are presented.
- A combination of support and critique, balancing trust building and collegiality on the one hand while engaging in critical inquiry and problem-solving on the other hand.

When it functions optimally, a professional learning community supports teachers' psychological needs. For instance, the learning community offers:

- Relatedness support, as it is a community founded on trust and partnership.
- Competence support, as it affords teachers opportunities to learn, develop new skills, and use both data and teamwork to solve difficult problems.
- Autonomy support, as it is a community focused on what teachers most value and deem as important, and it is a voluntary and self-chosen activity.

Here are two examples of a successful learning community in action.

Example #1: One of the national initiatives in Israel is "Hashkafa – Teachers as Leaders". It is a comprehensive nationwide initiative to improve the quality of teaching and learning by means of teacher-led learning communities. The communities engage with disciplinary and pedagogical matters and discuss professional dilemmas, authentic issues, motivation-promoting practices, the teaching-learning process, research findings, and more (Lefstein et al., 2020). As they do so, these communities use a variety of methods and learning tools, such as learning together in small groups or in the school plenary (mutual learning), learning through recorded lessons, observing colleagues' lessons or internet lessons, assessing and documenting one's teaching activities, engaging in reflective dialogue, and learning through books and articles (Mikulincer & Parzachevsky Amir, 2020).

Example #2: Tomer Elementary School in Beer Sheva, Israel is part of a network of SDT-based schools led by The Center for Motivation and Self-Determination at the Kaye Academic College of Education. The first years of the program were devoted to learning SDT's principles and constructing a need-supportive environment. The school's administration and teaching staff then developed a systemic educational approach based on the concept of agentic engagement (recall Chapter 21). This professional learning community developed a unique pedagogical and educational approach and a wide range of practices to promote self-determined, autonomously motivated, agentic students who can create a need-supportive environment for themselves. Additionally, the school has assimilated a heutagogical approach promoting self-determination and autonomous learning (Blaschke, Kenyon, & Hase, 2014; Kaplan, Bar-Tov, Glassner, & Back, 2021).

Here are some of the testimonies obtained in a study that accompanied the program (Kaplan et al., in press). In these testimonies, one student reports on her experience with a participating teacher, while two participating teachers report on their learning community, the benefits of an autonomy-supportive climate, and the learning outcomes gained.

STUDENT: "The teacher lets us be very free, think about all kinds of things we would like to do...a sense of 'you do what you want and if you make mistakes it's okay, mistakes happen'...to feel that what we do is in our hands and in no one else's hands and that kind of thing..."

TEACHER: "First of all, the atmosphere is of learning, one teacher learns from the other, none of us came here as an expert who dictates things, we think as a team. In collaboration, we think of an idea, a tool, and develop it. One gives a point to think about, another gives a different angle, from here we manage to develop something and then bring it out [...] each one also gives her point of view and together we manage to create a special plan, which fits our children."

TEACHER: "At first we didn't understand where we were really going...and each time there was a turn of direction while we were moving along. It's like streams of a river. There is a river that we flowed with and every time there was some stream that took us here or there...at the beginning we asked ourselves, where are we going? What are our needs and our students' needs [...] we sat and thought, and reached another destination and another one, and we saw that this had proved itself in our work with the students...we built everything together by thinking together."

CONCLUSION

Supporting teachers' autonomy is important from the training stage through the induction years and into one's work as a schoolteacher. For teachers to develop an autonomy-supportive teaching style, it is important that they experience a sense of autonomy themselves, preferably early in their careers. This can be done by creating a need-supportive environment for teachers. The core message is that teachers are the most significant agents of change in their own professional growth. Outside experts can help, but professional development is at its best when it is teacher-led, highly relevant to teachers' concerns, takes place where teachers work, and is a need-satisfying experience.

CHAPTER 23

Conclusion

In the end, what do we recommend? In one sense we recommend teachers become familiar with, learn about, and develop the skill necessary to enact seven autonomy-supportive instructional behaviors. In another sense, our recommendation is not so detailed. More succinctly, we recommend teachers learn three things—take the students' perspective, support intrinsic motivation, and support internalization. The seven recommended teaching practices are simply our specific answers to the teacher question of how to do these three things. But even that may be too fine-grained and formulaic. Essentially, what we recommend is that teachers strive toward one grand goal, which is to walk into the classroom to offer students an autonomy-supportive motivating style.

WHERE DO I BEGIN?

For those teachers who are interested in improving the quality of their classroom motivating style, the journey has a clear beginning, which is to take the students' perspective. We suggest teachers do this literally and mentally.

Literally, it helps to put yourself into the role of a student. Visit and sit in a classroom the way a student would visit and sit in a classroom. As the student, what is your experience? What goes through your mind? How do you feel? What do you want? If you could raise your hand to make a request of the teacher, what would it be? Wouldn't your experience as a learner be enhanced if the teacher was highly aware of your experience and was further both willing and able to adjust the lesson to speak to your concerns and preferences?

Mentally, trying to "take the students' perspective" exercises the mental capacity of a theory of mind (Estes & Bartsch, 2017). According to a theory of mind, we realize that other people have mental states, such as beliefs, desires, emotions, and intentions and, most importantly, that these ways of thinking, feeling, and wanting can be different from our own. Understanding this, we tend to become less egocentric (i.e., teacher focused) and more able to see things from a different frame of reference. We understand that there are always two valid perspectives within any social interaction.

As you work through these exercises in perspective taking, we can offer two catalysts to help you along the way: (1) Adopt a student focus and (2) adopt an understanding tone (as per Chapter 4). Together, a student focus, an understanding tone, and perspective taking help the teacher advance from "I understand" to "I care"

DOI: 10.4324/9781003091738-29

(e.g., I want to make things better for you). This is empathy and, with empathy, it becomes almost easy or natural to become more autonomy supportive. A teacher who walks into the classroom with perspective taking skill and empathic concern is off to an excellent start on the quest to become an autonomy-supportive teacher.

THE JOURNEY

The journey to become more autonomy supportive is a personal one. It is a professional journey, of course, because teaching is a profession, but it is also a personal one because the nature of the journey depends on where you start from. Some teachers already possess an in-tact autonomy-supportive motivating style. These teachers have the wind at their back throughout the journey. Other teachers, however, start with an indifferent or even a controlling motivating style. These teachers have the wind in their face, because they need to learn not only how to become more autonomy supportive but also how to replace existing indifferent or controlling instructional behaviors with autonomy-supportive substitutes. The journey also depends on the circumstances in which you teach. Teaching agentic kindergartners takes you in a different direction than does teaching passive high schoolers. It also matters if those around you (e.g., your colleagues, the principal, and parents) encourage and support (vs. criticize and resist) your journey to become more autonomy supportive.

Before you set off on your own personal journey, it can sometimes be helpful to hear the stories told by others who have already made this journey. The famous psychologist Carl Rogers explained how he learned to appreciate and support others (Rogers, 1969, p. 236, italics are original):

> I have come to think that one of the most satisfying experiences I know—and also one of the most growth-promoting experiences for the other person—is just fully to *appreciate* this individual in the same way that I appreciate a sunset. People are just as wonderful as sunsets if I can let them *be*. In fact, perhaps the reason we can truly appreciate a sunset is that we cannot control it. When I look at a sunset as I did the other evening I don't find myself saying, 'Soften the orange a little on the right hand corner, and put a bit more purple along the base, and use a little more pink in the cloud color'. I don't do that. I don't *try* to control a sunset. I watch it with awe as it unfolds. I like myself best when I can experience my staff member, my son, my daughter, my grandchildren, in this same way, appreciating the unfolding of a life.

Another who has made this same journey is self-determination theory co-founder Ed Deci. In his decades of work with professionals who had the responsibility of teaching, supervising, and caring for others (e.g., teachers, parents, coaches, managers, physicians, and politicians), Deci identified the question these professionals most wanted answered: "How can I motivate people?" In reply, he cautioned that this was not the best way to think about it (Deci, 1995, p. 236, italics are original):

> ...the answer to this important question can be provided only when the question is reformulated. The proper question is not, 'how can people motivate others?' but rather, '*how can people create the conditions within which others will motivate themselves?*'

Somewhere along your own personal journey, you too will likely discover that "How can I motivate my students?" is the wrong question to ask. It is off-center because it puts the teacher into a position of needing to take the lead and do something to students (e.g., offer an incentive, promise a reward, apply some pressure to steer students in the right direction, take charge in some way, or institute a policy that everyone needs to follow). The reformulated, "How can I create the conditions under which my students will motivate themselves?" is a better frame because it puts the teacher into a position of appreciating and finding ways to support the motivational resources that students already have. Those "conditions," Prof. Deci would say, are to "Provide autonomy support" (see the Youtube video: https://www.youtube.com/watch?v=m6fm1gt5YAM). Deci's primary learning was that high-quality motivation does not come from outside the student (i.e., external motivation created by the teacher) but, instead, is generated from within.

WHERE AM I TRYING TO GO?

Just as every journey has a beginning, every journey has a destination. This journey's destination is to discover and embrace what works—those "best practices" teachers can rely on to realize all those hoped-for student, teacher, and classroom climate benefits. Those best practices are epitomized by an autonomy-supportive motivating style (e.g., the mastery of the seven recommended autonomy-supportive instructional behaviors).

For a journey to be successful, it helps to have "this way" signs posted along the path. The figures in Chapter 15 (e.g., Figure 15.2) provide such road marks. These figures plotted the autonomy-supportive teaching scores of teachers who participated in the workshop (solid lines) against teachers who did not (dashed lines). Throughout Chapter 15, the focus was on the notable improvement in scores shown by teachers who participated in the workshop (i.e., the upwardly rising solid lines). But, here in the final chapter, we would like to expand the focus to highlight the scores of teachers who did not participate in the workshop (i.e., the flat horizontal lines).

Teachers in the no-workshop control condition began the semester or academic year with baseline scores of 4 or 5 (on a 1-7 scale), and these scores remained essentially stable and unchanged over the ensuring months, though a few scores did show a gradual deterioration. The quality of instruction reflected in these "4" and "5" scores was "okay." The instruction was not great, but it was "good enough." These teachers were moderately autonomy supportive, their students were moderately engaged, and teachers' job satisfaction and teaching efficacy were "pretty good." But the lesson to take away from all those flat horizontal lines throughout Chapter 15 is that the average teacher has meaningful room for improvement. Why not become a better teacher as the semester goes along? It can make quite a difference in terms of student, classroom, and teacher benefits when a teacher is able to increase a beginning-of-semester score of "4" up to an end-of-semester score of "6" (recall all the student, classroom, and teacher benefits identified in Chapters 17–19).

In the end, the purpose of this book has been to provide the reader with the knowledge ("What *specifically* could I do?") and the skill ("And *exactly* how do I do that?") needed to advance from "standard practice" up to "autonomy-supportive teaching." We have represented standard practice as the dashed horizontal lines of the control group, while we represent autonomy-supportive teaching as the solid upwardly sloped lines of the experimental group. We hope that we have been able to demystify this professional development journey enough to make the pathway a reasonably clear, appealing, and beneficial one. As you ready yourself to undertake your own personal journey, we can leave you with this assurance: When motivated, every journey is enjoyable.

Glossary of key terms

CHAPTER 1

None.

CHAPTER 2

Autonomy The psychological need to experience personal ownership during one's behavior.

Competence The psychological need to experience effectance during environmental transactions.

Extrinsic goal An outwardly focused pathway of goal pursuit to attain social approval, social status, or extrinsic reward.

Goal A future-focused mental representation of a desired end-state that guides present behavior.

Intrinsic goal An inwardly focused pathway of goal pursuit that opens up frequent opportunities to experience psychological need satisfaction.

Intrinsic motivation The motivation to engage in an activity out of interest and enjoyment; the inherent desire to seek out novelty and challenge, to explore, to take interest in activities, and to extend one's abilities.

Motivation An internal process (e.g., a need, goal, or value) that gives behavior its energy, direction, and persistence.

Psychological need An inherent condition within the central nervous system that must be satisfied for the person to experience personal growth, healthy development, and psychological well-being.

Relatedness The psychological need to experience acceptance and closeness in one's relationships.

Value A guiding principle about what is desirable and important in life.

CHAPTER 3

Professional development A structured learning opportunity (e.g., a workshop) schools provide to help teachers to improve some specific aspect of their teaching.

CHAPTER 4

Autonomy-supportive teaching The teacher adopts a student-focused attitude and an understanding interpersonal tone that enables the skillful enactment of seven autonomy-supportive instructional behaviors that serve two purposes—support intrinsic motivation and support internalization.

Behavioral control The teacher pressures and coerces students to perform prescribed behaviors (e.g., yelling).

Controlling teaching The teacher adopts a teacher-focused authoritarian attitude and an interpersonal tone of pressure to prescribe what students should think, feel, and do, irrespective of what students prefer.

Internalization The process of taking in a societal value, belief, or way of behaving and transforming it into one's own.

Intrinsic motivation The motivation to engage in an activity out of interest and enjoyment; the inherent desire to seek out novelty and challenge, to explore, to take interest in activities, and to extend one's abilities.

Motivating style The interpersonal tone and face-to-face behavior teachers rely on when they try to motivate their students to engage in the learning activities they provide.

Perspective taking The teacher sees and experiences classroom activities as if he or she were the students; the teacher adopts the students' frame of reference.

Psychological control The teacher intrudes on and manipulates students' thoughts and feelings so that students will pressure and coerce themselves into performing teacher-prescribed behaviors (e.g., guilt induction).

Student focus The teacher is curious about and open and attentive to students' interests, preferences, and goals.

Understanding tone The teacher shows that he or she cares about what students are feeling, is paying attention to their concerns, is listening, is "on their side," and is willing to make instructional adjustments to better provide what students want and prefer.

CHAPTER 5

Autonomy-supportive teaching The teacher adopts a student-focused attitude and an understanding interpersonal tone that enables the skillful enactment of seven autonomy-supportive instructional behaviors that serve two purposes—support intrinsic motivation and support internalization.

Controlling teaching The teacher adopts a teacher-focused authoritarian attitude and an interpersonal tone of pressure to prescribe what students should think, feel, and do, irrespective of what students prefer.

Motivating style The interpersonal tone and face-to-face behavior teachers rely on when they try to motivate their students to engage in the learning activities they provide.

CHAPTER 6

Autonomy-supportive dialogue A teacher-student conversation in which students express how they perceive and feel about classroom issues while the teacher listens to, understands, and sympathetically responds to those concerns.

Culturally responsive teaching The teacher connects students' culturally-rooted values and goals, home language, and life experiences to what students are learning and doing in the classroom.

Formative assessment Student-provided feedback that allows the teacher to evaluate what impact his or her instruction is having on students.

Interactive technology Technologies (e.g., smartphones, iPads, digital white-boards) that students can manipulate to gain the information they seek, produce products (e.g., drawings), and organize information (e.g., drag and drop).

Lesson plan A teacher's step-by-step plan of action for that day's classroom instruction, including an instructional goal, a strategy to attain that goal, and a way to measure how well the goal was attained.

Perspective taking The teacher sees and experiences classroom activities as if he or she were the students; the teacher adopts the students' frame of reference.

Student focus The teacher is curious about and open and attentive to students' interests, preferences, and goals.

Understanding tone The teacher shows that he or she cares about what students are feeling, is paying attention to their concerns, is listening, is "on their side," and is willing to make instructional adjustments to better provide what students want and prefer.

CHAPTER 7

Autonomy The psychological need to experience personal ownership during one's behavior.

Interest A psychological-emotional state in which the person is attracted to an activity, as by showing greater attention, concentration, and effort.

Intrinsic goal An inwardly focused pathway of goal pursuit that opens up frequent opportunities to experience psychological need satisfaction.

Intrinsic motivation The motivation to engage in an activity out of interest and enjoyment; the inherent desire to seek out novelty and challenge, to explore, to take interest in activities, and to extend one's abilities.

CHAPTER 8

Autonomy satisfaction Feeling free; feeling a sense of self-direction, personal ownership, and personal endorsement of one's behavior during activity engagement.

Competence satisfaction Feeling effective; feeling a sense of mastery, making progress, and a job well done during activity engagement.

Need satisfaction A sense of fulfillment that one is thriving and psychological well.

Relatedness satisfaction Feeling accepted; feeling a sense of warmth, closeness, and inclusion during an interpersonal interaction.

CHAPTER 9

Internalization The process of taking in a societal value, belief, or way of behaving and transforming it into one's own.

Intrinsic goal An inwardly focused pathway of goal pursuit that opens up frequent opportunities to experience psychological need satisfaction.

Rationale A verbal explanation as to why putting forth effort during an activity is a personally useful thing to do.

CHAPTER 10

None.

CHAPTER 11

Change-oriented feedback Post-performance information the teacher provides that students can use to improve or correct their poor performance or problematic behavior.

Informational language During conversation, the teacher provides the insights, tips, and strategies the student needs to better diagnose, understand, and solve a motivational problem.

Invitational language During conversation, the teacher supports students' initiative and volition by encouraging choice, self-direction, and autonomous self-regulation.

Motivational language A teacher's communication to inspire a student to take action.

Pitch How low vs. high a speaker's voice is perceived to be.

Pressuring language During conversation, the teacher demands students' compliance and immediate action by imposing pressure.

Speech content What the person says—the words spoken.

Speech prosody Tone of voice used while speaking.

CHAPTER 12

Autonomy support The teacher adopts a student-focused attitude and an understanding interpersonal tone that enables the skillful enactment of seven autonomy-supportive instructional behaviors that serve two purposes—support intrinsic motivation and support internalization.

Directive support The teacher offers how-to advice and guidance to help the student attain a goal or change a behavior.

Empathic listening The teacher actively listens to the students' words and feelings while trying to become aware of, understand, and vicariously experience that student input.

Impatience The teacher rushes in to take charge of diagnosing and solving the student's problem.

Laissez-faire Providing little or no guidance; the absence of directive support.

Patience The optimistic calmness a teacher shows as students struggle to start, adjust, or change their behavior.

CHAPTER 13

Competence The psychological need to experience effectance during environmental transactions.

Competence support The teacher offers an interpersonal tone of guidance to support students' effort to develop skill, perform well, and function adaptively; also referred to as "structure."

Discipline Training students to conform to a desired code of behavior, often by cultivating the students' self-control over that desired behavior.

Expectation A desired future achievement that the teacher would like to see the student attain.

Feedback Post-performance information about what one did well or poorly.

Guidance Step-by-step instruction as to how a student might make progress.

Structure The teacher's interpersonal tone of guidance that provides students with the information they need to develop skill, perform well, and function adaptively.

CHAPTER 14

Autonomy-supportive instructional behavior An act of instruction in which the teacher creates an opportunity for students to experience autonomy need satisfaction (e.g., providing a choice).

Dependent variable The condition that changes because of its exposure to the independent variable; the effect.

Independent variable The condition manipulated during an experiment; the cause.

Random assignment Each participant in an experiment has the same chance to be assigned to the experimental or the control condition.

Skill An ability to do something well.

Workshop A brief intensive educational program offered to a group of teachers to help them improve some specific aspect of their teaching.

CHAPTER 15

Dependent variable The condition that changes because of its exposure to the independent variable; the effect.

Effect size A statistic to communicate the magnitude to which an independent variable changed a dependent variable.

Independent variable The condition manipulated during an experiment; the cause.

CHAPTER 16

Conceptual change The cognitive process of changing a belief; a restructuring of one's knowledge so that an existing belief is fundamentally changed or replaced by a way of thinking that is more able to explain phenomena, solve problems, and teach effectively.

Intrinsic instructional goals The teacher's intention to provide instruction in a way that promotes students' personal growth or relationship growth.

Positive beliefs about autonomy-supportive teaching The teacher's conviction that autonomy-supportive teaching is effective, easy, and normative.

Teaching efficacy The teacher's confidence that he or she has "what it takes" to cope with the teaching situation in ways that bring about desired outcomes.

Teaching skill The teacher's mastery of a repertoire on instructional practices that can enhance students' motivation, engagement, and internalization.

CHAPTER 17

Amotivation A state of motivational apathy in which the student possesses little or no reason to invest the energy and effort necessary to learn or accomplish something; literally "without motivation."

Benefit A gain; something that promotes well-being.

Dual-process model A theoretical explanation of how students can simultaneously experience some degree of interpersonal support, need satisfaction, and adaptive functioning on the one hand as well as interpersonal control, need frustration, and maladaptive functioning on the other.

Internalization The process of taking in a societal value, belief, or way of behaving and transforming it into one's own.

Intrinsic motivation The motivation to engage in an activity out of interest and enjoyment; the inherent desire to seek out novelty and challenge, to explore, to take interest in activities, and to extend one's abilities.

Need frustration A sense of obstruction, floundering, and feeling psychological ill.

Need satisfaction A sense of fulfillment, thriving, and feeling psychological well.

CHAPTER 18

Antisocial behavior Volitional action students initiate to harm their classmates (e.g., hitting).

Autonomy-supportive teaching The teacher adopts a student-focused attitude and an understanding interpersonal tone that enables the skillful enactment of seven autonomy-supportive instructional behaviors that serve two purposes—support intrinsic motivation and support internalization.

Bullying Intentional and repeated acts of aggression and intimidation meant to inflict physical, verbal, or relational harm on a relatively powerless victim.

Classroom climate The norms, expectations, roles, priorities, and patterns of communication that prevail in a given classroom to guide students' behavior.

Prosocial behavior Volitional action students initiate to benefit their classmates (e.g., sharing).

Unit of analysis The level of interpretation one relies on to explain a phenomenon—an individual student analysis or a social group-based analysis.

CHAPTER 19

Agency Personal initiative to change one's surrounding environment for the better.

Job satisfaction An overall sense of fulfilment the teacher derives from being a teacher.

Passion Deep involvement in an activity that one loves, values, invests time and energy, and integrates into the personal identity.

Teaching self-concept The teacher's self-perception of how much ability he or she possesses in the domain of teaching.

Vitality The excess psychological energy the teacher feels; feeling "pumped up."

Well-being Feeling good and functioning well.

CHAPTER 20

Culture A society's values, expectations, norms, ideals, and definitions of success as to what is desirable and acceptable for its members.

Personality Stable teacher-to-teacher differences in their patterns of thinking, feeling, and behaving.

Professional development A structured learning opportunity (e.g., a workshop) schools provide to help teachers to improve some specific aspect of their teaching.

Skill An ability to do something well.

Value A guiding principle about what is desirable and important in life.

CHAPTER 21

Agentic engagement The student initiative to create a more favorable learning environment for oneself, including the quality of instruction one receives.

Conflict What one person does affects and harms what the other person does—and vice versa.

Independence What one person does affects little or no change in what the other person does.

Synchrony What one person does affects and benefits what the other person does—and vice versa.

CHAPTER 22

Learning community A group of teachers who come together to discuss their teaching concerns, such as how to provide effective instruction and resolve professional dilemmas.

Mentor An experienced and trusted advisor who provides support and special insights to facilitate the professional development of a less experienced colleague.

Professional development A structured learning opportunity (e.g., a workshop) schools provide to help teachers to improve some specific aspect of their teaching.

Teaching The process of attending to students' needs, experiences, and feelings, and intervening (e.g., listening, explaining, demonstrating, or informing) to promote their learning of something new.

Teacher-in-training A pre-service teacher; a teacher-to-be who is preparing to become a professional teacher by enrolling in an educational program.

CHAPTER 23

None.

References

Aelterman, N., Vansteenkiste, M., & Haerens, L. (2019). Correlates of students' internalization and defiance of classroom rules: A self-determination theory perspective. *British Journal of Educational Psychology*, *89*, 22–40.

Aelterman, N., Vansteenkiste, M., Haerens, L., Soenens, B., Fontaine, J., & Reeve, J. (2019). Toward an integrative and fine-grained insight into motivating and demotivating teaching styles: The merits of a circumplex approach. *Journal of Educational Psychology*, *111*, 497–521.

Ainley, M., Hidi, S., & Berndorff, D. (2002). Interest, learning, and the psychological processes that mediation their relationship. *Journal of Educational Psychology*, *94*, 545–561.

Altemeyer, B. (1998). The other "authoritarian personality". *Advances in Experimental Social Psychology*, *30*, 47–91.

Aronson, B., & Laughter, J. (2016). The theory and practice of culturally relevant education: A synthesis of research across content areas. *Review of Educational Research*, *86*(1), 163–206.

Assor, A. (2012). Allowing choice and nurturing an inner compass: Educational practices supporting students' need for autonomy. In S. L. Christenson, A. L. Reschly, & C. Wylie, (Eds.), *Handbook of research on student engagement* (pp. 421–438). New York, NY: Springer Science and Business Media, LLC.

Assor, A., Feinberg, O., Kanat-Maymon, Y., & Kaplan, H. (2018). Reducing violence in non-controlling ways: A change program based on self-determination theory. *Journal of Experimental Education*, *86*(2), 195–213.

Assor, A., Kaplan, H., Kanat-Maymon, Y., & Roth, G. (2005). Directly controlling teacher behaviors as predictors of poor motivation and engagement in girls and boys: The role of anger and anxiety. *Learning and Instruction*, *15*, 397–413.

Atlas, R. S., & Pepler, D. J. (1998). Observations of bullying in the classroom. *The Journal of Educational Research*, *92*(2), 86–99.

Baker-Doyle, K. (2012). First-year teachers' support networks: Intentional professional networks and diverse professional allies. *The New Educator*, *8*(1), 65–85. DOI: 10.1080/1547688X.2012.641870.

Baldwin, J. D., & Baldwin, J. I. (1986). *Behavior principles in everyday life* (2nd ed.). Englewood Cliffs, NJ: Prentice-Hall.

Bandura, A. (1983). Self-efficacy determinants of anticipated fears and calamities. *Journal of Personality and Social Psychology*, *45*(2), 464–469.

Bandura, A. (2006). Toward a psychology of human agency. *Perspectives on Psychological Science*, *1*, 164–180.

Bandura, A. (2018). Toward a psychology of human agency: Pathways and reflections. *Perspectives on Psychological Science*, *13*(2), 130–136.

Bao, X. H., & Lam, S. F. (2008). Who makes the choice? Rethinking the role of autonomy and relatedness in Chinese children's motivation. *Child Development*, *79*(2), 269–283.

Barber, B. K. (1996). Parental psychological control: Revisiting a neglected construct. *Child Development*, *67*(6), 3296–3319.

Bartholomew, K. J., Ntoumanis, N., Mouratidis, A., & Katartzi, E. (2018). Beware of your teaching style: A school-year long investigation of controlling teaching and student motivational experiences. *Learning and Instruction*, *53*, 50–63.

Bartholomew, K. J., Ntoumanis, N., Ryan, R. M., Bosch, J. A., & Thøgersen-Ntoumani, C. (2011). Self-determination theory and diminished functioning: The role of interpersonal control and psychological need thwarting. *Personality and Social Psychology*, *37*, 1459–1473.

Bartholomew, K. J., Ntoumanis, N., Ryan, R. M., & Thøgersen-Ntoumanis, C. (2011). Psychological need thwarting in the sport context: Assessing the darker side of athletic experience. *Journal of Sport & Exercise Psychology*, *33*, 75–102.

Beckhard, A. (1959). *Albert Einstein*. New York: Putnum.

Blaschke, L. M., Kenyon, C., & Hase, S. (Eds.) (2014), *Experiences in self-determined learning*. United States: Amazon.com Publishing. ISBN 1502785307

Boggiano, A. K., Barrett, M., Weiher, A. W., McClelland, G. H., & Lusk, C. M. (1987). Use of the maximal-operant principle to motivate children's intrinsic interest. *Journal of Personality and Social Psychology*, *53*, 866–879.

Boncquet, M., Soenens, B., Verschueren, K., Lavrijsen, J., Flamant, N., & Vansteenkiste, M. (2020). Killing two birds with one stone: The role of motivational resources in predicting changes in achievement and school well-being beyond intelligence. *Contemporary Educational Psychology*, *63*, 101905.

Borko, H. (2004). Professional development and teaching learning: Mapping the terrain. *Educational Researcher*, *33*(8), 3–15.

Bouwma-Gearhart, J. (2010). Pre-service educator attrition informed by self-determination theory: Autonomy loss in high-stakes education environments. *Problems of Education in the 21st Century*, *26*, 30–41.

Boyle, G. J., Borg, M. G., Falzon, J. M., & Baglioni, A. J. Jr. (1995). A structural model of the dimensions of teacher stress. *British Journal of Educational Psychology*, *65*, 49–67.

Caprara, G. V., Barbaranelli, C., Borgogni, L., & Steca, P. (2003). Efficacy beliefs as determinants of teachers' job satisfaction. *Journal of Educational Psychology*, *95*, 821–832.

Carpentier, J., & Mageau, G. A. (2013). When change-oriented feedback enhances motivation, well-being and performance: A look at autonomy-supportive feedback in sport. *Psychology of Sport and Exercise*, *14*(3), 423–435.

Carpentier, J., & Mageau, G. A. (2016). Predicting sport experience during training: The role of change-oriented feedback in athletes' motivation, self-confidence and needs satisfaction fluctuations. *Journal of Sport and Exercise Psychology*, *38*(1), 45–58.

Carver, C. S., & Scheier, M. F. (1998). *On the self-regulation of behavior*. Cambridge, UK: Cambridge University Press.

Central Bureau of Statistics (CBS) (2019). *Internal mobility and leaving the system among the educational system workers - 2000–2018*. Retrieved on 29.6.19 from: https://www.cbs.gov.il/he/mediarelease/Pages/2019/ (Hebrew or English).

Chao, R. K. (1994). Beyond parental control and authoritarian parenting style: Understanding Chinese parenting through the cultural notion of training. *Child Development*, *65*, 1111–1119.

Chen, B., Vansteenkiste, M., Beyers, W., Boone, L., Deci, E. L., Van der Kaap-Deeder, J., Duriez, B., Lens, W., Matos, L., Mouratidis, A., Ryan, R. M., & Sheldon, K. M. (2015). Basic psychological need satisfaction, need frustration, and need strength across four cultures. *Motivation and Emotion*, *39*, 216–236.

Chen, B., Vansteenkiste, M., Beyers, W., Soenens, B., & Van Petegem, S. (2013). Autonomy in family decision making for Chinese adolescents: Disentangling the dual meaning of autonomy. *Journal of Cross-Cultural Psychology*, *44*(7), 1184–1209.

Cheon, S. H., & Reeve, J. (2013). Do the benefits from autonomy-supportive PE teacher training programs endure?: A one-year follow-up investigation. *Psychology of Sport & Exercise*, *14*, 508–518.

Cheon, S. H., & Reeve, J. (2015). A classroom-based intervention to help teachers decrease students' amotivation. *Contemporary Educational Psychology*, *40*, 99–111.

Cheon, S. H., Reeve, J., Jang, H.-R., & Yu, T. H. (2021). *The path to passion: Becoming more autonomy supportive and adopting intrinsic instructional goals*. Manuscript under review.

Cheon, S. H., Reeve, J., Lee, J., & Lee, Y. (2015). Giving and receiving autonomy support in a high-stakes sport context: A field-based experiment during the 2012 London paralympic games. *Psychology of Sport and Exercise*, *19*, 59–69.

Cheon, S. H., Reeve, J., Lee, Y., & Lee, J.-W. (2018). Why autonomy-supportive interventions work: Explaining the professional development of teachers' motivating styles. *Teaching and Teacher Education*, *69*, 43–51.

Cheon, S. H., Reeve, J., Lee, Y., Ntoumanis, N., Gillet, N., Kim, B. R., & Song, Y.-G. (2019). Expanding autonomy psychological need states from two (satisfaction, frustration) to three (dissatisfaction): A classroom-based intervention study. *Journal of Educational Psychology*, *111*, 685–702.

Cheon, S. H., Reeve, J., & Marsh, H. (2021a). *How autonomy-supportive teaching enhances students' social functioning: A multilevel randomized control intervention to improve the classroom climate*. Paper under review.

Cheon, S. H., Reeve, J., & Marsh, H. (2021b). *A classroom climate bullying reduction program: An autonomy-supportive intervention to reduce bystander reinforcement*. Paper under review.

Cheon, S. H., Reeve, J., & Moon, I. S. (2012). Experimentally-based, longitudinally designed, teacher-focused intervention to help physical education teachers be more autonomy supportive toward their students. *Journal of Sport & Exercise Psychology*, *34*, 365–396.

Cheon, S. H., Reeve, J., & Ntoumanis, N. (2018). A needs-supportive intervention to help PE teachers enhance students' prosocial behavior and diminish antisocial behavior. *Psychology of Sport and Exercise*, *35*, 74–88.

Cheon, S. H., Reeve, J., & Ntoumanis, N. (2019). An intervention to help teachers establish a prosocial peer climate in physical education. *Learning and Instruction*. DOI:10.1016/j.learninstruc.2019.101223.

Cheon, S. H., Reeve, J., & Song, Y.-G. (2016). A teacher-focused intervention to decrease PE students' amotivation by increasing need satisfaction and decreasing need frustration. *Journal of Sport and Exercise Psychology*, *38*, 217–235.

Cheon, S. H., Reeve, J., & Song, Y.-G. (2019). Recommending goals and supporting needs: An intervention to help physical education teachers communicate their expectations while supporting students' psychological needs. *Psychology of Sport and Exercise*, *41*, 107–118.

Cheon, S. H., Reeve, J., & Song, Y.-G. (2021). An autonomy-supportive intervention to help students develop their life skills. Manuscript under review.

Cheon, S. H., Reeve, J., & Vansteenkiste, M. (2020, April). When teachers learn how to provide classroom structure in an autonomy-supportive way: Benefits to teachers and their students. *Teaching and Teacher Education*, *90*. Article 103004.

Cheon, S. H., Reeve, J., Yu, T. H., & Jang, H.-R. (2014). The teacher benefits from giving autonomy support during physical education instruction. *Journal of Sport and Exercise Psychology*, *36*, 331–346.

Chirkov, V. I., & Ryan, R. M. (2001). Parent and teacher autonomy support in Russian and U.S. adolescents: Common effects on well-being and academic motivation. *Journal of Cross-Cultural Psychology*, *32*, 618–635.

Chua, A. (2011). *Battle hymn of the tiger mom*. New York: Penguin.

Cizek, G. J. (2010). An introduction to formative assessment: History, characteristics, and challenges. In H. L. Andrade, & G. J. Cizek, (Eds.), *Handbook of formative assessment* (pp. 3–17). New York, NY: Routledge.

Cohen, J. (1988). *Statistical power analysis for the behavioral sciences* (2nd ed.). Mahwah, NJ: Erlbaum.

Cordova, D. I., & Lepper, M. R. (1996). Intrinsic motivation and the process of learning: Beneficial effects of contextualization, personalization, and choice. *Journal of Educational Psychology*, *88*, 715–730.

Curran, T., Hill, A., & Niemiec, C. (2013). A conditional process model of children's behavioral engagement and behavioral disaffection in sport based on self-determination theory. *Journal of Sport and Exercise Psychology*, *35*, 30–43.

deCharms, R. (1976). *Enhancing motivation: Change in the classroom*. New York: Irvington.

De Meyer, J., Soenens, B., Aelterman, N., De Bourdeaudhuij, I., & Haerens, L. (2016). The different faces of controlling teaching: Implications of a distinction between externally and internally controlling teaching for students' motivation in physical education. *Physical Education and Sport Pedagogy*, *21*(6), 632–652.

De Meyer, J., Tallir, I. B., Soenens, B., Vansteenkiste, M., Aelterman, N., Van den Berghe, L., Speleers, L., & Haerens, L. (2014). Does observed controlling teaching behavior relate to students' motivation in physical education? *Journal of Educational Psychology*, *106*(2), 541–554.

De Neve, D., & Devos, G. (2017). Psychological states and working conditions buffer beginning teachers' intention to leave the job. *European Journal of Teacher Education*, *40*(1), 6–27.

Deci, E. L. (1992). The relation of interest to the motivation of behavior: A self-determination theory perspective. In K. A. Renninger, S. Hidi, & A. Krapp, (Eds.), *The role of interest in learning and development* (pp. 43–70). Mahwah, NJ: Lawrence Erlbaum Associates, Inc.

Deci, E. L. (1995). *Why we do what we do: The dynamics of personal autonomy*. New York: Grosset/Putnam.

Deci, E. L., Eghrari, H., Patrick, B. C., & Leone, D. R. (1994). Facilitating internalization: The self-determination theory perspective. *Journal of Personality*, *62*, 119–142.

Deci, E. L., La Guardia, J. G., Moller, A. C., Scheiner, M. J., & Ryan, R. M. (2006). On the benefits of giving as well as receiving autonomy support: Mutuality in close friendships. *Personality and Social Psychology Bulletin*, *32*, 313–327.

Deci, E. L., Schwartz, A., Sheinman, L., & Ryan, R. M. (1981). An instrument to assess adult's orientations toward control versus autonomy in children: Reflections on intrinsic motivation and perceived competence. *Journal of Educational Psychology*, *73*, 642–650.

Downie, M., Koestner, R., ElGeledi, S., & Cree, K. (2004). The impact of cultural internalization and integration on well-being among tricultural individuals. *Personality and Social Psychology Bulletin*, *30*, 305–314.

Dweck, C. S. (2017). Needs, goals, and representations: Foundations for a unified theory of motivation, personality, and development. *Psychological Review*, *124*, 689–719.

Dweck, C. S., Dixon, M. L., & Gross, J. J. (2021). What is motivation, where does it come from, and how does it work? In M. Bong, S.-I. Kim, & J. Reeve (Eds.), *Motivation science: Controversies and insights*. Oxford, NY: Oxford University Press.

Eckes, A., Großmann, N., & Wilde, M. (2018). Studies on the effects of structure in the context of autonomy-supportive or controlling teacher behavior on students' intrinsic motivation. *Learning and Individual Differences*, *62*, 69–78.

Ericsson, K. A., Krampe, R. T., & Tesch-Romer, C. (1993). The role of deliberate practice in the acquisition of expert performance. *Psychological Review*, *100*, 363–406.

Estes, D., & Bartsch, K. (2017). Theory of mind: A foundational component of human general intelligence. *Behavior and Brain Sciences*, *40*, e201.

Evelein, F., Korthagen, F., & Brekelmans, M. (2008). Fulfillment of the basic psychological needs of student teachers during their first teaching experiences. *Teaching and Teacher Education*, *24*, 1137–1148.

Eyal, O., & Roth, G. (2011). Principals' leadership and teachers' motivation: Self-determination theory analysis. *Journal of Educational Administration*, *49*, 256–275.

Feather, N. T. (1995). Values, valences, and choice: The influence of values on the perceived attractiveness and choice of alternatives. *Journal of Personality and Social Psychology*, *68*(6), 1135–1151.

Fernet, C., Trépanier, S. G., Austin, S., & Levesque-Côté, J. (2016). Committed, inspiring, and healthy teachers: How do school environment and motivational factors facilitate optimal functioning at career start? *Teaching and Teacher Education*, *59*, 481–491.

Filak, V., & Sheldon, K. (2003). Student psychological need satisfaction and college teacher-course evaluations. *Educational Psychology*, *23*, 235–247.

Fitzpatrick, J., O'Grady, E., & O'Reilly, J. (2018). Promoting student agentic engagement through curriculum: Exploring the negotiated integrated curriculum initiative. *Irish Educational Studies*, *37*(4), 453–473.

Flowerday, T., & Schraw, G. (2000). Teacher beliefs about instructional choice: A phenomenological study. *Journal of Educational Psychology*, *92*, 634–645.

Flunger, B., Mayer, A., & Umbach, N. (2019). Beneficial for some or for everyone? Exploring the effects of an autonomy-supportive intervention in the real-life classroom. *Journal of Educational Psychology*, *111*(2), 210–234.

Fredrickson, B. L. (2009). *Positivity: Top-notch research reveals the 3-to-1 ratio that will change your life*. New York: Three Rivers Press.

Fresko, B., & Nasser-Abu Alhija, F. (2015) Induction seminars as professional learning communities for beginning teachers. *Asia-Pacific Journal of Teacher Education*, *43*(1), 36–48, DOI: 10.1080/1359866X.2014.928267

Froiland, J. M., & Oros, E. (2014). Intrinsic motivation, perceived competence and classroom engagement as longitudinal predictors of adolescent reading achievement. *Educational Psychology*, *34*, 119–132.

Froiland, J. M., & Worrell, F. C. (2016). Intrinsic motivation, learning goals, engagement, and achievement in a diverse high school. *Psychology in the Schools*, *53*(3), 321–336.

Galinsky, A. D., Ku, G., & Wang, C. S. (2005). Perspective-taking and self-other overlap: Fostering social bonds and facilitating social coordination. *Group Processes & Intergroup Relations*, *8*(1), 109–124.

Gaspard, H., Dicke, A.-L., Flunger, B., Brisson, B. M., Hafner, I., Nagengast, B., & Trautwein, U. (2015). Fostering adolescents' value beliefs for mathematics with a relevance intervention in the classroom. *Developmental Psychology*, *51*, 1226–1240.

Gorin, A. A., Powers, T. A., Koestner, R., Wing, R. R., & Raynor, H. A. (2014). Autonomy support, self-regulation, and weight loss. *Health Psychology*, *33*, 332.

Gottfried, A. E. (1985). Academic intrinsic motivation in elementary and junior high school students. *Journal of Educational Psychology*, *20*, 205–215.

Gregoire, M. (2003). Is it a challenge or a threat? A dual-process model of teachers' cognition and appraisal processes during conceptual change. *Educational Psychology Review*, *15*, 147–179.

Grolnick, W. S., Deci, E. L., & Ryan, R. M. (1997). Internalization within the family: The self-determination theory perspective. In J. E. Grusec & L. Kuczynski (Eds.), *Parenting and children's internalization of values: A handbook of contemporary theory* (pp. 135–161). Hoboken, NJ: John Wiley & Sons Inc.

Grolnick, W. S., & Pomerantz, E. M. (2009). Issues and challenges in studying parental control: Toward a new conceptualization. *Child Development Perspectives*, *3*(3), 165–170.

Haerens, L., Aelterman, N., Vansteenkiste, M., Soenens, B., & Van Petegem, S. (2015). Do perceived autonomy-supportive and controlling teaching relate to physical education students' motivational experiences through unique pathways? Distinguishing between the bright and the dark side of motivation. *Psychology of Sport and Exercise*, *16*, 26–36.

Haerens, L., Krijgsman, C., Mouratidis, A., Borghouts, L., Cardon, G., & Aelterman, N. (2018). How does knowledge about the criteria for an upcoming test relate to adolescents' situational motivation in physical education? A self-determination theory perspective. *European Physical Education Review*, *20*(11), 1–19.

Hargreaves, A., & Fullan, M. (2012). *Professional capital: Transforming teaching in every school*. New York, NY: Teachers College Press.

Harter, S. (1978). Pleasure derived from challenge and the effects of receiving grades on children's difficulty level choices. *Child Development*, *49*(3), 788–799.

Hawkins, D. L., Pepler, D. J., & Craig, W. M. (2001). Naturalistic observations of peer interventions in bullying. *Social Development*, *10*, 512–527.

Hein, V., & Koka, A. (2007). Perceived feedback and motivation in physical education and physical activity. In M. S. Hagger, & N. L. D. Chatzisarantis, (Eds.), *Intrinsic motivation and self-determination in exercise and sport* (pp. 127–140). Champaign, IL: Human Kinetics.

Hendrickx, M. M. H. G., Mainhard, M. T., Boor-Klip, H. J., Cillessen, A. H. M., & Brekelmans, M. (2016). Social dynamics in the classroom: Teacher support and conflict and the peer ecology. *Teaching and Teacher Education*, *53*, 30–40.

Hitlin, S. (2003). Values as the core of personal identity: Drawing links between two theories of self. *Social Psychology Quarterly*, *66*(2), 118–137.

Hodge, K., & Gucciardi, D. F. (2015). Antisocial and prosocial behavior in sport: The role of motivational climate, basic psychological needs, and moral disengagement. *Journal of Sport & Exercise Psychology*, *37*, 257–273.

Hodgins, H. S., Brown, A. B., & Carver, B. (2007). Autonomy and control motivation and self-esteem. *Self and Identity*, *6*(2–3), 189–208.

Holding, A., & Koestner, R. (2021). A self-determination theory perspective on how to choose, lose, and use personal goals. In A. O'Donnell, N. Barnes, & J. Reeve, (Eds.), *The Oxford handbook of educational psychology*. New York: Oxford University Press.

Hornstra, L., Mansfield, C., van der Veen, I., Peetsma, T., & Volman, M. (2015). Motivational teacher strategies: The role of beliefs and contextual factors. *Learning Environments Research*, *18*, 363–392.

Howe, E. R. (2006). Exemplary teacher induction: An international review. *Educational Philosophy and Theory*, *38*(3), 287–297. DOI:10.1111/j.1469-5812.2006.00195.

Hulleman, C. S., Godes, O., Hendricks, B. L., & Harackiewicz, J. M. (2010). Enhancing interest and performance with a utility value intervention. *Journal of Educational Psychology*, *102*, 880–985.

Hulleman, C. S., & Harackiewicz, J. M. (2009). Promoting interest and performance in high school science classes. *Science*, *326*, 1410–1412.

Hulleman, C. S., & Harackiewicz, J. M. (2020). The utility-value intervention. In G. W. Walton & A. Crum (Eds.). *Handbook of wise interventions: How social psychology can help people change (Chpt. 4)*. New York: Guilford Press.

Hulleman, C. S., Schrager, S. M., Bodmann, S. M., & Harackiewicz, J. M. (2010). A meta-analytic review of achievement goal measures: Different labels for the same constructs or different constructs with similar labels? *Psychological Bulletin*, *136*, 422–449.

Husman, J., & Hilpert, J. (2007). The intersection of students' perceptions of instrumentality, self-efficacy, and goal orientation in an online mathematics course. *Zeitschrift fur Padagogische Psychologie*, *21*, 229–239.

Ingersoll, R. (2012). Beginning teacher induction: What the data tell us. *Phi Kappan*, *93*(8), 47–51. http//www.kappanmagazine.org/content/234/

Ingersoll, R., Merrill, L., & May, H. (2014). *What are the effects of teacher education and preparation on beginning teacher attrition?* (Research report no. RR-82). Philadelphia: Consortium for Policy Research in Education, University of Pennsylvania.

Isen, A. M., & Reeve, J. (2005). The influence of positive affect on intrinsic and extrinsic motivation: Facilitating enjoyment of play, responsible work behavior, and self-control. *Motivation and Emotion*, *29*, 295–323.

Jang, H. (2008). Supporting students' motivation, engagement, and learning during an uninteresting activity. *Journal of Educational Psychology*, *100*, 798–811.

Jang, H., Kim, E. J., & Reeve, J. (2012). Longitudinal test of self-determination theory's motivation mediation model in a naturally-occurring classroom context. *Journal of Educational Psychology*, *104*, 1175–1188.

Jang, H., Kim, E.-J., & Reeve, J. (2016). Why students become more engaged or more disengaged during the semester: A self-determination theory dual-process model. *Learning and Instruction*, *43*, 27–38.

Jang, H., Reeve, J., & Halusic, M. (2016). A new autonomy-supportive way of teaching that increases conceptual learning: Teaching in students' preferred ways. *Journal of Experimental Education*, *84*, 686–701.

Jang, H., Reeve, J., Ryan, R. M., & Kim, A. (2009). Can self-determination theory explain what underlies the productive, satisfying learning experiences of collectivistically-oriented South Korean adolescents? *Journal of Educational Psychology*, *101*, 644–661.

Jang, H.-R. (2019). Teachers' intrinsic vs. extrinsic instructional goals predict their classroom motivating styles. *Learning and Instruction*, *60*, 286–300.

Jang, H.-R., & Reeve, J. (2021). Intrinsic instructional goal adoption increases autonomy-supportive teaching: A randomized control trial and intervention. *Learning and Instruction*.

Joesaar, H., Hein, V., & Hagger, M. S. (2012). Youth athletes' perception of autonomy support from the coach, peer motivational climate and intrinsic motivation in sport setting: One-year effects. *Psychology of Sport and Exercise*, *13*, 257–262.

Johnson, D. W., & Johnson, R. T. (2002). Learning together and alone: Overview and meta-analysis. *Asia Pacific Journal of Education*, *22*(1), 95–105.

Kaplan, H. (2021). Promoting optimal induction of beginning teachers using self-determination theory. *SAGE Open*, April–June, 1–14. https://doi.org/10.1177/21582440211015680

Kaplan, H. (2021) Suppression of psychological needs among beginning teachers: A self-determination theory perspective on the induction process in Bedouin schools. *Frontiers in Psychology*, *12*:621984. DOI: 10.3389/fpsyg.2021.621984

Kaplan, H. (2018). Teachers' autonomy support, autonomy suppression and conditional negative regard as predictors of optimal learning experience among high-achieving Bedouin students. *Social Psychology of Education*, *21*(1), 223–255.

Kaplan, H., & Assor, A. (2012). Enhancing autonomy-supportive I-Thou dialogue in schools: Conceptualization and socio-emotional effects of an intervention program. *Social Psychology of Education*, *15*(2), 251–269.

Kaplan, H., & Israel, V. (2021). *Autonomy-based Mentoring, The ABC-C Mentoring Model (Autonomy/Belongingness/Competence/Community)*. Unpublished manuscript. Kaye Academic College of Education, Growth Recourses Kaye Induction Unit. This paper is a result of Package I, led by Kaye College, within the Promentors international project of the European Union's Erasmus+ Program

Kaplan, H., Bar-Tov, I., Glassner, A., & Back, S. (2021). Promoting agentic engagement and heutagogy in Tomer elementary school in Beer Sheva, Israel. In L. M. Blaschke, & S. Hase (Eds.), *Harnessing the power of learner agency*. EdTech Books. https://edtechbooks.org/up

Kaplan, H., Glassner, A., & Adess, S. (2016). Support for basic psychological needs and the exploration of exploratory processes in novice teachers as a resource for the construction of a professional identity. *Dapim*, *63*, 130–165. MOFET Institute (Hebrew).

Kaplan, H., & Madjar, N. (2017). The motivational outcomes of psychological need-support among pre-service teachers: Multicultural and self-determination theory perspectives. *Frontiers in Education*, *2*(42), 1–14. https://doi.org/10.3389/feduc.2017.00042

Kasser, T., & Ryan, R. M. (1996). Further examining the American dream: Differential correlates of intrinsic and extrinsic goals. *Personality and Social Psychology Bulletin*, *22*, 280–287.

Katz, I., & Assor, A. (2007). When choice motivates and when it does not. *Educational Psychology Review*, *19*(4), 429–442.

Keller, J., & Bless, H. (2008). Flow and regulatory compatibility: An experimental approach to the flow model of intrinsic motivation. *Personality and Social Psychology Bulletin*, *34*, 196–209.

Koestner, R. (2008). Reaching one's personal goals: A motivational perspective focused on autonomy. *Canadian Psychology*, *49*(1), 60–67.

Koestner, R., Powers, T. A., Carbonneau, N., Milyavskaya, M., & Chua, S. N. (2012). Distinguishing autonomous and directive forms of goal support: Their effects on goal progress, relationship quality, and subjective well-being. *Personality and Social Psychology Bulletin*, *38*, 1609–1620.

Koestner, R., Powers, T. A., Milyavskaya, M., Carbonneau, N., & Hope, N. (2015). Goal internalization and persistence as a function of autonomous and directive forms of goal support. *Journal of Personality*, *83*, 179–190.

Koestner, R., Ryan, R. M., Bernieri, F., & Holt, K. (1984). Setting limits on children's behavior: The differential effects of controlling versus informational styles on children's intrinsic motivation and creativity. *Journal of Personality*, *54*, 233–248.

Krapp, A. (2002). An educational-psychological theory of interest and its relation to SDT. In E. L. Deci, & R. M. Ryan, (Eds.), *Handbook of self-determination research* (pp. 405–427). Rochester, NY: University of Rochester Press.

Krapp, A. (2005). Basic needs and the development of interest and intrinsic motivational orientations. *Learning and Instruction*, *13*, 381–395.

Ladson-Billings, G. (1994). *The dreamkeepers*. San Francisco, CA: Jossey-Bass.

Lansford, J. E., Malone, P. S., Dodge, K. A., Pettit, G. S., & Bates, J. E. (2010). Developmental cascades of peer rejection, social information processing biases, and aggression during middle childhood. *Development and Psychopathology*, *22*, 593–602.

Lee, W., & Reeve, J. (2017). Identifying the neural substrates of intrinsic motivation during task performance. *Cognitive, Affective, and Behavioral Neuroscience*, *17*, 939–953.

Lefstein, A., Vedder-Weiss, & Segal, A. (2020). Relocating research on teacher learning: Toward pedagogically productive talk. *Educational Researcher*, *49*(5), 360–368.

Legault, L., Green-Demers, I., & Pelletier, L. G. (2006). Why do high school students lack motivation in the classroom? Toward an understanding of academic amotivation and the role of social support. *Journal of Educational Psychology*, *98*, 567–582.

Lillard, A. S. (2019). Shunned and admired: Montessori, self-determination, and a case for radical school reform. *Educational Psychology Review*, *31*, 939–965.

LoCasale-Crouch, J., Davis, E., Wiens, P., & Pianta, R. (2012). The role of the mentor in supporting new teachers: Associations with self-efficacy, reflection, and quality. *Mentoring and Tutoring Partnership in Learning*, *20*(3), 303–323. http://dx.doi.org/10.1080/13611267.2012.701959

Marsh, H. W., Dicke, T., & Pfeiffer, M. (2019). A tale of two quests: The (almost) non-overlapping research literatures on students' evaluations of secondary-school and university teachers. *Contemporary Educational Psychology*, *58*, 1–18.

Marsh, H. W., & Martin, A. J. (2011). Academic self-concept and academic achievement: Relations and causal ordering. *British Journal of Educational Psychology*, *81*(1), 59–71.

Marsh, H. W., Nagengast, B., Morin, A. J. S., Parada, R. H., Craven, R. G., & Hamilton, L. R. (2011). Construct validity of the multidimensional structure of bullying and victimization: An application of exploratory structural equation modeling. *Journal of Educational Psychology*, *103*(3), 701–732.

Martela, F., & Ryan, R. M. (2016). The benefits of benevolence: Basic psychological needs, beneficence, and the enhancement of well-being. *Journal of Personality*, *84*(6), 750–764.

Matos, L., Reeve, J., Herrera, D., & Claux, M. (2018). Students' agentic engagement predicts longitudinal increases in perceived autonomy-supportive teaching: The squeaky wheel gets the grease. *Journal of Experimental Education*, *86*(4), 592–609.

Meng, H. Y., & Wang, J. W. C. (2016). The effectiveness of an autonomy-supportive teaching structure in physical education. *RICYDE: Revista Internacional de Ciencias del Deporte*, *43*(12), 5–28.

Meyer, B., Enström, M. K., Harstveit, M., Bowles, D. P., & Beevers, C. G. (2007). Happiness and despair on the catwalk: Need satisfaction, well-being, and personality adjustment among fashion models. *The Journal of Positive Psychology*, *2*(1), 2–17.

Mikami, A. Y., Lerner, M. D., & Lun, J. (2010). Social context influences on children's rejection by their peers. *Child Development Perspectives*, *4*, 123–130.

Mikulincer, M., & Parzachevsky Amir, R. (Eds.) (2020). *Optimal management of professional development and training in the education system: Status report and recommendations*. Yozma, Center for knowledge and Research in Education, The Israel Academy of Sciences and Humanities. Report of the committee on optimal management of professional development and training in the education system, Jerusalem.

Mouratidis, A., Lens, W., & Vansteenkiste, M. (2010). How you provide corrective feedback makes a difference: The motivating role of communicating in an autonomy- supportive way. *Journal of Sport and Exercise Psychology*, *32*, 619–637.

Mouratidis, A., Vansteenkiste, M., Sideridis, G., & Lens, W. (2011). Vitality and interest – enjoyment as a function of class-to-class variation in need-supportive teaching and pupils' autonomous motivation. *Journal of Educational Psychology*, *103*(2), 353–366.

Mynard, J., & Shelton-Strong, S. J. (Eds.) (2021). *Autonomy support beyond the language learning classroom: A self-determination theory perspective*. Bristol, UK: Multilingual Matters.

Nalipay, M. J. N., King, R., & Cai, Y. (2020). Autonomy is equally important across East and West: Testing the cross-cultural universality of self-determination theory. *Journal of Adolescence*, *78*, 67–72.

Newberry, M., & Allsop, Y. (2017). Teacher attrition in the USA: The relational elements in a Utah case study. *Teaching and Teacher Education*, *23*, 863–880.

Newby, T. J. (1991). Classroom motivation: Strategies of first-year teachers. *Journal of Educational Psychology*, *83*(2), 195–200.

Ng, F. F. Y., Pomerantz, E. M., & Deng, C. (2014). Why are Chinese mothers more controlling than American mothers? "My child is my report card". *Child Development*, *85*, 355–369.

Niemiec, C. P., Ryan, R. M., & Deci, E. L. (2009). The path taken: Consequences of attaining intrinsic and extrinsic aspirations in post-college life. *Journal of Research in Personality*, *43*, 291–306.

Noddings, N. (2012). The caring relation in teaching. *Oxford Review of Education*, *38*, 771–781.

Ntoumanis, N., & Vazou, S. (2005). Peer Motivational climate in youth sport: Measurement development and validation. *Journal of Sport and Exercise Psychology*, *27*, 432–455.

Orland-Barak, L., & Maskit, D. (2011). Novices 'in story': What first-year teachers' narratives reveal about the shady corners of teaching. *Teachers and Teaching*, *17*(4), 435–450.

Owen, S. (2016). Professional learning communities: Building skills, reinvigorating the passion, and nurturing teacher wellbeing and "flourishing" within significantly innovative schooling contexts. *Educational Review*, *68*(4), 403–419.

Ozer, E. M., & Bandura, A. (1990). Mechanisms governing empowerment effects: A self-efficacy analysis. *Journal of Personality and Social Psychology*, *58*, 472–486.

Pan, Y., Gauvain, M., & Schwartz, S. J. (2013). Do parents' collectivistic tendency and attitudes toward filial piety facilitate autonomous motivation among young Chinese adolescents? *Motivation and Emotion*, *37*, 701–711.

Patall, E. A. (2013). Constructing motivation through choice, interest, and interestingness. *Journal of Educational Psychology*, *105*(2), 522–534.

Patall, E. A., Cooper, H., & Robinson, J. C. (2008). The effects of choice on intrinsic motivation and related outcomes: A meta-analysis of research findings. *Psychological Bulletin*, *134*(2), 270–300.

Patall, E. A., Dent, A. L., Oyer, M., & Wynn, S. R. (2013). Student autonomy and course value: The unique and cumulative roles of various teacher practices. *Motivation and Emotion*, *37*, 14–32.

Patall, E. A., Linnenbrink-Garcia, L., Liu, P. P., Zambrano, J., & Yates, N. (2021). Education practices that support adaptive motivation, engagement, and learning. In A. M. O'Donnell, N. Barnes, & J. Reeve (Eds.), *Handbook of educational psychology*. New York: Oxford University Press.

Patall, E. A., Pituch, K. A., Steingut, R. R., Vasquez, A. C., Yates, N., & Kennedy, A. A. U. (2019). Agency and high school science students' motivation, engagement, and classroom experiences. *Journal of Applied Developmental Psychology*, *62*(1), 77–92.

Patall, E. A., Steingut, R. R., Vasquez, A. C., Trimble, S. R., Pituch, K. A., & Freeman, J. L. (2018). Daily autonomy supporting or thwarting and students' motivation, engagement, and disaffection in the high school science classroom. *Journal of Educational Psychology*, *110*(2), 268–288.

Patall, E. A., Vasquez, A. C., Steingut, R. R., Trimble, S. S., & Pituch, K. A. (2016). Daily interest, engagement, and autonomy support in the high school science classroom. *Contemporary Educational Psychology*, *46*, 180–194.

Patall, E. A., & Zambrano, J. (2019). Facilitating student outcomes by supporting autonomy: Implications for practice and policy. *Policy Insights from the Behavioral and Brain Sciences*, *6*(2), 115–122.

Patall, E. A., & Zambrano, J. (2021). *Promoting an agentic orientation: An intervention in university psychology and physical science courses*. Manuscript under review.

Patton, K., Parker, M., & Tannehill, D. (2015). Helping teachers help themselves: Professional development that makes a difference. *NASSP Bulletin SAGE*, *99*(1), 26–42.

Pekrun, R., Goetz, T., Titz, W., & Perry, R. P. (2002). Achievement emotions in students' self-regulated learning and achievement: A program of qualitative and quantitative research. *Educational Psychologist*, *37*(2), 91–106.

Pelletier, L., Seguin-Levesque, C., & Legault, L. (2002). Pressure from above and pressure from below as determinants of teachers' motivation and teaching behaviors. *Journal of Educational Psychology*, *94*, 186–196.

Pineda-Baez, C., Manzuoli, C. H., & Sanchez, A. V. (2019). Supporting student cognitive and agentic engagement: Students' voices. *International Journal of Educational Research*, *96*, 81–90.

Prendergast, M., Podus, D., Pinney, J., Greenwell, L., & Roll, J. (2006). Contingency management for treatment of substance use disorders: A meta-analysis. *Addiction*, *101*(11), 1546–1560.

Radel, R., Sarrazin, P., & Pelletier, L. (2009). Evidence of subliminally primed motivational orientations: The effects of unconscious motivational processes on the performance of a new motor task. *Journal of Sport and Exercise Psychology*, *31*, 657–674.

Reeve, J. (1998). Autonomy support as an interpersonal motivating style: Is it teachable? *Contemporary Educational Psychology*, *23*, 312–330.

Reeve, J. (2009). Why teachers adopt a controlling motivating style toward students and how they can become more autonomy supportive. *Educational Psychologist*, *44*, 159–178.

Reeve, J. (2013). How students create motivationally supportive learning environments for themselves: The concept of agentic engagement. *Journal of Educational Psychology*, *105*, 579–595.

Reeve, J. (2015). Giving and summoning autonomy support in hierarchical relationships. *Social and Personality Psychology Compass*, *9*(8), 406–418.

Reeve, J. (2016). Autonomy-supportive teaching: What it is, how to do it. In J. C. K. Wang, W. C. Liu, & R. M. Ryan's, (Eds.), *Building autonomous learners: Perspectives from research and practice using self-determination theory* (pp. 129–152). New York: Springer.

Reeve, J., & Cheon, S. H. (2016). Teachers become more autonomy supportive after they believe it is easy to do. *Psychology of Sport and Exercise*, *22*, 178–189.

Reeve, J., & Cheon, S. H. (2020). Sociocultural influences on teachers' reactions to an intervention to help them become more autonomy supportive. In G. A. D. Liem, & D. M. McInerney, (Eds.), *Promoting motivation and learning in contexts: Sociocultural perspectives on educational interventions* (pp. 13–36). Greenwich, CT: Information Age Publishing.

Reeve, J., & Cheon, S. H. (2021). Autonomy-supportive teaching: Its malleability, benefits, and potential to improve educational practice. *Educational Psychologist*, *56*, 54–77.

Reeve, J., Cheon, S. H., & Jang, H. (2020). How and why students make academic progress: Reconceptualizing the student engagement construct to increase its explanatory power. *Contemporary Educational Psychology*, *62*, Article 101899. https://doi.org/10.1016/j.cedpsych.2020.101899.

Reeve, J., Cheon, S. H., & Yu, T. H. (2020). An autonomy-supportive intervention to develop students' resilience by boosting agentic engagement. *International Journal of Behavioral Development*, *44*(4), 325–338.

Reeve, J., & Jang, H. (2006). What teachers say and do to support students' autonomy during learning activities. *Journal of Educational Psychology*, *98*, 209–218.

Reeve, J., Jang, H., Carrell, D., Jeon, S., & Barch, J. (2004). Enhancing high school students' engagement by increasing their teachers' autonomy support. *Motivation and Emotion*, *28*, 147–169.

Reeve, J., Jang, H., Hardre, P., & Omura, M. (2002). Providing a rationale in an autonomy-supportive way as a motivational strategy to motivate others during an uninteresting activity. *Motivation and Emotion*, *26*, 183–207.

Reeve, J., Jang, H.-R., & Jang, H. (2018). Personality-based antecedents of teachers' autonomy-supportive and controlling motivating styles. *Learning and Individual Differences*, *62*, 12–22.

Reeve, J., Jang, H.-R., Shin, S., Ahn, J. S., Matos, L., & Gargurevich, R. (2021). When students show some initiative: Two experiments on the benefits of greater agentic engagement. *Learning and Instruction*.

Reeve, J., & Lee, W. (2014). Students' classroom engagement produces longitudinal changes in classroom motivation. *Journal of Educational Psychology*, *106*, 527–540.

Reeve, J., Lee, W., & Won, S. (2015). Interest as emotion, as affect, and as schema. In K. A. Renninger, M. Nieswandt, & S. Hidi, (Eds.), *Interest in mathematics and science learning* (pp. 79–92). Washington DC: American Educational Research Association.

Reeve, J., Nix, G., & Hamm, D. (2003). The experience of self-determination in intrinsic motivation and the conundrum of choice. *Journal of Educational Psychology*, *95*, 375–392.

Reeve, J., & Shin, S. H. (2020). How teachers can support students' agentic engagement. *Theory into Practice*, *59*(2), 150–161.

Reeve, J., & Tseng, C.-M. (2011a). Cortisol reactivity to a teacher's motivating style: The biology of being controlled versus supporting autonomy. *Motivation and Emotion*, *35*, 63–74.

Reeve, J., & Tseng, C.-M. (2011b). Agency as a fourth aspect of students' engagement during learning activities. *Contemporary Educational Psychology*, *36*, 257–267.

Renninger, K. A., & Hidi, S. E. (2016). *The power of interest for motivation and engagement*. New York, NY: Routledge.

Richardson, V. (1990). Significant and worthwhile change in teaching. *Educational Researcher*, *19*, 10–18.

Richter, D., Kunter, M., Lüdtke, O., Klusmann, U., Anders, Y., & Baumert, J. (2013). How different mentoring approaches affect beginning teachers' development in the first years of practice. *Teaching and Teacher Education*, *36*, 166–177.

Rodkin, P. C., & Hodges, E. V. E. (2003). Bullies and victims in the peer ecology: Four questions for psychologists and school professionals. *School Psychology Review*, *32*(3), 384–400.

Rogat, T. K., Witham, S. A., & Chinn, C. A. (2014). Teachers' autonomy relevant practices within an inquiry-based science curricular context: Extending the range of academically significant autonomy supportive practices. *Teachers College Record*, *116*(7), 1–46.

Rogers, C. R. (1961). *On becoming a person*. Boston, MA: Houghton Mifflin.

Rogers, C. R. (1969). *Freedom to learn: A view of what education might become*. Columbus, OH: Merrill.

Rokeach, M. (1973). *The nature of human values*. New York: Free Press.

Roth, G. (2014). Antecedents and outcomes of teachers' autonomous motivation: A self-determination theory analysis. In P. W. Richardson, H. M. G. Watt, & S. A. Karabenick, (Eds.), *Teacher motivation: Theory and practice* (pp. 36–51). New York, NY: Routledge.

Roth, G., Assor, A., Kanat-Maymon, Y., & Kaplan, H. (2007). Autonomous motivation for teaching: How self-determined teaching may lead to self-determined learning. *Journal of Educational Psychology*, *99*(4), 761–774.

Roth, G., Assor, A., Niemiec, C. P., Ryan, R. M., & Deci, E. L. (2009). The emotional and academic consequences of parental conditional regard: Comparing conditional positive regard, conditional negative regard, and autonomy support as parenting practices. *Developmental Psychology*, *45*, 1119–1142.

Rots, I., Aelterman, A., Vlerick, P., & Vermeulen, K. (2007). Teacher education, graduates' teaching commitment and entrance into the teaching profession. *Teaching and Teacher Education*, *23*(5), 543–556.

Ryan, R. M. (1982). Control and information in the intrapersonal sphere: An extension of cognitive evaluation theory. *Journal of Personality and Social Psychology*, *43*, 450–461.

Ryan, R. M., & Deci, E. L. (2000). Self-determination theory and the facilitation of intrinsic motivation, social development, and well-being. *American Psychologist*, *55*, 68–78.

Ryan, R. M., & Deci, E. L. (2017). *Self-determination theory: Basic psychological needs in motivation, development, and wellness*. New York, NY: Guilford Press.

Ryan, R. M., & Frederick, C. M. (1997). On energy, personality, and health: Subjective vitality as a dynamic reflection of well-being. *Journal of Personality*, *65*, 529–565.

Ryan, R. M., Huta, V., & Deci, E. L. (2008). Living well: A self-determination theory perspective on eudaimonia. *Journal of Happiness Studies*, *9*(1), 139–170.

Ryan, R. M., Stiller, J. D., & Lynch, J. H. (1994). Representations of relationships to teachers, parents, and friends as predictors of academic motivation and self-esteem. *The Journal of Early Adolescence*, *14*(2), 226–249.

Salmivalli, C. (2010). Bullying and the peer group: A review. *Aggression and Violent Behavior*, *15*, 112–120.

Sameroff, A. (Ed.) (2009). *The transactional model of development: How children and contexts shape each other*. Washington, DC: American Psychological Association.

Sarrazin, P. G., Tessier, D. P., Pelletier, L. G., Trouilloud, D. O., & Chanal, J. P. (2006). The effects of teachers' expectations about students' motivation and teachers' autonomy-supportive and controlling behaviors. *International Journal of Sport and Exercise Psychology*, *4*, 283–301.

Savard, A., Joussemet, M., Pelletier, L. G., & Mageau, G. A. (2013). The benefits of autonomy support for adolescents with severe emotional and behavioral problems. *Motivation and Emotion*, *37*, 688–700.

Schunk, D. H., Meece, J. R., & Pintrich, P. R. (2014). *Motivation in education: Theory, research, and applications* (4th ed.). Englewood Cliffs, NJ: Pearson Higher Education.

Sheldon, K. M., Elliot, A. J., Kim, Y., & Kasser, T. (2001). What is satisfying about satisfying events? Testing 10 candidate psychological needs. *Journal of Personality and Social Psychology*, *80*, 325–339.

Schneider, S., Nebel, S., Beege, M., & Rey, G. D. (2018). The autonomy-enhancing effects of choice on cognitive load, motivation and learning with digital media. *Learning and Instruction*, *58*, 161–172.

Skinner, E. A., & Belmont, M. J. (1993). Motivation in the classroom: Reciprocal effects of teacher behavior and student engagement across the school year. *Journal of Educational Psychology*, *85*, 571–581.

Skinner, E. A., Kindermann, T. A., & Furrer, C. (2009). A motivational perspective on engagement and disaffection: Conceptualization and assessment of children's behavioral and emotional participation in academic activities in the classroom. *Educational and Psychological Measurement*, *69*, 493–525.

Skinner, E. A., Pitzer-Graham, J., Brule, H., Rickert, N., & Kindermann, T. A. (2020, May). "I get knocked down but I get up again": Integrative frameworks for studying the development of motivational resilience in school. *International Journal of Behavioral Development*, *44*(4), 290–300. https://doi.org/10.1177/0165025420924122

Smith, P. K. (2016). Bullying: Definition, types, causes, consequences and intervention. *Social and Personality Psychology Compass*, *10*(9), 519–532.

Soenens, B., Elliot, A. J., Goossens, L., Vansteenkiste, M., Luyten, P., & Duriez, B. (2005). The intergenerational transmission of perfectionism: Parents' psychological control as intervening variable. *Journal of Family Psychology*, *19*, 358–366.

Soenens, B., Sierens, E., Vansteenkiste, M., Dochy, F., & Goossens, L. (2012). Psychologically controlling teaching: Examining outcomes, antecedents, and mediators. *Journal of Educational Psychology*, *104*(1), 108–120.

Soenens, B., & Vansteenkiste, M. (2010). A theoretical upgrade of the concept of parental psychological control: Proposing new insights on the basis of self-determination theory. *Developmental Review*, *30*(1), 74–99.

Solomon, D., Watson, M. S., Delucchi, K. L., Schaps, E., & Battistich, V. (1988). Enhancing children's prosocial behavior in the classroom. *American Educational Research Journal*, *25*(4), 527–554.

Sparks, C., Dimmock, J., Whipp, P., Lonsdale, C., & Jackson, B. (2015). "Getting connected": High school physical education teacher behaviors that facilitate students' relatedness support perceptions. *Sport, Exercise, and Performance Psychology*, *4*, 219–236.

Sparks, C., Lonsdale, C., Dimmock, J. A., & Jackson, B. (2017). An intervention to improve teachers' interpersonally-involving instructional practices in high school physical education: Implications for student relatedness support and in-class experiences. *Journal of Sport & Exercise Psychology*, *39*, 120–133.

Sperling, D. (2015). *Teacher dropout around the world: Information survey*. Tel Aviv: MOFET Institute (Hebrew).

Steingut, R., Patall, E. A., & Trimble, S. (2017). The effect of rationale on motivation and performance outcomes: A meta-analysis. *Motivation Science*, *3*, 19–50.

Stewart, S. M., Bond, M. H., Kennard, B. D., & Zaman, R. M. (2002). Does the Chinese construct of guan export to the West? *International Journal of Psychology*, *37*, 74–82.

Tan, C. (2013). *Learning from Shanghai: Lessons on achieving educational success*. New York: Springer Science.

Taylor, I. M., & Lonsdale, C. (2010). Cultural differences in the relationships among autonomy support, psychological need satisfaction, subjective vitality, and effort in British and Chinese physical education. *Journal of Sport & Exercise Psychology*, *32*(5), 655–673.

Taylor, I. M., Ntoumanis, N., & Standage, M. (2008). A self-determination theory approach to understanding the antecedents of teachers' motivational strategies in physical education. *Journal of Sport & Exercise Psychology*, *30*, 75–94.

Tschannen-Moran, M., & Woolfolk Hoy, A. (2001). Teacher efficacy: Capturing an elusive construct. *Teaching and Teacher Education*, *17*, 783–805.

Tschannen-Moran, M., & Woolfolk Hoy, A. (2007). The differential antecedents of self-efficacy beliefs of novice and experienced teachers. *Teaching and Teacher Education*, *23*, 944–956.

Tettegah, S., & Anderson, C. J. (2007). Pre-service teachers' empathy and cognitions: Statistical analysis of text data by graphical models. *Contemporary Educational Psychology*, *21*(1), 48–82.

Thomas, T., Tuytens, M., Moolenaar, N., Devos, G., Kelchtermans, G., & Vanderlinde, R. (2019). Teachers' first year in the profession: The power of high-quality support. *Teachers & Teaching*, *25*(2), 166–188.

Tilga, H., Kalajas-Tilga, H., Hein, V., Raudsepp, L., & Koka, A. (2020). 15-month follow-up on the web-based autonomy-supportive intervention program for PE teachers. *Perceptual and Motor Skills*, *127*(1), 5–7.

Trouilloud, D., Sarrazin, P., Bressoux, P., & Bois, J. (2006). Relations between teachers' early expectations and students' later perceived competence in physical education classes: Autonomy-supportive climate as a moderator. *Journal of Educational Psychology*, *98*, 75–86.

Tsai, Y.-M., Kunter, M., Ludtke, O., Trautwein, U., & Ryan, R. M. (2008). What makes lessons interesting? The role of situational and individual factors in three school subjects. *Journal of Educational Psychology*, *100*(2), 460–472.

Turner, J. C. (2010). Unfinished business: Putting motivation theory to the "classroom test". In T. C. Urdan & S. A. Karabenick (Eds.), The decade ahead: Applications and contexts of motivation and achievement. *Advances in motivation and achievement* (Vol. 16B, pp. 109–138). Bingley, UK: Emerald Group Publishing Limited.

Turner, J. C., Warzon, K. B., & Christensen, A. (2011). Motivating mathematics learning: Changes in teachers' practices and beliefs during a nine-month collaboration. *American Educational Research Journal*, 48, 718–762.

Vallerand, R. J. (2010). On passion for life activities: The dualistic model of passion. *Advances in experimental social psychology*, *42*, 97–193.

Vallerand, R. J. (2015). *The psychology of passion: A dualistic model*. New York, NY: Oxford University Press.

Vallerand, R. J., Fortier, M. S., & Guay, F. (1997). Self-determination and persistence in a real-life setting: Toward a motivational model of high school dropout. *Journal of Personality and Social Psychology*, 72, 1161–1176.

Van den Berghe, L., Soenens, B., Vansteenkiste, M., Aelterman, N., Cardon, G., Tallir, I., & Haerens, L. (2013). Observed need-supportive and need-thwarting teaching behavior in physical education: Do teachers' motivational orientations matter? *Psychology of Sport and Exercise*, *14*, 650–661.

Van den Berghe, L., Tallir, I., Cardon, G., Aelterman, N., & Haerens, L. (2015). Student (dis) engagement and need-supportive teaching behavior: A multi-informant and multilevel approach. *Journal of Sport and Exercise Psychology*, *37*, 353–366.

Van Petegem, S., Vansteenkiste, M., Soenens, B., Zimmerman, G., Antonietti, J.-P., Baudat, S., & Audenaert, E. (2017). When do adolescents accept or defy to material prohibitions? The role of social domain and communication style. *Journal of Youth and Adolescence*, *46*, 1022–1037.

Vansteenkiste, M., Aelterman, N., De Muynck, G.-J., Haerens, L., Patall, E., & Reeve, J. (2018). Fostering personal meaning and self-relevance: A self-determination theory perspective on internalization. *Journal of Experimental Education*, *86*, 30–49.

Vansteenkiste, M., Aelterman, N., Haerens, L., & Soenens, B. (2019). Seeking stability in stormy educational times: A need-based perspective on (de)motivating teaching grounded in self-determination theory. In E. N. Gonida & M. S. Lemos (Eds.), *Motivation in education at a time of global change: Theory, research, and implications for practice* (Vol. 20, pp. 53–80). Bingley, UK: Emerald.

Vansteenkiste, M., & Ryan, R. M. (2013). On psychological growth and vulnerability: Basic psychological need satisfaction and need frustration as a unifying principle. *Journal of Psychotherapy Integration*, *23*(3), 263–280.

Vansteenkiste, M., Ryan, R. M., & Soenens, B. (2020). Basic psychological need theory: Trends, critical themes, and future directions. *Motivation and Emotion*, *44*, 1–31.

Vansteenkiste, M., Simons, J., Lens, W., Sheldon, K. M., & Deci, E. L. (2004). Motivation learning, performance and persistence: The synergistic effects of intrinsic goal contents and autonomy-supportive contexts. *Journal of Personality and Social Psychology*, *87*, 246–260.

Vansteenkiste, M., Simons, J., Lens, W., Soenens, B., & Matos, L. (2005). Examining the motivational impact of intrinsic versus extrinsic goal framing and autonomy-supportive versus internally controlling communication style on early adolescents' academic achievement. *Child Development*, *76*, 483–501.

Vansteenkiste, M., Simons, J., Soenens, B., & Lens, W. (2004). How to become a persevering exerciser? The importance of providing a clear, future intrinsic goal in an autonomy-supportive manner. *Journal of Sport and Exercise Psychology*, *26*, 232–249.

Vansteenkiste, M., Timmermans, T., Lens, W., Soenens, B., & Van den Broeck, A. (2008). Does extrinsic goal framing enhance extrinsic goal-oriented individuals' learning and performance? An experimental test of the match perspective versus self-determination theory. *Journal of Educational Psychology*, *100*, 387–397.

Vasconcellos, D., Parker, P. D., Hilland, T., Cinelli, R., Owen, K. B., Kapsal, N., Lee, J., Antczak, D., Ntoumanis, N., Ryan, R. M., & Lonsdale, C. (2020). Self-determination theory applied in physical education: A systematic review and meta-analysis. *Journal of Educational Psychology*, *112*(7), 1444–1469. https://doi.org/10.1037/edu0000420

Waterschoot, J., Vansteenkiste, M., & Soenens, B. (2019, December). The effects of experimentally induced choice on elementary school children's intrinsic motivation: The moderating role of indecisiveness and teacher–student relatedness. *Journal of Experimental Child Psychology*, *188*, Article 104692. https://doi.org/10.1016/j.jecp.2019.104692

Weinstein, N., & Ryan, R. M. (2010). When helping helps: Autonomous motivation for prosocial behavior and its influence on wellbeing for the helper and recipient. *Journal of Personality and Social Psychology*, *98*, 222–244.

Weinstein, N., Zougkou, K., & Paulmann, S. (2018). You 'have' to hear this: Using tone of voice to motivate others. *Journal of Experimental Psychology: Human Perception and Performance*, *44*(6), 898–913.

Weinstein, R. S., Madison, S. M., & Kuklinski, M. R. (1995). Raising expectations in schooling: Obstacles and opportunities for change. *American Educational Research Journal*, *32*, 121–159.

Williams, G. C., & Deci, E. L. (1996). Internalization of biopsychosocial values by medical students: A test of self-determination theory. *Journal of Personality and Social Psychology*, *70*, 767–779.

Williams, S. (1998). An organizational model of choice: A theoretical analysis differentiating choice, personal control, and self-determination. *Genetic, Social & General Psychology Monographs*, *124*, 465–492.

Yu, S., Chen, B., Levesque-Bristol, C., & Vansteenkiste, M. (2018). Chinese education examined via the lens of self-determination. *Educational Psychology Review*, *30*, 177–214.

Zach, S., Sivan, T., Harari, I., Stein, H., & Nabel-Heller, N. (2015). Success as a springboard for novice physical education teachers in their efforts to develop a professional career. *Journal of Teaching in Teacher Education*, *34*(2), 278–296.

Zhou, M., Ma, W. J., & Deci, E. L. (2009). The importance of autonomy for rural Chinese children's motivation for learning. *Learning and Individual Differences*, *19*(4), 492–498.

Zougkou, K., Weinstein, N., & Paulmann, S. (2017). ERP correlates of motivating voices: Quality of motivation and time-course matters. *Social Cognitive and Affective Neuroscience*, *12*, 1687–1700.

Author Index

Subject Index

Made in the USA
Middletown, DE
10 February 2023